This Call to Abide

Abiding in the Presence, Growing in Grace, and Living in His Word

Table of Contents

This Call to Abide

A 365 Day Devotional by Starrla Riordan

Abiding in the Presence, Growing in **Grace**, and Living in His Word

Printed and bound in the United States of America First Edition 2025

Dedication

For Austin, Emily, Jaedon, Anika, Aubree, Caleb, and Nolen.

May your heart always find rest in **His Presence***, strength in* **His Word***, and purpose in His Calling. May your lives be a reflection of His Faithfulness from*

generation to generation.

Foreword:
This Call to Abide

In a world filled with distractions, uncertainty, and shifting priorities, there remains a steadfast invitation from the heart of the Father: to abide in Him. This devotion, born from moments of reflection, revelation, and reverence, is both a guide and a call to a deeper connection with the One Who knows us intimately and loves us unconditionally. Through these pages, you will find reflections, scriptures, and prophetic insights that encourage you to lean into God's Presence, trust His Promises, and walk boldly in the identity He has given you. This is not merely a collection of words but a spiritual journey, a call to step away from the noise, embrace His Truth, and align your heart with His.

As you engage with each reflection, let them lead you into prayer, worship, and a renewed sense of His nearness. Whether you are in a season of joy, challenge, or transition, these words are meant to anchor you in the unchanging love of Christ and inspire you to live a life rooted in His Grace and Truth.

The path of abiding is not always easy, but it is always worth it. As you embark on this journey, may you experience the depths of His Love, the clarity of His Voice, and the fullness of His Peace. Abide in Him, for in Him, you will find everything you need.

The Rhythm of Renewal: Wind, Fire, and Water
A movement of the Spirit within Faith and Expectation

Within the rhythm of faith comes a Divine progression: the breath that awakens, the fire that refines, and the living water that restores. These pages trace the holy movement of the Spirit as He breathes, burns, and flows through every surrendered heart. Each element carries His Presence: the wind to stir, the fire to purify, and the water to refresh. Together they reveal one Truth that the God Who begins the work is faithful to complete it.

"By the Word of the Lord were the heavens made; and all the host of them by the breath of His Mouth."

- Psalm 33:6 KJV

About the Author

Starrla Riordan is a woman after God's own heart; a writer, intercessor, and encourager whose words flow from a life of abiding in His Presence. Through seasons of refining and revelation, she has learned that true strength is found in stillness, and that healing begins where surrender leads. Each devotion in This Call to Abide was birthed from prayer, tested through faith, and anchored in the unwavering Truth of God's Word. Her desire is simple yet profound to see hearts healed, faith restored, and lives transformed by the power of intimacy with Jesus Christ.

When Starrla is not writing or ministering encouragement, she finds joy in her family, her community, and every opportunity to remind others that abiding is not passive; it is powerfully alive in His Presence.

May every word in this book draw you nearer to the heart of our **Heavenly Father** and **deepen your call to abide.**

This collection was born from seasons of waiting, trusting, and learning to rest in the hands of my Heavenly Father. I discovered that abiding isn't about doing more, it's about being still and allowing Him to work through me. May these words remind you that His timing is perfect, His Plans are good, and His Presence is enough.

Starrla Riordan

Section One:
Trust In God

Day 1
The Call to Abide

Scripture:

"I am the vine, ye are the branches: He that abideth in Me, and I in him, the same bringeth forth much fruit: for without Me ye can do nothing."

John 15:5 (KJV)

Reflection:

Every journey with God begins with an invitation to Abide.

To abide is more than believing; it is choosing to remain, to stay close, to dwell in continual communion with the One Who is life itself. The world pushes, rushes, and demands constant movement, but the abiding heart learns a different rhythm: the rhythm of Grace. In His Presence, striving ceases, anxieties loosen their grip, and trust begins to rise like breath in the soul.

Fruitfulness is never produced by human effort; it flows naturally from connection. The branch does not strain to bear fruit; it simply stays connected to the Vine. In the same way, the more deeply we dwell in Christ, the more freely His Life, His Strength, and His Peace flow through us.

To abide is to breathe in His Presence and exhale surrender. It is to quiet the noise long enough to hear His whisper. It is waking with the awareness, Lord, I cannot do this without You, and walking through the day anchored by His Love.

Abiding transforms the heart from a state of survival to overflow. It shapes character, fuels purpose, and positions us to receive every Grace He pours out. It is not a one-time moment, but a continual posture of closeness choosing to dwell, not merely visit, the Presence of Jesus. The call to abide is the call to life itself.

Prayer:

Lord Jesus, teach me to abide. Slow my soul and settle my heart in Your Presence. Let every part of my life be rooted in Your Love and nourished by Your Word. Draw me into deeper communion with You moment by moment, breath by breath. May my heart learn to dwell, not just visit, in the sweetness of Your Presence. In Your Holy Name, Amen.

True trust begins when we choose to abide.

Day 2
The God Who Sees Me

Scripture:

"And she called the name of the Lord that spake unto her Thou God seest me."

Genesis 16:13 (KJV)

Reflection:

Before trust can bloom, the heart must first know it is seen. Hagar wounded, rejected, and wandering in the wilderness felt invisible to the world around her. Yet in that lonely place, she discovered a life-changing truth: God had never taken His eyes off her. He is El Roithe God Who sees.

When life feels hidden, overlooked, or devalued, remember this: His gaze is upon you not with judgment, but with unwavering love. He sees your effort when no one else notices. He sees your pain when others misunderstand. He sees your waiting, your endurance, your quiet obedience, and the courage it takes to hold on when your heart is weary.

The tears you cry in silence are not invisible to Him. The prayers you whisper in the dark are heard in the throne room of Heaven. His seeing is not distant observation; it is intimate care. His attention is not passive; it is protective, intentional, and filled with compassion.

El Roi does not simply notice you; He knows you. He is with you. And His gaze brings healing to places where loneliness once lived. The God Who saw Hagar in the desert sees you in every season of your life and His Presence turns barren places into holy ground.

Prayer:

Father, thank You for seeing me even in the wilderness places of my life. When I feel unseen or forgotten by others, remind me that I am fully known and deeply loved by You. Let Your tender gaze heal the wounds of loneliness and strengthen my heart with the comfort of Your watchful love. Teach me to rest in the assurance that You are El Roi, the God Who sees me. In Jesus' Name, Amen.

Trust grows in the heart that knows it is seen.

Day 3
Still Waters

Scripture:

"He maketh me lie down in green pastures: He leadeth me beside the still waters."

Psalm 23:2 (KJV)

"In returning and rest shall ye be saved; in quietness and in confidence shall be your strength."

Isaiah 30:15 KJV

Reflection:

God's leading is never frantic. Heaven does not hurry, panic, or push. Even when life feels chaotic, the Shepherd's Voice draws you toward stillness, not the stillness of inactivity, but the stillness of peaceful confidence in Him.

Still waters are where your soul exhales. They are the sacred spaces where anxiety loses its grip, where clarity rises, and where your heart remembers Who is truly in control. Trust is learning to match the Shepherd's pace, not the world's pressure. He never drives you. He gently leads you. When your mind races and your heart feels restless, His invitation remains the same:

Come. Lie down. Breathe. Let Me restore you.

Rest is not weakness; it is worship. It is the surrender that says, Lord, You lead I follow. And the same Shepherd who brings you to quiet waters is the One Who walks beside you in the valley, guiding you with unwavering love. Still waters are not a place you visit, they are a posture you carry when you remain near Him.

Prayer:

Shepherd of my soul, lead me today to still waters. Quiet the noise around me and the noise within me. Calm every anxious thought and steady every restless place in my heart. Let Your peace restores my soul and Your Presence refresh my strength. Teach me to walk at Your pace and to trust Your Timing, even when I cannot see the full path ahead. Lead me into rest that strengthens, faith that anchors, and peace that endures. In Jesus' Name, Amen.

Trust is found beside the still waters of His Peace.

Day 4
Leaning on the Everlasting Arms

Scripture:

"The eternal God is thy refuge, and underneath are the everlasting arms."

Deuteronomy 33:27 (KJV)

Reflection:

There are days when the weight feels too heavy and your own strength seems to slip through your fingers. Seasons when you stand, but barely… when faith feels stretched thin and your heart wonders how much more it can hold. Yet even in those fragile places, God's everlasting arms remain beneath you.

You may not always sense His grip, but His hold is sure. You may feel shaken, but you are never in danger of falling beyond His reach. The same arms that shaped the heavens, steadied the prophets, carried the cross, and broke the power of the grave are the very arms that carry you now.

Trust doesn't mean you never tremble; it means you lean into the only One Who cannot fail. Deep trust is born in the moments when you have nothing left to stand on but the character of God. And there resting on everlasting strength you discover a refuge that cannot be moved and a love that will not let you go.

Prayer:

Lord, thank You that Your everlasting arms never shift, weaken, or let go. When I feel small, tired, or overwhelmed, teach me to lean fully into Your strength. Quiet every fear with the assurance of Your unfailing love. Help me release the need to control and instead find my rest in who You are my refuge, my fortress, my eternal support. Hold me close and carry me through every season. In Jesus' Name, Amen.

Every fall becomes a flight when we are caught by His everlasting arms.

Day 5
The Gift of Dependence

Scripture:

"Trust in the Lord with all thine heart; and lean not unto thine own understanding."

Proverbs 3:5 (KJV)

Reflection:

There are seasons when strength fails, courage shakes, and faith feels thin. Life can press hard enough to make even the strongest heart tremble. Yet even in those moments, especially in those moments God's everlasting arms remain beneath you. You may not always feel His hold, but you will never fall beyond His reach.

His arms are eternal; they do not weaken, slip, or withdraw. They have carried prophets through wildernesses, lifted weary saints through trials, and held generations through storms. These are the same arms that carried the cross, bore the weight of sin, and conquered the grave. If they were strong enough to redeem the world, they are more than strong enough to carry you.

Trust grows deepest in the moments when we lean hardest. Leaning is not a sign of weakness; it is a declaration of dependence on the One Who cannot fail. God never asked you to stand in your own strength; He invites you to rest in His.

To trust is not to never tremble; it is to know Who holds you when you do. His arms are underneath your fears, your questions, your pain, and your uncertainty. They uphold you when you cannot hold yourself. They steady you when life becomes unsteady. They are your refuge, your shelter, and your everlasting support. When everything else feels shaky, His arms remain sure.

Prayer:

Lord, thank You that Your everlasting arms never let me go. When I feel weak or overwhelmed, teach me to lean fully into Your strength. Let my security rest not in what I can control, but in who You are my refuge, my foundation, my eternal support. Calm my trembling heart with the assurance of Your unfailing love, and carry me through every season with Your mighty embrace. In Jesus' Name, Amen.

Dependence is not defeat; it is a Divine partnership.

Day 6
In the Waiting

Scripture:

"Rest in the Lord, and wait patiently for Him."

Psalm 37:7 (KJV)

Reflection:

Waiting is holy ground, a sacred place where God slows the pace of your life so He can strengthen the posture of your heart. Seasons of waiting are not wasted seasons; they are seasons where God works beneath the surface, arranging what you cannot see, preparing what you cannot yet hold, and maturing what you are becoming. In the waiting, God is not inactive. He is intentional. He uses stillness as a sculptor uses clay forming you, stretching you, softening what has grown rigid, and strengthening what has grown weary. Waiting reveals where trust lives and where it still needs to be planted. It exposes the impatience of the flesh and invites the endurance of the Spirit. The enemy wants you to interpret waiting as a sign of abandonment. But waiting is not evidence that God is far; waiting is proof that He is near enough to be working inside you. When you surrender the desire to hurry God, peace enters the room. When you let go of timelines and outcomes, rest becomes your worship. And when you stop striving to make something happen, you begin to see His fingerprints all over what He is preparing. Waiting is not passive. Waiting is active trust. Waiting is believing God's not yet is still good. Waiting is worship in slow motion. And when the season shifts, you will not step into your blessing anxious or exhausted; you will step into it ready, refined, and rooted.

Prayer:

Lord, teach me the beauty of Your Timing. Quiet every anxious thought that wants to rush ahead of You. Help me to rest not just with my body, but with my mind, my emotions, and my spirit. Let patience rise within me like fruit watered by Your Presence. When I start to fear delay, remind me that You are never late. When I feel unseen, remind me that You are working in the unseen. When I feel forgotten, remind me that You are preparing something worth waiting for. Strengthen me to trust Your pace. Refine me in the stillness. Shape me into a vessel who can steward the blessing when it comes. May my waiting glorify You, and may my faith remain steady until Your Promise unfolds. In Jesus' Name, Amen.

Waiting with faith is a form of worship in motion.

Day 7
Anchored in Promise

Scripture:

"Which hope we have as an anchor of the soul, both sure and steadfast."

Hebrews 6:19 (KJV)

Reflection:

Storms reveal what truly anchors you. When the winds of uncertainty whip around your life, when circumstances shake what once felt steady, the promises of God hold you firm. His Word does not drift with emotion, fray under pressure, or fail in adversity. It stands unmoved, unchanging, and utterly dependable. Trust becomes the rope that ties your soul to His Truth, keeping you from being pulled away by fear or doubt.

The promises of God were never given to tease or torment you; they were given to train you. Each promise strengthens your endurance, shapes your perspective, and anchors your heart in who He is. As you hold to His Word, you learn the steady rhythm of hope. You learn that His character remains constant, even when circumstances do not.

Life's storms may rise suddenly and fiercely, but they cannot uproot what is anchored in Christ. The tide may swell, the waves may roar, but the soul fastened to God's Promises will not be swept away. Hope is not fragile; it is sure and steadfast because its foundation is the unchanging God Himself.

Keep your hope anchored, beloved. The storm may rage, but your anchor holds.

Prayer:

Father, thank You for every promise You've spoken over my life. Anchor me in Your Truth when waves of doubt or fear arise. Strengthen my trust so that my heart remains steady and secure in Your unchanging Word. Let my hope be firm, my faith unmovable, and my confidence rooted in who You are. In Jesus' Name, Amen.

An anchored soul cannot be carried away by the storm.

Day 8
The God Who Provides

Scripture:

"And Abraham called the name of that place Jehovah Jireh: as it is said to this day, In the mount of the Lord it shall be seen."

Genesis 22:14 (KJV)

Reflection:

Provision is often revealed on the mount of surrender. Abraham didn't encounter God as Jehovah-Jireh at the bottom of the mountain; he discovered Him at the top, in the place where obedience came at a cost. When Abraham lifted the knife of obedience, God revealed the ram of mercy. Trust led him to the very place where fear ended, and faith finally saw.

God's provision rarely arrives early, but it is never late. He waits until your dependence on Him is complete until your heart says, Even if not, I will trust You. It is in that sacred, trembling moment of surrender that Heaven unveils what was prepared long before you could see it.

Jehovah-Jireh doesn't simply respond to needs; He anticipates them. Long before Abraham climbed the mountain, the ram was already caught in the thicket. Long before you face your own mountain, God has already arranged the provision. Your role is obedience. His role is supply.

Surrender creates the space where faith becomes sight. On the mount of trust, what once looked impossible becomes the place where God's faithfulness is revealed in full. The God Who provided for Abraham is the same God Who provides for you perfectly, precisely, and personally.

Prayer:

Jehovah-Jireh, my Provider, thank You that You see my need long before I speak it. Strengthen my trust to obey even when the path is unclear and the mountain is steep. Help me place everything on the altar with confidence in Your faithfulness. Let my surrender become the place where Your provision is revealed, and let my faith testify that You are always enough. In Jesus' Name, Amen

Where trust is tested, provision is revealed.

Day 9
Under His Wings

Scripture:

"He shall cover thee with His feathers, and under His wings shalt thou trust."

Psalm 91:4 (KJV)

Reflection:

There is no safer place than beneath His wings. Trust brings you close to the very heart of God into the shelter where fear cannot follow, and threats lose their power. Like a loving mother bird shielding her young from danger, God gathers you near and covers you with His unfailing protection. His Love becomes your refuge, and His Faithfulness becomes your fortress. To dwell under His wings is not an escape from life's storms; it is an invitation to endure them in supernatural peace. The winds may howl, the thunder may shake the sky, and circumstances may swirl around you, but the soul hidden in Him remains steady. When you are close enough to hear His Heartbeat, the noise of fear grows faint.

Every worry that drives you to His Presence becomes a doorway to worship. Every wave that pushes you toward Him becomes a reminder of His nearness. He does not simply shield you. He embraces you. The closer you stay, the quieter the storm feels. Under His wings, you are not forgotten. You are fiercely loved. And the more you trust, the more you rest held, covered, and carried by the One Who cannot fail.

Prayer:

Lord, thank You for covering me with Your wings. Hide me in Your Presence when fear rises and surround me with the peace that comes only from You. Draw me close until every anxious whisper is silenced and trust becomes the song of my heart. Keep me near Your side, sheltered in Your Love and steady in Your care. In Jesus' Name, Amen.

Peace is found in the Shadow of His wings.

Day 10
The Unfailing Love of God

Scripture:

"The Lord hath appeared of old unto me, saying, Yea, I have loved thee with an everlasting love: therefore, with loving kindness have I drawn thee."

Jeremiah 31:3 (KJV)

Reflection:

All trust begins with love. You can only rest in a heart you know will never turn away. God's love is not measured by moods, moments, or merit; it is marked by eternity. His Love does not rise and fall with your performance. It does not dim when you struggle or lessen when you question. It remains constant, steady, and unchanging.

When life wounds you and people disappoint you, His Love becomes the thread that gently pulls you back to peace. When everything else feels uncertain, His everlasting love becomes the one Truth you can anchor to without fear. He doesn't just love you. He draws you, woos you, and welcomes you with kindness that melts fear and softens resistance.

The more you trust His Love, the less you fear His Plans. A heart that knows it is deeply loved can surrender fully. It can release the need to control, to predict, or to understand everything. Every act of surrender becomes a response to the love that refuses to let you go, love that reaches into your past, covers your present, and secures your future. His Love is not only reliable, it is everlasting. It is the first Truth that steadies your heart and the final Truth that carries your soul.

Prayer:

Father, thank You for loving me with an everlasting, unchanging love. Draw me daily with the sweetness of Your kindness and steady my heart in the certainty of Your faithfulness. Let Your Love become the foundation of all my trust, the anchor of my peace, and the song that carries me through every season. May I rest in the beauty of knowing I am fully known, fully seen, and fully loved by You. In Jesus' Name, Amen.

Everlasting love births everlasting trust.

Day 11
Faithful in the Fire

Scripture:

"If it be so, our God whom we serve is able to deliver us from the burning fiery furnace, and He will deliver us out of thine hand, O king. But if not, be it known unto thee, O king, that we will not serve thy gods."

Daniel 3:17 - 18 (KJV)

Reflection:

Trust is proven in the fire. It is one thing to believe God can deliver it is another to remain faithful when you haven't yet seen how. The three Hebrew men were not spared from entering the furnace, but they were spared from being destroyed by it. Their faith did not rest on whether they would be delivered, it rested on Who God is.

They stepped into the flames declaring, God is able… but even if He doesn't, we are His.

That is the essence of unshakable faith. Sometimes God does not remove the heat; He reveals His Presence within it. The miracle was not merely that they survived the fire, it was that Jesus Himself walked with them in it. The furnace became the place where the invisible God became undeniably seen. True faith does not demand escape, it declares allegiance. It says, My obedience is not for sale, my worship is not negotiable, and my trust does not depend on outcomes. Whether deliverance comes immediately or ultimately, His Faithfulness never changes, and neither should your devotion.

The fire is not your end; it is your refining. What burns away is bondage. What remains is faith made pure, steadfast, and proven.

Prayer:

Lord, give me the courage to stand firm in the fire. Strengthen my heart so that my faith does not waver when trials come. Let me find You walking beside me in every flame, reminding me that I am never alone. Purify my heart until fear burns away and only trust in Your Goodness remains. In Jesus' Name, Amen.

The fire refines what fear cannot destroy.

Day 12
The God Who Speaks

Scripture:

"My sheep hear My voice, and I know them, and they follow Me."

John 10:27 (KJV)

Reflection:

The heart that trusts learn to listen. God has never been silent. His Voice weaves through Scripture, breathes through prayer, and settles into the soul as a quiet, steady peace. The Shepherd knows your name. He calls you, not with the harshness of command, but with the closeness of communion. When life grows loud, His Voice often grows soft not because He is distant, but because He draws you closer. The world shouts demand, but the Spirit whispers direction. He does not compete with the noise; He invites you into stillness. In that sacred quiet, clarity rises and fear begins to fade.

God will never speak in contradiction to His Word. His Voice is consistent with His Character, pure, life-giving, and full of truth. When He speaks, heaviness lifts, confusion clears, courage strengthens, and love is felt. Every word from His mouth carries life. Every whisper carries light. Every nudge carries love. To trust Him is to follow Him even when the next step is unseen. Faith isn't about having the map; it's about following the Guide. And the Shepherd Who speaks is the Shepherd Who leads, protects, and loves without failing. His Voice is your compass. His Presence is your assurance. And His Word is your anchor.

Prayer:

Speak, Lord, for Your servant is listening. Quiet every competing sound and let Your Voice rise above the noise. Calm my confusion, steady my heart, and direct my steps. Help me discern Your Word and follow where You lead. Teach me to trust what You say more than what I see. In Jesus' Name, Amen.

The Shepherd's Voice leads hearts that trust.

Day 13
When I Am Afraid

Scripture:

"What time I am afraid, I will trust in Thee."

Psalm 56:3 (KJV)

Reflection:

Faith has never required the absence of fear; it requires a choice in the presence of it. David did not pretend he was fearless; he refused to let fear have the final word. He acknowledged the trembling in His Heart, but he anchored his confidence in the unfailing character of God.

Every time fear tries to rise within you, you are invited into a holy decision: to stare at the threat or to look toward the One Who is greater than anything that threatens you. Fear begins to lose its power the moment you remember who holds your life, your future, and your every breath.

God is not disappointed by your trembling; He is moved by your trust. Even the weakest whisper of I trust You, Lord carries weight in Heaven. And as trust is spoken, peace begins its gentle descent settling the storm within long before the storm around you changes.

Prayer:

Father, when fear tries to overwhelm me, remind me of Your nearness. Lift my eyes from what threatens me and fix them on who You are my refuge, my strength, and my constant help. Turn my fear into faith, my anxiety into worship, and my trembling into trust. Let Your perfect love cast out all fear and fill my heart with courage and peace. In Jesus' Name, Amen.

Faith whispers peace where fear once shouted doubt.

Day 14
The Strength of Surrender

Scripture:

"And He said unto me, My Grace is sufficient for thee: for My strength is made perfect in weakness."

2 Corinthians 12:9 (KJV)

Reflection:

The world teaches that strength is found in control, in pushing harder, in proving that you can handle everything on your own. But Heaven reveals a different truth: strength is discovered not in striving, but in surrender. Paul did not encounter God's power by becoming stronger, but by yielding to the reality of his own weakness.

Your weakness does not diminish God's ability; it becomes the very place where His Power shines brightest. When you stop trying to carry what only God can hold, you create room for **Grace** to flow freely. Surrender isn't defeat; it is releasing the burden from yourself and entrusting it to Him. It is the holy exchange where your insufficiency meets His abundance.

Trust grows deepest when pride grows quiet. You are not called to be enough; you are called to rely on the One Who has always been more than enough. In surrender, you find strength. In weakness, you discover the power that only God can supply.

Prayer:

Lord, I surrender every weakness, burden, and limitation into Your Hands. Let Your strength rest upon me and Your Grace sustain me in every place I feel insufficient. Quiet my pride and teach my heart to depend fully on You. May Your power be revealed not through my ability, but through my surrender. In Jesus' Name, Amen.

Surrender is the soil where true strength takes root.

Day 15
The Secret Place

Scripture:

"He that dwelleth in the secret place of the Most High shall abide under the Shadow of the Almighty."

Psalm 91:1 (KJV)

Reflection:

Trust is what leads you into intimacy. The secret place is not a physical location; it is a posture of the heart. It is the quiet determination to choose presence over performance, prayer over panic, stillness over striving. It is the inward turning of the soul toward God with a whisper that says, You are enough for me.

In that sacred space, you may not always receive the answers you seek, but you will always find the assurance you need. The secret place becomes the meeting point between your weakness and His Strength, between your questions and His Peace.

Every moment spent with Him becomes protection, not escape from life's pressures. Dwelling under the Shadow of the Almighty does not shield you from reality; it covers you with His reality. His Shadow is not darkness; it is Divine covering. In that hidden place:

- Fear cannot find you.
- Chaos cannot shake you.
- Circumstances cannot uproot you.
- The enemy cannot overthrow you.

To dwell in the secret place is to live tucked beneath the wings of God's Presence, surrounded by a peace too deep to disrupt and a strength too strong to break. It is where your soul learns to breathe again.

Prayer:

Father, draw me into the secret place of Your Presence. Teach me to dwell, not only visit. Let Your Peace over Shadow every worry and Your Presence surround every corner of my heart. In the stillness, remind me that You are my refuge, my strength, and my hiding place. Keep me close beneath the Shadow of the Almighty. In Jesus' Name, Amen.

Abiding in His Shadow brings the brightest peace.

Day 16
The Path of Peace

Scripture:

"And the work of righteousness shall be peace; and the effect of righteousness quietness and assurance forever."

Isaiah 32:17 (KJV)

Reflection:

Peace is not found by avoiding storms, it is discovered by walking righteously with God through them. When your steps align with His will, peace begins to follow you like a faithful companion. Even when uncertainty surrounds you, a heart that is right before Him stands on steady ground. God's Peace is not fragile. It remains unbroken by chaos and unmoved by what you cannot yet understand. His Peace is forged in trust that releases control, surrenders agendas, and chooses His leading over your own impulses. When you stop forcing outcomes and start following His Spirit, peace rises like a quiet river within you. Every detour holds purpose; every delay carries design. Nothing in the hands of God is wasted. The path He leads you on may not be the shortest, but it is always the safest for your soul. It is marked by righteousness, shaped by wisdom, and sustained by His Presence.

Allow the Spirit of peace to guide you, rather than pressure, fear, or comparison. His Peace whispers direction when confusion tries to speak. His Peace anchors you when emotions shift. His Peace quiets the noise so you can hear His Voice clearly. To walk the path of peace is to walk the path of trust step by step, led by the assurance that He is good and He is guiding you.

Prayer:

Lord, guide me on the path of peace. Let righteousness govern my decisions and Your Spirit order my steps. Silence the noise of doubt and steady my heart with Your quiet assurance. Lead me where You desire to take me, and give me Grace to follow without fear. Wherever You lead, I will follow. In Jesus' Name, Amen.

Peace is the fruit of a heart walking in His way.

Day 17
The Promise Keeper

Scripture:

"There hath not failed one word of all His good promise."

1 Kings 8:56 (KJV)

Reflection:

God's Promises are not wishful ideas; they are the guarantees of a faithful Father. His Word is not fragile, and His covenant does not crumble under the weight of time. From generation to generation, every promise He has spoken has stood firm. Seasons may shift, circumstances may change, and emotions may rise and fall, but His Word has never failed not once.

Time may test your patience, but it will never diminish His Truth. When you cannot see the outcome, hold tightly to what He said. Promises often bloom in hidden soil long before the first signs of fruit appear. What looks like silence is often God working beneath the surface, aligning details, preparing hearts, and setting the stage for fulfillment.

Every word He Speaks carries the power to fulfill itself. His Promises do not depend on your strength, your timing, or your understanding; they depend on His Faithfulness. Trust is not measured by what you already hold in your hands, but by what you are willing to wait for because He spoke it. The Promise Keeper is not slow. He is perfect. He is not hesitant. He is intentional. And when the right moment comes, His Promise will unfold with a beauty that reveals why it had to take the time it did. Hold fast, beloved. Every word He has spoken over your life is alive, active, and appointed for its time.

Prayer:

Faithful God, thank You that not one of Your Promises has ever failed. Strengthen me to wait with patience, confidence, and unwavering trust. Help me remember that Your Word cannot return void and that every promise carries Your Power. Let my life become a testimony of Your faithfulness and of promises fulfilled by Your hand. In Jesus' Name, Amen.

The promise is sure because the Promiser is faithful.

Day 18
Still I Will Praise

Scripture:

"Though the fig tree shall not blossom, neither shall fruit be in the vines… yet I will rejoice in the Lord, I will joy in the God of my salvation."

Habakkuk 3:17 18 (KJV)

Reflection:

Praise in seasons of plenty is gratitude. Praise in seasons of loss is trust. When what you hoped for seems delayed, denied, or completely gone, praise becomes something deeper; it becomes a declaration: God is still good, and I am still His. The kind of faith that worships in the dark is the faith that has truly seen the light. It knows that God is not defined by what He gives but by Who He is. Habakkuk looked at barren fields, empty vines, and stripped-away blessings yet his response was worship. Not because the situation changed, but because his confidence in God did not.

Every yet I will rejoice, push back the night and invites Heaven into the very places where despair once tried to settle. Praise in pain becomes warfare. Praise in uncertainty becomes victory. Praise in disappointment becomes a seed that will one day bloom again. True trust does not praise God because circumstances are good, it praises Him because His character is unchanging. He remains faithful even when the field is empty. He remains worthy even when your hands feel empty. And He remains present even when your heart feels heavy. This kind of praise is not born of emotion it is born of revelation.

Prayer:

Lord, teach me to praise You when the harvest is bare and the answers feel far away. Let my worship rise as an act of faith, not feeling. Strengthen me to rejoice in who You are, even when I cannot see what You are doing. May my song in the valley be as loud as my shout on the mountain. You are always worthy. In Jesus' Name, Amen.

Praise is the language of unwavering trust.

Day 19
The Hand of Providence

Scripture:

"The steps of a good man are ordered by the Lord: and he delighteth in His way."

Psalm 37:23 (KJV)

Reflection:

Nothing in your life is random when it rests in God's Hands. His providence stitches together the invisible threads, the delays you didn't expect, the detours you didn't want, the closed doors you didn't understand, and the Divine connections you could never have orchestrated. What feels like a setback in the moment is often the very setup God is using to position you for a greater story.

God wastes nothing. Not a step, not a season, not a struggle. Even when life feels scattered, His Hand is steady. Even when the path feels uncertain, His Plan is sure. His ordering is not mechanical it is deeply personal, crafted with wisdom, love, and infinite foresight.

Trust looks backward and sees His Fingerprints; it looks forward and expects His Faithfulness. You don't have to understand every detail to rest in His direction. The same God Who led you before will lead you again. The same God Who protected you in past seasons is guiding you in this one.

The One Who orders your steps does not miscalculate. He does not lose track. He does not make mistakes. Every twist in the road carries intention. Every pause carries purpose. Every step is held within the sovereign choreography of a God Who delights in guiding you.

Your life is not wandering; it is being woven.

Prayer:

Lord, thank You for ordering my steps even when I cannot see the pattern. Help me walk by faith and not by sight. Strengthen my trust in Your perfect providence, and teach me to rest in the assurance that You are guiding every detail of my journey. Let my path become a testimony of Your sovereign hand at work in my life. In Jesus' Name, Amen.

Providence turns detours into Divine appointments.

Day 20
The Unseen Way

Scripture:

"Thy way is in the sea, and Thy path in the great waters, and Thy footsteps are not known."

Psalm 77:19 (KJV)

Reflection:

There are moments when God's path cannot be traced only trusted. The sea hides His footsteps, yet the waters still part at His command. His Ways are higher than your understanding, His thoughts deeper than your reasoning, and His methods often cloaked in mystery. But His Heart toward you? That remains unchanging.

Sometimes God leads you into places where visibility is limited and clarity seems absent not to confuse you, but to anchor you in trust. The unseen way is not abandonment; it is Divine direction veiled in wisdom. What feels hidden to you is fully known to Him.

When you cannot see what God is doing, you can still trust who He is. His silence is not His absence. His mystery is not His distance. Even when the path disappears beneath the waves, His Presence goes before you like an invisible compass. The Red Sea did not part until Moses stepped forward. The miracle waited on movement. The path appeared after obedience. This is the paradox of faith: sometimes you must move when the way is not yet visible. Sometimes your step of trust becomes the very thing that reveals God's direction. Where there seems to be no way, He is already making one. The unseen way is often the holiest one of all.

Prayer:

Lord, when I cannot see the way, remind me that You are the Way. Strengthen my heart to trust the invisible path You lay before me. Teach me to walk by faith into Your Promises, even when my eyes see no evidence. Let every hidden step draw me closer to Your Heart and deeper into Your purpose. In Jesus' Name, Amen.

When you can't trace His Hand, trust His Heart.

Day 21
The Anchor of Hope

Scripture:

"Which hope we have as an anchor of the soul, both sure and steadfast, and which entereth into that within the veil."

Hebrews 6:19 (KJV)

Reflection:

Hope is the steady hand that grips trust when the winds of uncertainty rise. It does not deny the storm it defies its pull. Hope is not wishful thinking; it is a spiritual anchor driven deep into the character of God. While circumstances shift and emotions waver, the God Who holds you does neither. Anchored hope rests in who He is unchanging, unfailing, and eternally faithful.

When your heart begins to drift, hope holds. When prayers seem delayed, hope whispers, He's still faithful. When fear tries to pull you into deep waters, hope keeps your soul from sinking. It is the quiet strength that refuses to let despair have the final word.

Behind the veil beyond what your natural eyes can see, God is already at work. His Promises are the weight that keeps your spirit grounded. His Presence is the rope that ties your soul to truth. Hope enters places you cannot, securing you to a reality higher than what you feel.

Hope does not depend on visible outcomes; it depends on the invisible God Who has never broken a promise. And because He is steadfast, your hope can be too.

Prayer:

Lord, be my anchor when the waters rise and my soul feels unsteady. Remind me that my hope is not fragile but firmly founded in Your unchanging Word. Hold me sure, steadfast, and unmovable in the midst of uncertainty. Keep my heart anchored in Your faithfulness, knowing You will never let me go. In Jesus' Name, Amen.

Hope holds firm when everything else feels uncertain.

Day 22
God of the Hills and Valleys

Scripture:

"The Lord God is my strength, and He will make my feet like hinds' feet, and He will make me to walk upon mine high places."

Habakkuk 3:19 (KJV)

Reflection:

The same God Who meets you on the mountain walks with you through the valley. His Strength does not rise and fall with your circumstances. Elevation may change, seasons may shift, emotions may fluctuate but His Presence remains constant. Trusting God means learning to praise Him in triumph and in trial, to recognize His Goodness in the Shadow as clearly as in the sunlight.

When the path climbs steep and feels overwhelming, He steadies your steps and strengthens your footing. Like a sure-footed deer navigating rugged terrain, God equips you to move with confidence where you once felt fearful. When the path descends into a valley, He holds you close, reminding you that you are never alone, not for a moment.

The valleys refine your dependence, teaching you to lean into His Heart. The mountaintops reveal perspective, allowing you to see the bigger picture of His Faithfulness. Both are necessary. Both are purposeful. And both are guided by the same faithful hand.

Every season becomes sacred when you walk it with Him. Whether heights or depths, joy or testing, gain or loss His Strength is your constant. His Presence is your assurance. And His Love   is your stability in every place.

Prayer:

Lord, thank You for being with me in every season on the mountain of joy and in the valley of testing. Strengthen my steps and make me sure-footed in faith. Help me trust Your guidance when the path is steep and Your comfort when the way is low. Let my praise rise from every place You lead me, knowing You are faithful through it all. In Jesus' Name, Amen.

Trust climbs higher and walks deeper when it sees God in both the hills and valleys.

Day 23
Streams in the Desert

Scripture:

"Behold, I will do a new thing; now it shall spring forth; shall ye not know it? I will even make away in the wilderness, and rivers in the desert."

Isaiah 43:19 (KJV)

Reflection:

God specializes in bringing life to barren places. When your surroundings feel dry and your strength feels drained, God leans close and whispers, I am doing a new thing. Deserts are not dead ends, they are the birthplaces of miracles. They strip away what is unnecessary so you can clearly see what only God can do.

The wilderness may feel endless, but it is never purposeless. Trust invites vision where sight is limited. Faith sees potential where the natural eye sees only sand. Beneath the surface of your desert, living water is already flowing. Beneath the disappointment, hope is rising. Beneath the exhaustion, renewal is preparing to break forth.

God never wastes wilderness seasons. He uses them to deepen your dependence, sharpen your discernment, and grow your expectations. What feels barren today will become tomorrow's testimony. The very ground that seemed lifeless will soon spring forth with His Glory.

When God says He will make rivers in the desert, He is promising not just survival but newness, refreshing, and abundance in the very place that once felt empty. He meets you in your desert not to leave you there, but to transform it into a place of encounter.

Prayer:

Father, thank You for the promise of newness in dry and weary places. Refresh my faith and water my soul where it feels depleted. Let Your Presence spring up within me like streams in the desert, bringing renewal, hope, and life to every barren area of my heart. Do a new thing in me, Lord, and let it spring forth in Your Perfect Timing. In Jesus' Name, Amen.

The desert blooms for those who trust the rainmaker.

Day 24
Perfect Peace

Scripture:

"Thou wilt keep him in perfect peace, whose mind is stayed on Thee: because he trusteth in Thee."

Isaiah 26:3 (KJV)

Reflection:

Peace is not found by changing what surrounds you, it is found by fixing your gaze on the One Who dwells within you. When your mind is anchored in God, fear cannot overthrow you. Anxiety may knock at the door, but it cannot take residence in a heart guarded by trust. Perfect peace is not the product of perfect circumstances; it is the fruit of perfect trust.

Every anxious thought is not condemnation; it is an invitation. An invitation to realign your focus, to shift your gaze, to steady your soul on the Truth of who God is. When you choose to meditate on His Word instead of the what-ifs, His Voice becomes louder than your worry.

His Peace doesn't merely calm the troubled heart, it guards it. It fortifies your mind, protects your emotions, and strengthens your spirit. It becomes a shield against fear and a sanctuary from turmoil. This Peace is not temporary, fragile, or fleeting. It flows from the unchanging character of God. And as you keep your mind fixed, focused, and settled on Him, peace becomes not just an experience, but a lifestyle. Perfect peace is not the absence of storms, it is the Presence of God within them.

Prayer:

Lord, steady my thoughts on You. Keep my heart in perfect peace as I trust in Your unfailing care. Quiet every fear with the strength of Your Presence, and renew my confidence in Your Goodness. Teach me to fix my mind on You until peace becomes the natural rhythm of my soul. In Jesus' Name, Amen.

Peace reigns where the mind remains on God.

Day 25
The Weight of Glory

Scripture:

"For our light affliction, which is but for a moment, worketh for us a far more exceeding and eternal weight of Glory."

2 Corinthians 4:17 (KJV)

Reflection:

Every trial carries a hidden Glory, and every burden holds a Divine purpose. What feels unbearably heavy today is producing something eternal within you, something far greater than the pain of the moment. Trust lifts your eyes beyond what hurts to what is being shaped. Faith sees not just the hardship, but the holy work happening behind it.

The refining fire does not diminish your worth, it reveals it. Just as gold is purified in flames, so the believer is formed in seasons of pressure. Heaven measures value differently than earth; what we call affliction, God calls preparation. What we label as loss, He identifies as increase. What feels like breaking becomes the ground where Glory is born.

God is not wasting your suffering. He is working in it producing depth, endurance, compassion, and strength you could not gain any other way. These momentary afflictions are not the end of your story; they are the chisels shaping you for eternity.

When you choose trust in the middle of hardship, you are being fitted for Glory that will never fade. The weight you feel now is light compared to the brilliance He is preparing. And when the story is complete, you will see that every tear, every trial, and every moment of endurance was woven into something breathtakingly beautiful.

Prayer:

Lord, help me to see my trials through the lens of eternity. Let every hardship draw me nearer to Your Heart and shape me more into Your likeness. Strengthen me to trust that every weight I carry is producing something far greater in Your plan. Refine me, Lord, and let the Glory You are forming within me shine for Your Name's sake. In Jesus' Name, Amen.

Present pain cannot compare to the Glory it produces.

Day 26
Faith That Moves Mountains

Scripture:

"For verily I say unto you, That whosoever shall say unto this mountain, Be thou removed, and be thou cast into the sea; and shall not doubt in His Heart, but shall believe that those things which he saith shall come to pass; he shall have whatsoever he saith."

Mark 11:23 (KJV)

Reflection:

Faith does not deny the mountain it speaks to it. Trusting God doesn't mean pretending obstacles aren't real; it means believing that His Power is greater than anything that stands in front of you. The God Who spoke creation into existence has placed His Word in your mouth and His authority in your spirit. He invites you not just to endure mountains, but to confront them. Mountains move when hearts align with Heaven. When your prayers are shaped by belief rather than fear, they carry Divine weight. When your words echo God's Promises instead of your uncertainties, the spiritual atmosphere begins to shift. Faith-filled declarations are not arrogance, they are agreement with God.

The Voice of faith doesn't need to shout; it needs to stand. It is anchored, unwavering, and rooted in conviction. It speaks God's Truth until every opposing thing must bow to it. Mountains may look immovable, but they cannot resist the authority of God released through a believing heart. Faith speaks. Faith stands. Faith sees beyond the natural. And faith moves what once seemed impossible.

Prayer:

Lord, increase my faith to believe beyond what I see. Teach me to speak Your Word with holy confidence and to trust that You can move every obstacle in Your perfect time and perfect way. Strengthen my heart so that my prayers echo Your Power and my words release Your Will. Let every mountain before me bow to Your Authority. In Jesus' Name, Amen.

Faith moves what fear magnifies.

Day 27
The Unshaken Heart

Scripture:

"He only is my rock and my salvation: He is my defence; I shall not be greatly moved."

Psalm 62:2 (KJV)

Reflection:

Trust doesn't prevent storms, it anchors you through them. The heart that stands upon the Rock of Ages may feel the wind, but it will not fall. When everything else shifts, God remains unshaken. Stability is not found in controlling the storm but in clinging to the One Who commands it.

You are not called to calm the waves you are called to stand on the Rock. Each wave that crashes become another testimony of His steady strength. Trust reminds you that no circumstance can undo what His Hand has secured. Your footing is not your own; it is held firm by the God Who never moves.

Prayer:

Father, be my Rock when the earth trembles and my defense when fear rises. Let my heart remain unshaken because it rests in You alone. Strengthen me to stand firm and trust that Your Word endures forever. In Jesus' Name, Amen.

An anchored heart remains unmoved by changing tides.

Day 28
The Potter's Hands

Scripture:

"But now, O Lord, Thou art our father; we are the clay, and Thou our potter; and we all are the work of Thy hand."

Isaiah 64:8 (KJV)

Reflection:

The hands that carved mountains, flung galaxies into the heavens, and breathed life into dust are the same hands shaping you. The molding process may feel like pressure, stretching, and reshaping, but every movement is precise and every touch is guided by perfect love. The Potter never harms His clay; He forms it with intention, knowing exactly what He is crafting it to become.

Trust means staying on the wheel even when it spins faster than you understand. The shaping seasons may feel uncomfortable or uncertain, but the Potter's hands never leave you. What feels like breaking is often the refining that brings forth beauty. What feels like being undone is actually being remade. And what looks like delay is often His preparation for greater purpose.

The Potter sees the finished vessel long before the clay recognizes its own potential. He is committed to forming you until your life reflects His Glory, carries His Presence, and fulfills the purpose He envisioned from the beginning. You are not abandoned in the process; you are held, shaped, and loved into becoming.

Prayer:

Lord, I yield myself to Your hands. Shape me according to Your Will and mold me into the vessel You desire. Smooth the rough places, refine the broken pieces, and form in me a heart that reflects Your Character. Let every part of my life carry Your beauty, reveal Your workmanship, and fulfill Your purpose. In Jesus' Name, Amen.

Trust is staying on the wheel until the Potter's work is complete.

Day 29
God's Timing Is Perfect

Scripture:

"He hath made everything beautiful in His time."

Ecclesiastes 3:11 (KJV)

Reflection:

Trust is deeply connected to timing. God's timing, not ours, is the thread that weaves beauty through every chapter of our lives. The unfolding of His Plan is often hidden in the waiting in-between seasons where nothing appears to be changing, yet everything is being aligned behind the scenes. When things seem delayed, Heaven is arranging details you cannot see and preparing outcomes you would not imagine.

The God Who authored your story knows the exact moment to bring each promise into bloom. Impatience tries to rush what faith is still preparing. But when you place the clock in God's Hands, you begin to discover peace in the process, not just in the outcome. Every promise has an appointed season, and the One Who sets the times and seasons never arrives early and never comes late. His timing is not merely good, it is perfect.

Your waiting is not wasted. Your delays are not denials. And the beauty God is preparing will be worth every moment of trust.

Prayer:

Father, teach my heart to rest in Your Perfect Timing. When impatience rises or fear whispers that I am falling behind, remind me that You are never late and never unaware. Align my desires with Your Will and steady my spirit in seasons of waiting. Help me trust that Your Timing is preparing something beautiful, and make me content to wait until Your purpose unfolds. In Jesus' Name, Amen.

What God begins in promise, He perfects in time.

Day 30
The Refuge of His Presence

Scripture:

"Thou art my hiding place; Thou shalt preserve me from trouble; Thou shalt compass me about with songs of deliverance."

Psalm 32:7 (KJV)

Reflection:

When life becomes overwhelming, the safest place is not found in escape, distraction, or self-reliance; it is found in the Presence of God. He never promised a life without trouble, but He has promised Himself as your covering, your peace, and your place of refuge. When fear presses in, trust steps beneath His wings and listens for the song Heaven sings over the weary soul.

The Presence of God is not limited to a sanctuary or a set moment it dwells in every surrendered heart. You carry a refuge with you because you carry Him. When anxiety rises, when pressure closes in, you are invited to run not away, but into His Presence. There, you find your fortress, your comfort, your shield, your peace, your song.

His Peace becomes a barrier that trouble cannot break through. His nearness becomes the deliverance that steadies your heart. The refuge of His Presence is not just a place you visit; it is the place where you are held, preserved, strengthened, and set free.

Prayer:

Lord, You are my hiding place and my refuge. Cover me with Your Peace and surround me with the nearness of Your Presence. When fear draws close, remind me that I am safe in You. Let Your songs of deliverance rise within me driving out every shadow, calming every storm, and filling me with Your unshakable peace. In Jesus' Name, Amen.

The safest place in every storm is the presence of God.

Day 31
The Keeper of My Soul

Scripture:

"The Lord shall preserve thy going out and thy coming in from this time forth, and even forevermore."

Psalm 121:8 (KJV)

Reflection:

Trust is knowing that God never loses sight of you not for a moment, not in a single step, not in any season. You are never unattended. The One Who guards the galaxies also guards your going out and your coming in. His care is constant, deliberate, and deeply personal.

Every detail of your journey matters to Him: the paths you walk, the decisions you face, the nights you lie awake, and the mornings you rise with new strength. When the road ahead feels uncertain or the days feel unsteady, remind yourself of this unchanging truth: He is the Keeper of your soul.

His Hand shields you from what you cannot see. His Mercy preserves you from what could have overwhelmed you. His Love upholds you when your own strength falters. You are never beyond His reach, never outside the circle of His protection, and never forgotten. The Keeper of your soul does not sleep, does not grow weary, and does not abandon what He treasures and He treasures you.

Prayer:

Lord, thank You for watching over my life with unfailing love and steady care. Keep my heart anchored in Your faithfulness and my steps aligned with Your path. When uncertainties arise, let me rest in the assurance that You preserve me in every season, in every moment, and in every place. Hold me close and keep me always in the safety of Your Presence. In Jesus' Name, Amen.

The One Who called you will also keep you.

Day 32
The Benefits of Prayer

Scripture:

"When we draw near to God, prayer becomes the bridge that carries our hearts into His Presence. Draw nigh to God, and He will draw nigh to you."

James 4:8 (KJV)

Reflection:

Prayer is not a ritual; it is communion with our Creator. It draws us closer to the heart of the Father, aligning our desires with His will. Through prayer, peace replaces anxiety, and His Presence becomes our dwelling place. Every whispered word is heard, and every heart cry is met with His tender mercy. Prayer builds us up, strengthens us in times of temptation, and clothes us in spiritual armor to stand in victory.

Prayer:

Heavenly Father, thank You for the privilege of prayer. Teach me to come before You with reverence, gratitude, and expectancy. Let my prayers be filled with faith, guided by Your Spirit, and rooted in Your Will. Draw me closer to You each day, and let my life reflect the peace that comes from abiding in Your Presence. In Jesus' Name, Amen.

Day 33
Hidden Blessings

Scripture:

"And we know that all things work together for good to them that love God, to them who are the called according to His Purpose."

Romans 8:28 (KJV)

Reflection:

Some blessings do not arrive looking like blessings at all. They come wrapped in difficulty, disguised as delay, disappointment, or detours you never expected. Yet trust lifts the veil and teaches the heart to see deeper   to recognize that God is working even when the process feels painful.

God wastes nothing. Not the tears you've cried, not the prayers you prayed in the dark, not the losses that still ache when remembered. Every moment   even the ones that felt like breaking are being folded into His design for good. He is the Master Weaver, threading mercy through trials, hope through heartache, and purpose through every season that felt unclear.

You may not always understand the pattern, but you can trust the One Who holds the threads. In time, the pieces that once looked broken will reveal a beauty that only Heaven could orchestrate. What confused you then will comfort you later. What felt hidden will shine with purpose. And what seems to hinder you will be the very thing God uses to shape you.

Prayer:

Father, thank You for working all things together for my good, even in the moments I do not understand. Open my eyes to see Your Hand in the hidden places. Strengthen my trust when I cannot see the full picture, and anchor my heart in the confidence that Your purpose is always good, always faithful, and always perfect. In Jesus' Name, Amen.

Even unseen blessings are perfectly placed by His Hand.

Day 34
Safe in His Hands

Scripture:

"And I give unto them eternal life; and they shall never perish, neither shall any man pluck them out of My Hand."

John 10:28 (KJV)

Reflection:

There is no safer place than the hand of God. The same hands that shaped galaxies and formed the foundations of the earth now cradle your life with unwavering care. His grip is not fragile. His hold is not temporary. No trial, no failure, no attack of the enemy can pull you from the security of His Love. Trust means resting, not striving in His hold. Even when the path feels steep or uncertain, you are not hanging on to God by your own strength; He is holding you by His. You don't have to cling in fear, because the One Who carries you cannot lose what He has claimed.

- His Hand is your protection when danger surrounds.
- His Hand is your guidance when decisions feel unclear.
- His Hand is your comfort when the night feels long.
- His Hand is your assurance that you are never abandoned.

To be in His Hand is to be enveloped in love, covered in Grace, and guarded by a strength greater than anything you face.

Prayer:

Lord, thank You for holding me so securely in Your Hands. When fear tries to steal my peace, remind me that I am Yours and nothing can separate me from Your Love. Strengthen my faith to rest fully in Your unfailing protection, Your steady grip, and Your tender care. Keep my heart anchored in the safety of Your presence. In Jesus' Name, Amen.

The hand that holds you will never let you go.

Day 35
The Faithfulness of God

Scripture:

"It is of the Lord's mercies that we are not consumed, because His compassions fail not. They are new every morning: great is Thy faithfulness."

Lamentations 3:22 - 23 (KJV)

Reflection:

Every sunrise is a sermon of God's faithfulness. Before your feet touch the ground, mercy has already met you. Before a single word is spoken, compassion is already covering you. Before the day unfolds, Grace is already going ahead of you. Trust grows when you remember yesterday's deliverance and recognize today's provision.

God never forgets, never falters, and never fails. His compassion does not run out not on your weary days, not on your stumbling days, not on your broken days. His Faithfulness renews like the dawn steady, gentle, consistent, and sure. Even when life feels unpredictable, He remains the One Who changes not.

The heart that trusts doesn't wonder if God will be faithful; it rests securely knowing He already is. His record is flawless. His Love is unwavering. His Presence is constant. And His Mercy meets you every morning as a reminder: He has not forgotten you. He has not abandoned you. He is faithful, always.

Prayer:

Lord, thank You for Your unending faithfulness. Each morning declares that You are the same yesterday, today, and forever. Let my life reflect the steadiness of Your mercy and the strength of Your truth. Teach me to trust Your Heart in every season and to rest in the renewal You give each day. In Jesus' Name, Amen.

Faith finds rest in the unchanging faithfulness of God.

Day 36
The Substance of Things Hoped For

Scripture:

"Now faith is the substance of things hoped for, the evidence of things not seen."

Hebrews 11:1 (KJV)

Reflection:

Faith is not wishful thinking; it is confident knowing. Hope imagines what could be, but faith steps forward as if it already is. Faith does not float in emotion; it stands with substance. It gives form, shape, and weight to what the heart expects from God. To believe before you see is not denial, it is Divine alignment with Heaven's reality.

Faith pulls unseen promises into visible manifestation. It walks in obedience long before the evidence appears. It stands firm when circumstances offer no proof, because God's Word is its proof. When doubt whispers, What if it doesn't happen? faith responds with quiet authority, God said, therefore it will.

Faith refuses to be swayed by what the natural eye cannot detect. It sees with the spirit. It holds with conviction. It rests in the Truth that what God has spoken is already settled in eternity. The unseen becomes certain when anchored in His unfailing truth.

Faith is not fragile, it is the confident assurance that every promise will take shape exactly as God has declared.

Prayer:

Father, thank You for the gift of faith. Strengthen me to believe beyond what my eyes can see and to trust what You have spoken more than what I feel. Let my hope take form through obedience, and let my heart remain steadfast in every promise You have made. Shape my expectations to match Your Word, and teach me to rest in the certainty of Your truth. In Jesus' Name, Amen.

Faith gives form to what hope can only imagine.

Day 37
A Heart That Believes

Scripture:

"Jesus said unto him, If thou canst believe, all things are possible to him that believeth."

Mark 9:23 (KJV)

Reflection:

Faith does not begin with sight, it begins with surrender. A believing heart is not one that has every answer; it is one that has made the choice to trust even when understanding falls short. God moves through those who dare to believe Him before they see Him work. Faith is not the absence of questions, it is the refusal to let questions overrule trust.

Doubt builds walls around the heart, but belief opens doors to the impossible. The miracle is never found in human striving; it is discovered in yielded confidence that nothing is too hard for the Lord. When you choose to believe, you step into the realm where Heaven responds.

The measure of faith is not how much you understand, how much you feel, or how much you can figure out. The measure of faith is how much you are willing to trust the One Who knows all, sees all, holds all, and loves without limits. A believing heart becomes the vessel through which God reveals His Power.

Prayer:

Lord, I believe help my unbelief. Strengthen every place where my faith wavers and breathe courage into the corners of my heart. Let belief rise where fear once lived, and let trust take root where doubt once spoke loudly. Make my heart a resting place for Your Truth and a doorway for Your Power to move. In Jesus' Name, Amen.

The heart that believes is the soil where miracles grow.

Day 38
Divine Appointments

Scripture:

"The steps of a good man are ordered by the Lord: and he delighteth in His way."

Psalm 37:23 (KJV)

Reflection:

Faith walks into what God has already prepared. Nothing in the Kingdom is coincidence; every moment is woven with purpose. There are Divine appointments hidden inside ordinary days, sacred connections tucked within what seems routine. God is always aligning hearts, timing, and paths to fulfill His greater plan.

When you live with expectation, interruptions no longer frustrate you; they invite you. Delays stop feeling like detours, they become directions. Closed doors become protection. Unexpected moments become assignments. The believer who walks by faith understands that every step is sacred and every encounter intentional.

God wastes nothing. Not a moment. Not a meeting. Not a delay. Not a conversation.

He orders everything with precision and love. Even when you cannot see the full picture, Heaven is arranging every detail around your obedience. You are never simply going through your day, you are walking through a Divinely scripted path where God has already gone before you. Open your heart, lift your eyes, and expect Him. Every step is a setup for destiny.

Prayer:

Father, thank You for the Divine appointments You place along my path. Open my eyes to recognize Your Hand in every detail and every encounter. Teach me to walk with purpose, sensitivity, and expectation, trusting that each step I take is guided by Your wisdom. Lead me into the places You've prepared and align my heart with Your perfect direction. In Jesus' Name, Amen.

Faith sees providence where others see coincidence.

Day 39
Stepping Out of the Boat

Scripture:

"And Peter answered Him and said, Lord, if it be Thou, bid me come unto Thee on the water. And He said, Come."

Matthew 14:28 - 29 (KJV)

Reflection:

Faith will always call you beyond comfort. The boat represents what is familiar, predictable, and safe but miracles are never found where fear keeps you still. Peter didn't walk on water; he walked on the Word. One word Come became the bridge between doubt and destiny. The same Voice that calmed the sea is the Voice that calls you forward.

To step out is to declare that obedience is safer than security, because safety is not found in the boat it is found in Jesus. Waves may rise, winds may howl, and fear may whisper, but Jesus never lets the faithful sink. The water that threatens becomes the pathway to His Presence.

Every step of courage brings you closer to Him and further from fear. Faith is not the absence of trembling it is the choice to move toward the One Who stands above the storm. When your eyes are fixed on Jesus, the impossible becomes your invitation and the supernatural becomes your steady ground. He is still whispering Come to every heart willing to trust Him.

Prayer:

Lord, call me out where faith is required. Give me courage to leave the familiar and step toward You. When the waves roar, steady my steps and strengthen my focus. Lift my eyes above the storm until I find myself walking with You in the impossible. In Jesus' Name, Amen.

Faith begins where comfort ends.

Day 40
Eyes Fixed on the Promise

Scripture:

"Looking unto Jesus the author and finisher of our faith."

Hebrews 12:2 (KJV)

Reflection:

Faith follows focus. What you fix your eyes on determines what grows within you. When your gaze is set on the promise instead of the problem, your perspective shifts from fear to confidence. Jesus is not only the Author who writes the first line of your story He is the Finisher who completes it with purpose and victory. He initiates your faith, sustains your faith, and perfects your faith.

Distraction dilutes faith. It pulls your attention toward what is temporary instead of what is eternal. But devotion strengthens it. Every time you choose to look to Jesus above the noise, above the pressure, above the circumstance your faith deepens and your courage rises.

The One you look to never loses sight of you. His eyes are fixed on every detail of your journey. He sees the beginning from the end, and He guides with precision and love. The promise will come to pass, not because you hold tightly to Him, but because He holds faithfully to you. Keep looking to Jesus. Where your eyes rest, your faith will follow.

Prayer:

Lord, fix my eyes on You. When distractions arise and doubts try to pull me away, draw my gaze back to Your Word and Your Presence. Help me trust the story You are writing and follow You with unwavering focus. Strengthen my heart until the promise You spoke becomes the promise I see. In Jesus' Name, Amen.

Faith grows when eyes remain fixed on Jesus.

Day 41
Prepared for the Promise

Scripture:

"For the vision is yet for an appointed time, but at the end it shall speak, and not lie: though it tarry, wait for it; because it will surely come, it will not tarry."

Habakkuk 2:3 (KJV)

Reflection:

God's Promises always arrive dressed in preparation. Before the vision is fulfilled, the vessel must be formed. Waiting seasons are not wasted seasons; they are workshops of faith, classrooms of trust, and sanctuaries of transformation. God does not delay to disappoint He delays to develop.

When what He spoke feels distant or slow, remember: He is not just preparing the promise; He is preparing you to carry it. There is a weight to every blessing and a responsibility attached to every fulfilled word. The waiting is where He strengthens your character, sharpens your discernment, and deepens your dependence.

What you cultivate in the quiet determines how you will steward the blessing when it comes. Patience produces stability. Humility protects purpose. Surrender purifies motives. Trust strengthens vision.

The vision will speak clearly, loudly, undeniably. And when it does, it will testify of a faith that chose to wait well, a heart that refused to grow weary, and a life shaped by the God Who finishes what He starts.

Prayer:

Lord, thank You for the promises You've spoken over my life. Teach me to prepare with patience and to grow in the waiting. Strengthen my faith to remain steadfast when the vision feels far away. Shape my character so I can carry the blessing well. And when the appointed time arrives, let Your Word come to pass in fullness and Glory. In Jesus' Name, Amen.

The promise delays only until you're ready to receive it.

Day 42
Faith That Speaks

Scripture:

"We having the same spirit of faith, according as it is written, I believed, and therefore have I spoken; we also believe, and therefore speak."

2 Corinthians 4:13 (KJV)

Reflection:

Faith is never silent; it speaks what it believes long before it sees results. The tongue of faith does not echo fear; it declares truth. It does not repeat what circumstances say; it proclaims what God has already spoken. When you speak God's Word with confidence, Heaven aligns with what has been decreed in eternity.

Words shape the world around you. Faith-filled speech carries spiritual authority. When you confess His Promises, you open the door for their manifestation. When you agree with Heaven, you silence hell. Faith speaks life where the enemy whispers death. It speaks hope where despair tries to settle. It speaks light into places where shadows linger.

Your voice becomes a vessel of victory not because of your power, but because it carries His Word, His Truth, and His authority. What you release from your mouth reveals what you believe in your heart. Let your confession match your expectation. Let your words align with His will.

Speak boldly. Speak biblically. Speak with the spirit of faith and watch mountains move.

Prayer:

Lord, let my words agree with Your Word. Teach me to speak life, blessing, and Truth over every situation. Silence every seed of doubt within me and let the spirit of faith rise until my confession matches Your Promise. Use my voice as an instrument of Your Authority and a carrier of Your Victory. In Jesus' Name, Amen.

Faith finds its strength when belief becomes declaration.

Day 43
When Heaven Delays

Scripture:

"But they that wait upon the Lord shall renew their strength; they shall mount up with wings a eagles; they shall run, and not be weary; and they shall walk, and not faint."

Isaiah 40:31 (KJV)

Reflection:

Delay is not denial, it is Divine pacing. God's timing is intentional, precise, and always purposeful, even when it feels painfully slow. In the waiting, faith is stretched, strengthened, and refined. Delay becomes the sacred place where endurance is born, and endurance produces a maturity that cannot be cultivated any other way.

The waiting season does not weaken you; it renews you. It peels away self-reliance and teaches you to lean wholly on Him. Heaven's delay is often the testing ground of expectation where your hope is purified, your vision clarified, and your trust deepened.

When your heart grows weary, remember: the eagle does not fight the wind; it rises on it. The very resistance that appears to oppose you may be the lift that carries you higher. What feels like delay is often the wind beneath your wings, positioning you for greater altitude, clearer sight, and deeper dependence on God. Trust the wind beneath your waiting. God is not late. He is preparing you to soar.

Prayer:

Lord, when Heaven seems silent and answers feel distant, renew my strength. Lift my heart above discouragement and teach me to soar instead of struggle. Help me wait with worship instead of worry, and trust that Your Timing is perfecting my faith. Let the wind of Your Spirit carry me higher while I wait on You. In Jesus' Name, Amen.

Delays refine faith until it shines like gold.

Day 44
The God Who Finishes

Scripture:

"Being confident of this very thing, that He which hath begun a good work in you will perform it until the day of Jesus Christ."

Philippians 1:6 (KJV)

Reflection:

God never abandons what He begins. The same hands that formed you, called you, and started your story will be the hands that bring it to completion. He is not a halfway God. He is the God Who finishes. Faith becomes the bridge between His Promise and its fulfillment. When you feel unfinished, uncertain, or incomplete, remember this simple truth: the Author is still writing.

Progress may feel slow, but His Plan is never off track. What looks like delay is often alignment. What feels like a detour is often direction. God's work in you doesn't stall when life becomes difficult; instead, He weaves every moment, every joy, every tear, every stretch into His perfect design.

You are not unfinished because you lack something, you are unfinished because He is still shaping something. The God Who began your good work isn't improvising as He goes; He is perfecting purpose with precision. Trust the process, even when it feels unclear. Trust the timeline, even when it feels long. What He starts in Grace, He always completes in Glory.

Prayer:

Faithful Father, thank You that You finish what You begin. Strengthen my confidence in Your ongoing work within me. Let every unfinished place in my life become a canvas for Your faithfulness. Help me trust Your Timing, Your process, and Your perfect plan until Your work in me is complete. In Jesus' Name, Amen.

What God begins in mercy, He completes in majesty.

Day 45
The Power of Expectation

Scripture:

"And blessed is she that believed: for there shall be a performance of those things which were told her from the Lord."

Luke 1:45 (KJV)

Reflection:

Expectation is the birthplace of manifestation. Mary did not strive; she simply believed. She received God's Word with a heart open to the impossible, and Heaven brought it to pass. What you believe about God shapes what you experience from Him. Faith opens the door, but expectation prepares the room.

Expectation draws the supernatural into the natural. It is the stance of a heart that says, God is moving even when I cannot see it. Expectation watches for Him. It prepares for Him. It makes space for Him. When you anticipate God's movement, you align your life with His Promise and posture your heart for fulfillment. Faith declares, It will happen. Expectation adds, And it could happen today.

This holy anticipation is not wishful thinking; it is rooted in the character of a God Who never lies and never fails. Expectation shifts the atmosphere. It fuels hope. It silences doubt. It magnifies the God Who performs what He promises. The blessing is not simply in believing it is in believing with expectation.

Prayer:

Lord, fill me with holy expectation. Help me believe that every word You have spoken is already in motion. Let my faith attract the performance of Your Promises, and let my heart remain ready to receive all that You have prepared. Stir within me a confident anticipation that You are working even now. In Jesus' Name, Amen.

Expectation positions you for Divine performance.

Section Two:
Faith And Expectation

Day 46
Faith in the Fire

Scripture:

"When thou walkest through the fire, thou shalt not be burned; neither shall the flame kindle upon thee."

Isaiah 43:2 (KJV)

Reflection:

Faith doesn't flee the fire, it walks through it with assurance. God never promised the absence of trials, but He did promise His Presence in the midst of them. The flames that should have consumed you become the very light that reveals His Glory resting upon your life.

Fire purifies what fear contaminates. It burns away self-reliance, pride, and anything unstable, until trust remains unshaken. What feels like the fiercest heat often becomes the place where God's nearness becomes unmistakable. The fire that threatened to destroy you becomes the furnace where your faith is strengthened beyond measure.

When everything around you shakes, your faith becomes a testimony not to your strength, but to the God Who keeps His Word. You don't simply survive the fire, you shine through it. The flames refine, but they cannot define. The trial tests, but it cannot triumph over the one held by God. Your faith in the fire becomes a beacon that declares, He is with me, and He is faithful.

Prayer:

Lord, thank You for walking with me through the fire. When I face heat and hardship, remind me that Your presence is my protection and Your Promise is my peace. Let the flames refine me, not define me. Remove what hinders and strengthen what remains, until my faith reflects Your Glory alone. In Jesus' Name, Amen.

Faith doesn't burn, it glows brighter in the fire.

Day 47
The Sound of Rain

Scripture:

"And Elijah said unto Ahab, Get thee up, eat and drink; for there is a sound of abundance of rain."

1 Kings 18:41 (KJV)

Reflection:

Faith hears what the natural ear cannot detect. Long before a cloud formed, Elijah heard rain. He discerned breakthrough before it appeared, because expectation tunes the spirit to Heaven's frequency. Faith listens beyond circumstances and catches the whisper of what God is about to do.

When faith listens, it begins to prepare. Elijah didn't wait for the sky to darken; he built an altar in the middle of the drought. He worshiped before the wind shifted. He bowed before a single drop fell. Likewise, you prepare in praise even when the atmosphere around you feels barren. Your altar becomes the place where drought ends and expectation rises.

God always sends rain to the heart that believes in His coming abundance. Even when the sky looks empty, Heaven is gathering clouds. Even when the wait feels long, the sound of provision is already moving toward you. The promise precedes the manifestation.

Faith hears the rain before it falls. Faith looks up when others look down. Faith prepares the ground for what God has promised. If you listen closely, you'll hear the sound of something new, something full, something God-sized drawing near.

Prayer:

Lord, let me hear the sound of Your coming rain. Tune my heart to the frequency of Heaven so I recognize breakthrough before it arrives. Help me prepare in faith long before I see results, and let my worship call forth what You have promised. May my expectation water the ground for miracles. In Jesus' Name, Amen.

Faith hears the rain before clouds ever form.

Day 48
The God Who Makes a Way

Scripture:

"Thus saith the Lord, which maketh a way in the sea, and a path in the mighty waters."

Isaiah 43:16 (KJV)

Reflection:

When there is no way, God creates one. The Red Sea stood as an impossible barrier until faith stepped forward. What looked like a dead end became the very platform where God revealed His unmatched power. Your greatest obstacles are often the stages where Heaven writes its most breathtaking stories.

God specializes in paths no one else can see. Long before you face the barrier, He has already carved the route. Long before you reach the impossibility, He has already arranged the miracle. The God Who carved a highway through the sea still opens doors that no man can shut, softens hearts that seemed unmovable, and orchestrates opportunities that only His Hand could prepare.

Faith doesn't need to see the entire route; it only needs to trust the Waymaker. You may not know how He will do it, when He will do it, or which direction He will lead, but you can rest in His Truth: He always goes ahead of you. And wherever He walks, a way is formed.

The sea obeys Him. The storm recognizes Him. The impossible yields to Him. Your only task is to follow in faith.

Prayer:

Lord, thank You for being the God Who makes a way where there seems to be none. Strengthen my faith to move forward even when the path is hidden. Let every obstacle become an opportunity for Your Glory. Guide my steps into the way You have prepared and show Yourself strong on my behalf. In Jesus' Name, Amen.

Where faith steps, God makes a way.

Day 49
Unwavering Faith

Scripture:

"He staggered not at the promise of God through unbelief; but was strong in faith, giving Glory to God."

Romans 4:20 (KJV)

Reflection:

Faith that glorifies God stands firm when logic falters. Abraham didn't remain steady because he understood the promise he remained steady because he was persuaded by the character of the One Who spoke it. Faith is not built on evidence but on the unchanging nature of God. When your heart becomes convinced of who He is, wavering loses its power.

Unwavering faith is not dramatic or loud, it is consistent. It whispers praise when progress is invisible. It worships when signs are absent. It stands firm when everything else around you collapses. This kind of faith doesn't depend on emotion; it depends on endurance. It is strengthened not by what it sees but by what it knows: God is faithful, and His Word cannot fail.

Unwavering faith is forged in the waiting, refined in the testing, and revealed in the standing. It honors God not only when the promise arrives, but long before when all you have is His Word and the confidence that He cannot lie.

Faith that refuses to stagger becomes faith that gives Him Glory.

Prayer:

Lord, strengthen my faith to remain steady. When doubts arise, anchor my heart in Your Word. Teach me to praise You even before the promise manifests, and to trust Your Character above my circumstances. Let my unwavering confidence honor You in all things and reveal the steadfastness of Your Love. In Jesus' Name, Amen.

Faith that refuses to waver gives God the greatest Glory.

Day 50
The Dawn of Promise

Scripture:

"For His anger endureth but a moment; in His favour is life: weeping may endure for a night, but joy cometh in the morning."

Psalm 30:5 (KJV)

Reflection:

Every promise has a dawn. Nights may feel long, heavy, and unending, but darkness has a limit it cannot outlast the light of God's faithfulness. Faith endures the night not with despair, but with quiet assurance that joy is already on its way. Even when you cannot see the horizon, Heaven is preparing the light.

Morning always comes for the believer who waits in worship. The tears that fall in the night do not fall in vain; they water the ground of your promise. The prayers you whispered in brokenness become the dew that nourishes new beginnings. God turns your midnight cries into the melodies of a new morning.

The promise will rise not because of your strength, but because of His Mercy. Not because you held on perfectly, but because He held you. Not because you could see the way forward, but because He is the Light that leads you. No night lasts forever. No sorrow is permanent. Joy is not an emotion you chase; it is a promise that pursues you. And when the morning breaks, it carries the unmistakable glow of God's unfailing love.

Prayer:

Lord, thank You that every night of sorrow gives way to a morning of joy. Strengthen me to trust You in the waiting and to worship even in the dark. When the dawn breaks, let my heart rejoice in the brightness of Your faithfulness. Let the light of Your Promise renew my **hope** and restore my joy. In Jesus' Name, Amen.

Faith holds on through the night until promise greets the morning.

Day 51
The Waiting Heart

Scripture:

"I waited patiently for the Lord; and He inclined unto me, and heard my cry."

Psalm 40:1 (KJV)

Reflection:

Waiting is not idleness, it is trust in motion. A waiting heart does not withdraw; it leans in. It listens. It yields. Every moment of silence becomes a sacred exchange where God bends low, hears deeply, and strengthens quietly. Waiting is not a pause in God's Plan, it is part of the plan.

When your heart aches for answers, remember this: He hears before you finish speaking. His attention is immediate even when His action is unfolding in unseen places. Heaven's response is never late; it always arrives wrapped in wisdom.

The wait stretches your faith not to break it, but to expand its capacity for blessing. Patience is the melody faith hums while Heaven arranges the harmony. The waiting heart is refined, steadied, and deepened in ways that only stillness can accomplish.

What seems like delay is often Divine preparation. What feels like silence is often God speaking in ways you're learning to discern. Trust the slow work of God. He is never idle in the stillness.

Prayer:

Lord, teach me to wait with peace and confidence in Your Perfect Timing. Calm the restlessness within me and remind me that delay is not distance. Incline Your ear to my cry and steady my heart in Your Presence. Let my waiting bring You Glory and shape me for the blessing You have prepared. In Jesus' Name, Amen.

A waiting heart is a worshiping heart.

Day 52
Faith That Pleases God

Scripture:

"But without faith it is impossible to please Him: for he that cometh to God must believe that He is, and that He is a rewarder of them that diligently seek Him."

Hebrews 11:6 (KJV)

Reflection:

Faith is the language Heaven understands. It pleases God because it declares trust in His character before you see His outcome. Faith honors who He is even when circumstances are unclear. It says, God, I trust Your Heart even when I cannot trace Your Hand.

To believe that He is that's recognition. To believe that He rewards that relationship. Faith that pleases God is not shallow optimism or positive thinking. It is deep, unwavering conviction that:

- His nature is faithful
- His motives are pure
- His Promises are true
- His timing is perfect
- His Heart is good

This kind of faith doesn't wait for proof; it rests in promise. It seeks God not for what He can give, but for who He is. And God delights in the heart that seeks Him with confidence, hunger, and expectation.

Faith that pleases Him is faith that says:

You are my reward. You are my source. You are my confidence.

Prayer:

Lord, I desire to please You with my faith. Strengthen me to believe beyond what I can see and to trust Your Heart in every circumstance. Let my confidence in You bring joy to Your Heart and Glory to Your Name. Teach me to seek You diligently, trust You completely, and walk with You faithfully all my days. In Jesus' Name, Amen.

Faith that pleases God begins with believing who He is.

Day 53
The Power of Agreement

Scripture:

"Again I say unto you, That if two of you shall agree on earth as touching any thing that they shall ask, it shall be done for them of My Father which is in heaven."

Matthew 18:19 (KJV)

Reflection:

Faith multiplies in agreement. When believers unite their hearts in prayer, Heaven responds to their harmony. Agreement does not demand sameness; it calls for unity of spirit, unity of purpose, and unity of faith.

There is a supernatural strength released when two or more stand together, not in personal opinion, but in alignment with God's Word. The power of agreement is the merging of faith streams until they become a river strong enough to move mountains.

Division weakens prayer; unity amplifies it. The enemy fears agreement because united believers carry the authority of Heaven. When hearts align with the will of God and with one another, miracles move quickly and breakthrough comes with force.

Agreement says: We believe together. We stand together. We expect together. And Heaven answers

Prayer:

Lord, teach me to walk in true agreement with those who seek Your Heart. Remove every trace of pride, fear, and division within me. Let unity mark my relationships and strengthen my prayers. May our voices rise as one before Your throne, carrying the faith that Heaven recognizes and responds to. In Jesus' Name, Amen.

Unity strengthens faith; agreement invites miracles.

Day 54
Worship Before the Walls Fall

Scripture:

"And it came to pass, when the people heard the sound of the trumpet, and the people shouted with a great shout, that the wall fell down flat."

Joshua 6:20 (KJV)

Reflection:

Faith doesn't wait for victory to worship it worships into victory. The walls of Jericho didn't fall because Israel had the perfect plan; they fell because Israel had the right posture. Breakthrough didn't come from their march, it came from their surrender expressed through praise.

Worship is not a response to what God has done; it is a declaration of trust in what God is about to do. It is the sound of faith rising above fear, expectation rising above obstacles, and obedience rising above impossibility.

Every shout of praise sends a signal to Heaven that your confidence is in the God Who never fails. And often, the walls standing before you begin to tremble long before you ever see them fall. When you worship in advance, you align your spirit with Heaven's victory and weaken the strongholds around you. Keep praising your breakthrough is already shaking loose beneath your feet.

Prayer:

Lord, let my worship be louder than my worry. Teach me to praise You before the walls fall, trusting that You are already working behind the scenes. Fill my heart with expectancy and my mouth with victory. Let my worship become the sound that ushers in the breakthrough You have ordained. In Jesus' Name, Amen.

Worship is the weapon of those who trust the outcome to God.

Day 55
The Blessing of Believing

Scripture:

"Jesus saith unto him, Thomas, because thou hast seen Me, thou hast believed: blessed are they that have not seen, and yet have believed."

John 20:29 (KJV)

Reflection:

Belief without proof is the purest form of faith. Thomas needed sight, but Jesus reserved a special blessing for those willing to trust Him without visible evidence. Heaven places honor on the heart that says, Your Word is enough for me.

Faith is not blindness, it is Divine confidence rooted in the nature of God. To believe before you see is to step into the rhythm of eternity, where God's Word always precedes His works. It is to trust that every promise He speaks already carries the seed of fulfillment.

The blessing is not found in what becomes visible; it is found in who is trusted before anything appears. When you choose faith over feelings, Scripture over circumstance, and trust over sight, you enter the realm where miracles are born.

Blessed are they who believe even in the silence. Blessed are they who trust even in the waiting. Blessed are they who cling to His Word even when nothing around them confirms it. This is the faith Jesus celebrates.

Prayer:

Lord, thank You for blessing those who believe before they see. Strengthen my heart to trust Your Word even when the results are hidden. Quiet every doubt and deepen my confidence in who You are. Let my life be marked by a faith that honors You and a belief that glorifies Your Name. In Jesus' Name, Amen.

The blessing belongs to those who believe beyond sight.

Day 56
Faith That Endures

Scripture:

"Knowing this, that the trying of your faith worketh patience. But let patience have her perfect work, that ye may be perfect and entire, wanting nothing."

James 1:3 - 4 (KJV)

Reflection:

Faith that endures is not formed in comfort; it is forged in the fire of testing. Every trial becomes a classroom where trust matures and spiritual strength is shaped. God never tests to break you; He tests to build you. He strengthens what already belongs to Him so it will stand firm in every season.

Patience is the posture of enduring faith. It doesn't crumble under pressure, complain in the process, or retreat in weariness. Instead, it grows more stable, more surrendered, and more anchored with time. Patience is faith stretched, refined, and purified until it becomes unshakable.

When you persevere through pain, Heaven is perfecting something within you, something lasting, whole, and gloriously complete. What feels like delay is often the deep work of God preparing you for blessing, purpose, and spiritual maturity.

Enduring faith does not merely survive the trial, it is strengthened through it.

Prayer:

Lord, help me to endure with Grace. When my faith is tested, let patience rise within me until Your perfect work is complete. Strengthen me to trust You even when progress feels slow and the process feels heavy. Refine my heart, deepen my resilience, and let my endurance bring Glory to Your Name. In Jesus' Name, Amen.

Enduring faith stands firm until the promise speaks.

Day 57
The Power of the Word

Scripture:

"So then faith cometh by hearing, and hearing by the word of God."

Romans 10:17 (KJV)

Reflection:

Faith feeds on the Word. Every verse is a seed planted into the soil of your heart, and every promise is a breath from Heaven restoring life, courage, and clarity to your spirit. When you fill yourself with Scripture, doubt loses its authority, fear loses its edge, and Truth begins to take a deep, immovable root.

The Word of God does not merely inform it transforms. It renews your mind, strengthens your will, stabilizes your emotions, and aligns your perspective with Heaven's. The Word confronts lies, breaks strongholds, and awakens spiritual sight. It shifts you from feeling to faith, from confusion to clarity, from weakness to strength.

Faith grows wherever the Word is welcomed. The more you listen, meditate, speak, and obey His Word, the louder the Voice of faith rises within you. Scripture becomes the soundtrack of your spirit, and as it fills your inner life, faith becomes bold, anchored, and unshakable. Strong faith is not accidental; it is cultivated by a heart consistently nourished by the Word of God.

Prayer:

Lord, let Your Word dwell richly in me. Feed my spirit with Your Truth until faith overflows. Silence every Voice that contradicts Your Promises and sharpen my hearing to recognize Your Voice. Help me to believe, meditate on, and act upon what You have spoken, knowing that Your Word cannot fail. Strengthen me through Scripture until my life reflects Your truth. In Jesus' Name, Amen.

The Word sustains what faith begins.

Day 58
When God Is Silent

Scripture:

"Be still, and know that I am God."

Psalm 46:10 (KJV)

Reflection:

Silence is not absence. When God grows quiet, He is never withdrawing. He is inviting. In the stillness, He often speaks the loudest, not through words but through presence. His silence is not rejection; it is refinement. It draws you beyond emotion, beyond immediate answers, and into a deeper knowing of who He is.

When Heaven seems quiet, it may mean in ways your eyes cannot yet see. His silence can be a shelter, a season of strengthening, or the gentle tuning of your spiritual hearing. In quiet seasons, God is often repositioning your heart so that when He does speak, you recognize His Voice with clarity and confidence.

Stillness becomes sacred when you cease striving to force a word and instead rest in the certainty of His nearness. Trust listens even when nothing is said. Faith grows roots in the silence. And in that holy quiet, you come to know Him not just as the God Who speaks, but as the God Who stays.

Prayer:

Lord, teach me to trust You in the silence. Calm my restless heart and remind me that Your Presence is near, even when Your Voice is still. Deepen my faith beyond my feelings and anchor my trust in who You are. Let the quiet draw me closer to Your Heart and strengthen my confidence in Your unfailing love. In Jesus' Name, Amen.

God's silence often hides His greatest work.

Day 59
The Joy of Believing

Scripture:

"Whom having not seen, ye love; in whom, though now ye see Him not, yet believing, ye rejoice with joy unspeakable and full of Glory."

1 Peter 1:8 (KJV)

Reflection:

Faith finds joy in unseen realities. True belief does not simply trust it celebrates. It rejoices before manifestation, before evidence, before understanding. This is why Scripture calls it joy unspeakable and full of Glory because it comes from Heaven, not earth.

Joy is the fragrance of faith. It rises from a heart convinced of God's goodness and confident in His Promises. It fills the atmosphere with hope that Heaven recognizes and responds to. Joy is not tied to circumstance; it is tied to Christ. It flows from loving a Savior you have never seen, yet know deeply.

When you believe, joy becomes your strength. The enemy cannot steal a heart that rejoices in faith. Every moment you choose joy in the waiting, you testify that the promise is already yours in spirit. Rejoicing is not denial of reality, it is alignment with Divine truth.

Joy says:

I trust Him. I believe Him. I expect Him. And Heaven calls that faith glorious.

Prayer:

Lord, thank You for the joy that fills my heart as I believe. Let my faith be marked by praise, not complaint. Teach me to celebrate Your Promises long before they unfold, and to carry joy as a banner of victory. May my rejoicing honor You and strengthen me for every step ahead. In Jesus' Name, Amen.

Joy is faith's celebration before the promise appears.

Day 60
Wind of God

Scripture:

"And suddenly there came a sound from heaven as of a rushing mighty wind, and it filled all the house where they were sitting".

Acts 2:2 (KJV)

"The wind bloweth where it listeth, and thou hearest the sound thereof, but cans tnot tell whence it cometh, and whither it goeth: so is every one that is born of the Spirit."

John 3:8 (KJV)

"Then said He unto me, Prophesy unto the wind, prophesy, son of man, and say to the wind, Thus saith the Lord God; Come from the four winds, O breath, and breathe upon these slain, that they may live. So I prophesied as He commanded me, and the breath came into them, and they lived, and stood up upon their feet, an exceeding great army."

Ezekiel 37:9 - 10 (KJV)

Reflection:

The Wind of God cannot be contained or controlled; it moves with Divine purpose, carrying life, direction, and power wherever it goes. When the wind of His Spirit begins to move, everything that was still begins to awaken. Dry bones begin to rattle, weary hearts are revived, and the stagnant places are stirred once more by the breath of Heaven. There is nothing ordinary about His Wind. It carries healing in its flow, direction in its current, and revival in its sound. When the Wind of God enters your situation, it announces change a holy stirring that testifies that God is still moving, still breathing, and still faithful. Faith does not resist His movement; it leans into it. To abide in Him is to yield to allow His Wind to lift you beyond fear and into the rhythm of His Spirit. You don't have to understand where the wind comes from or where it's going; you only have to trust the One Who sends it.

Prayer:

Holy Spirit, breathe upon me again. Let Your wind move through every place that has grown still within my soul. Awaken what has fallen asleep, and carry me where You desire me to go. May Your breath restore, renew, and reignite my heart until I am fully aligned with the movement of Heaven. In Jesus' Name, Amen.

When His Wind moves, everything changes.

Day 61
Small Wind with His Great Fire

Scripture:

"No weapon that is formed against thee shall prosper; and every tongue that shall rise against thee in judgment thou shalt condemn. This is the heritage of the servants of the Lord, and their righteousness is of me, saith the Lord."

Isaiah 54:17 (KJV)

"Wherefore we receiving a kingdom which cannot be moved, let us have Grace, whereby we may serve God acceptably with reverence and godly fear: For our God is a consuming fire."

Hebrews 12:28 - 29 (KJV)

"And suddenly there came a sound from heaven as of a rushing mighty wind, and it filled all the house where they were sitting. And there appeared unto them cloven tongues like as of fire, and it sat upon each of them. And they were all filled with the Holy Ghost."

Acts 2:2 - 4 (KJV)

Reflection:

There are times when the wind seems small when prayers are whispered rather than shouted, when faith feels fragile rather than fierce. Yet in the Kingdom of God, even a small wind can carry a great fire. What begins as a gentle stirring in your spirit i s often the breath of Heaven prepares to ignite something powerful. God does not require your strength to make His Presence known; He only asks for your surrender. When His breath meets your obedience, His consuming fire falls. Every storm that once opposed you becomes a testimony of His Power at work within you. His fire refines, purifies, and reveals consuming what was sent to destroy, and leaving behind the brilliance of His Glory.

Prayer:

Lord, even when my strength feels small, let Your Spirit move mightily within me. Breathe upon my faith until Your Holy Fire burns away all fear, doubt, and distraction. Let Your consuming Presence refine me and cause my life to bear witness of Your Power and Glory. In Jesus' Name, Amen.

Even the smallest wind carries the greatness of His fire.

Day 62
Let the Rivers of Living Water Flow

Scripture:

"He that believeth on me, as the scripture hath said, out of his belly shall flow rivers of living water."

John 7:38 (KJV)

"Then He brought me back to the door of the temple; and there was water, flowing from under the threshold of the temple toward the east, for the front of the temple faced east; the water was flowing from under the right side of the temple, south of the altar."

Ezekiel 47:1 (NKJV)

"And he shewed me a pure river of water of life, clear as crystal, proceeding out of the throne of God and of the Lamb."

Revelation 22:1 (KJV)

Reflection:

The Presence of God is never stagnant; it moves, refreshes, and restores. When Jesus spoke of rivers of living water, He was revealing the life of the Spirit flowing within every believer who abides in Him. These waters cleanse what has been polluted by pain and refresh what has grown weary in waiting. When the rivers flow, they carry healing to the barren places of the heart. They bring joy where sorrow once lingered and strength where fear once lived. The same Spirit that hovered over the waters in creation now dwells in you a well that never runs dry, a flow that cannot be stopped by circumstance. You are not meant to merely contain His Presence; you are meant to release it. Let the rivers flow. Speak His Word, worship in His Truth, and yield to His Spirit for where the river flows, everything lives.

Prayer:

Lord, let Your living water flow through me today. Wash away all dryness and restore the places that have been parched by disappointment or delay. Let Your Presence overflow in my heart until every word, every step, and every act of love becomes a stream of Your life to others. In Jesus' Name, Amen.

The river of His Spirit refreshes everything it touches.

Day 63
Streams in the Wilderness

Scripture:

"I will open rivers in high places, and fountains in the midst of the valleys: I will make the wilderness a pool of water, and the dry land springs of water."

Isaiah 41:18 (KJV)

Reflection:

In February 2024, I found myself searching for a home after my daughter's accident, in a season when my living situation had become unreconcilable. I was weary, yet I chose to keep trusting in God's faithfulness. When I pulled onto the street to view a house, the address 4118 immediately caught my attention. After learning the rent, I told the owner I would pray about it. That night, in prayer, I said, Lord, if this is meant to be, please let the rent be $200 less. That's the only way I can manage with medical bills and appointments for my daughter. The next day, I called the owner back to explain I couldn't commit. Yet, as I drove past the house one last time, 4118 drew my eyes again, stirring something deep within me.

Two days later, the owner and his wife called to say they both felt the house should be mine and they lowered the rent by exactly $200. I had never spoken that number aloud, only to God in prayer. In tears, I drove back to the house, once again drawn to 4118. I asked, Lord, what Am I missing? And in that still, small voice, He whispered: Isaiah 41:18. At that moment, I knew He had been guiding every step. The house wasn't just a home; it was a promise. God was reminding me that He can make rivers flow in the desert and springs rise up in dry places. Even when circumstances seem barren, His provision never runs dry.

Prayer:

Lord, You are the One Who brings life to the wilderness and hope to the weary heart. Thank You for showing me that You are not limited by my circumstances. Let Your living waters flow in every dry place of my life, and may Your faithfulness continues to refresh my spirit and renew my trust. In Jesus' Name, Amen.

Even in the wilderness, His rivers still flow.

Day 64
Faith That Overcomes

Scripture:

"For whatsoever is born of God overcometh the world: and this is the victory that overcometh the world, even our faith."

1 John 5:4 (KJV)

Reflection:

Faith is Heaven's victory language. You were not created to barely survive, you were born of God, and therefore born to overcome. The same resurrection power that raised Christ from the grave now lives within you, enabling you to stand firm when everything around you is shaking.

Faith is not denial of hardship; it is dominion in hardship. It looks straight into the face of storms and silently declares, You will not define me, and you will not defeat me. Overcoming faith doesn't pretend trials aren't real; it simply refuses to bow to them. It believes that God's Word holds greater authority than anything the world can send against you. When faith leads, defeat loses its grip. Fear cannot rule a heart convinced of victory. The One Who believes walks in the confidence that triumph is not merely possible it's already promised. Every battle becomes a platform for God's power, and every obstacle becomes the material for a testimony. Overcoming faith doesn't wait for the victory to appear; it carries the victory within.

Prayer:

Lord, thank You that my victory is secure in You. Strengthen my faith to stand in every battle. Let Your overcoming power rise within me until every obstacle becomes a testimony of triumph. Teach me to walk in the confidence of One Who is born of God and destined to overcome. In Jesus' Name, Amen.

Faith does not escape the battle, it wins it.

Day 65
Speak to the Promise

Scripture:

"Death and life are in the power of the tongue: and they that love it shall eat the fruit thereof."

Proverbs 18:21 (KJV)

Reflection:

Faith speaks life where fear speaks lack. Your tongue is the gatekeeper of manifestation. What you consistently speak sets the direction of your faith. Words are not empty; they are seeds. And every seed you sow with your mouth grows into fruit you will eventually eat. Your words shape your reality. Confession aligns your world with the Word. When you speak what God has said, you give Heaven permission to move in the earth through your agreement.

God created the world with His Voice, and He placed that same creative authority within you through faith. When you declare His Promises, you are not commanding God You are aligning with Him. You are echoing His Truth until your atmosphere agrees with what Heaven has already decreed. Speak to the promise, not the problem. Speak to the future, not the fear. Speak to the mountain, not the moment. Watch how the atmosphere shifts when your voice matches God's Word.

Your declaration becomes the doorway through which His fulfillment enters.

Prayer:

Lord, let the words of my mouth agree with the Truth of Your Word. Teach me to speak faith over every situation and silence every word of doubt and fear. Let my declarations carry life, authority, and expectation. Fill my mouth with promises, not problems, truth, not turmoil. In Jesus' Name, Amen.

Faith filled words prepare the way for promise to come forth.

Day 66
The God Who Rewards

Scripture:

"But without faith it is impossible to please Him: for he that cometh to God must believe that He is, and that He is a rewarder of them that diligently seek Him."

Hebrews 11:6 (KJV)

Reflection:

Faith not only believes that God is, it believes that God is good. True faith expects His reward, not out of entitlement, but out of intimacy. To trust Him fully is to trust His character, His generosity, and His desire to bless His children.

God takes delight in rewarding those who seek Him with persistence, purity of heart, and unwavering devotion. The One Who pursues Him finds not only answers, but transformation; not only blessings, but breakthrough; not only gifts, but the Giver Himself. The reward is not always immediate, but it is always certain. Sometimes it arrives as an answered prayer. Sometimes as peace that surpasses understanding. Sometimes as an unexpected provision, direction, or strength you didn't know you needed. The God Who sees your faithfulness is never unjust to overlook it. He is the Rewarder because He is the Father. And every reward He gives leads your heart closer to Him.

Prayer:

Father, thank You that You are the Rewarder of those who seek You. Help me to pursue You not for what You can give, but for who You are. Let my faith remain steadfast, trusting that Your rewards are perfect and Your Timing is flawless. Draw me deeper into intimacy with You, and let every reward point me back to Your Heart. In Jesus' Name, Amen.

The greatest reward of faith is finding more of Him.

Day 67
Faith That Sees

Scripture:

"While we look not at the things which are seen, but at the things which are not seen: for the things which are seen are temporal; but the things which are not seen are eternal."

2 Corinthians 4:18 (KJV)

Reflection:

Faith has vision beyond the visible. It looks past what is and beholds what will be. It peers through the fog of circumstance and fixes its gaze upon the eternal. The eyes of faith do not deny reality; they simply discern a greater one. They recognize that what is seen is temporary, shifting, fragile… but what God speaks is unshakable and everlasting.

When your focus shifts from what surrounds you to Who sustains you, Heaven's perspective becomes your peace. Faith refuses to be ruled by what the natural eye sees. It chooses to see through the lens of promise rather than the lens of pressure.

The natural eye sees obstacles; the spiritual eye sees opportunity. The natural eye sees delay; the spiritual eye sees development. The natural eye sees impossibility; the spiritual eye sees the God Who makes all things possible.

What you behold, you begin to mirror. Lift your eyes higher, beloved above the fear, above the waiting, above the noise. Look to the unseen, and you will see that God has already gone before you, preparing a path that your natural eyes could never perceive.

Faith is sight that begins where vision ends.

Prayer:

Lord, open the eyes of my spirit to see beyond the temporary. Teach me to perceive Your Promises with clarity and to look beyond what my natural eyes can discern. Anchor my perspective in eternity and let faith become my focus. Strengthen my sight until I see every situation through the Truth of Your Word. In Jesus' Name, Amen.

Faith sees what sight cannot.

Day 68
Relentless Authority in Christ

Scripture:

"Behold, I give unto you power to tread on serpents and scorpions, and over all the power of the enemy: and nothing shall by any means hurt you."

Luke 10:19 (KJV)

"As for God, His way is perfect: the word of the Lord is tried: He is a buckler to all those that trust in Him."

Psalm 18:30 (KJV)

Reflection:

Every battle fought in faith refines the authority we walk in. True authority in Christ is not born from ease, but from endurance from facing the storm and declaring, It is written, until the waves obey His Word. The believer who has been tested and found standing is not just strong; they are established. When the enemy comes in like a flood, they rise with the confidence of One Who knows the Word is tried and proven. They have seen God keep His Promises, heal what was broken, and restore what was lost. Their authority is not arrogance; it is the fruit of abiding in the One whose power has never failed. To walk in relentless authority is to speak with Heaven's assurance: the victory has already been won, and every promise of God stands undefeated. Trials may roar, but the tried Word of God roars louder. A reminder that trials reveal the power and authority of those who stand on the proven Word of God.

Prayer:

Heavenly Father, thank You for the battles that taught me to trust Your Word. When the enemy whispers doubt, remind me that Your Promises have been tried and proven in my life. Clothe me in the authority of Jesus Christ not to boast, but to boldly declare Your Victory. Let my words carry the weight of Heaven, and may my life testify that Your Word always prevails. In Jesus' mighty Name, Amen.

Tried and proven His Word still stands.

Day 69
Great Wonders Are Coming!

Scripture:

"Sanctify yourselves: for tomorrow the Lord will do wonders among you."

Joshua 3:5 (KJV)

"For the earth shall be filled with the knowledge of the Glory of the Lord, as the waters cover the sea."

Habakkuk 2:14 (KJV)

Reflection:

The Spirit of God is stirring in the earth, and Heaven is preparing to display great wonders once again. These will not merely be signs and miracles for spectacle's sake, but demonstrations of His holiness, justice, and mercy through a people made ready. Before every Divine outpouring, there is a Divine cleansing. The Lord is purifying His Bride-separating her from the noise of the world so that His Glory can be revealed without mixture.

Do not be disheartened by shaking or pruning; both precede the unveiling of His Power. As the Church surrenders pride for purity, comfort for calling, and fear for faith, the atmosphere of Heaven will invade the earth. You were not born for complacency - you were born to carry Glory. God is preparing to move in ways that will silence doubt and ignite awe. What He does next will not just change circumstances; it will change hearts. Stand ready, sanctified, and steadfast for great wonders are coming, and they will flow through those who have learned to abide. A reminder that God is preparing to reveal His Power and Glory through a purified and obedient Church.

Prayer:

Father, thank You for the promise of Your coming wonders. Purify my heart and prepare my life as a vessel of Your Glory. Let Your Presence move through me in power, humility, and holiness. Use me to carry the fire of revival into every place You send me. In Jesus' Name, Amen.

I am consecrated, I am ready, and I will behold His wonders.

Day 70
The Overflow of Belief

Scripture:

"Out of his belly shall flow rivers of living water."

John 7:38 (KJV)

Reflection:

Faith was never meant to be contained or kept still. When you truly believe, the Spirit moves through you with power refreshing, renewing, and restoring everything He touches. His Presence doesn't trickle; it flows. It washes over the hidden places, revives what has grown weary, and brings life where dryness once ruled. Unbelief dammed the flow, but faith tears down every barrier. When you open your heart fully to Him, the living water of His Spirit begins to rise, filling every empty place and spilling over into the lives of those around you. This overflow is not accidental; it is the natural evidence of a heart anchored in Jesus.

You were not created to simply hold faith, you were created to release it. Your testimony carries water. Your obedience carries water. Your worship carries water. Every act of belief becomes a river through which God refreshes the world around you. And as you pour out, He pours in ensuring that the flow never runs dry. Let your life be a stream of Grace that points others back to the Source.

Prayer:

Lord, let faith rise within me like a river fed by Your Spirit. Remove every hindrance that blocks the flow of Your Presence in my life. Let living water pour out of me to refresh the weary, restore the broken, and awaken hope in those around me. Make my life a vessel that carries Your Glory into every dry and thirsty place. Keep me overflowing in strength, in love, and in unwavering trust. In Jesus' Name, Amen.

Faith that overflows transforms everything it touches.

Day 71
The Strength of Believing

Scripture:

"Abraham staggered not at the promise of God through unbelief; but was strong in faith, giving Glory to God."

Romans 4:20 (KJV)

Reflection:

Strength in faith does not come from striving harder, trying to force belief, or willing ourselves to be strong. It flows from resting in the unshakable character of God. Abraham's confidence wasn't built on what he could see but on Who he knew. His circumstances shouted impossible, yet his spirit whispered God is faithful. That is the strength of believing. Faith matures when it stops asking how and simply agrees with God's yes. It grows when we shift our focus from the size of the problem to the strength of the Promise Keeper. Every promise God gives invites us into endurance. Waiting becomes the place where spiritual muscle is formed. The longer the wait, the deeper the roots of trust grow.

There will always be moments when doubt tries to creep in, when what you see seems to contradict what God said. But each time you choose faith over fear, trust over questioning, and praise over worry, you rise stronger than before. Praise becomes the weight you lift in the gym of waiting. It builds strength where anxiety once drained you. Like Abraham, your belief honors God not because you understand the process, but because you trust the One writing your story.

Prayer:

Father, strengthen my faith as I hold to the promises You have spoken. Teach me to stand firm even when I cannot see the outcome. Let my confidence rest not in my ability to figure things out, but in Your unfailing character and unchanging Word. Help me give You Glory in the waiting with a heart anchored in trust and a spirit strengthened by Your Presence. Make my belief unshakable, my praise constant, and my hope steadfast. In Jesus' Name, Amen

Faith grows strong through continual surrender.

Day 72
Faith That Moves Forward

Scripture:

"Speak unto the children of Israel, that they go forward."

Exodus 14:15 (KJV)

Reflection:

Faith is never stagnant; it carries movement, momentum, and direction. When Israel stood trapped between the Red Sea and an approaching enemy, everything in the natural said stop, fear, or turn back. But God's command was simple and bold: Go forward. Their miracle did not meet them where they stood; it met them where they stepped.

Before the waters parted, their feet had to move. Before the pathway appeared, their faith had to respond. This is the rhythm of Divine partnership: God speaks, we move and heaven manifests what obedience activates.

Fear freezes the heart, convincing us that standing still is safer than stepping into the unknown. But faith refuses to be paralyzed. Faith lifts its foot even when the ground isn't visible yet. Faith believes that the God Who calls you forward will not let you drown in the waters He told you to approach. Every step of obedience pushes back resistance. Every act of trust opens new territory. And every moment you choose to move rather than shrink back declares THIS Truth: God has already gone before you. Forward is not just a direction, it is a declaration. A declaration that you trust His Voice more than your surroundings, His Promise more than your fear, and His Power more than your past. The same God Who stood with Israel stands with you and the path you need will reveal itself as you walk toward it.

Prayer:

Lord, give me holy courage to move forward even when the way seems closed. Strengthen my heart to obey Your Voice above every fear and every obstacle. Help me remember that every step of faith leads me closer to the breakthrough You have already prepared for me. Clear the path as I walk in obedience, and let my movement honor You. In Jesus' Name, Amen.

Faith advances even when the path is unseen.

Day 73
Promise in the Process

Scripture:

"Being confident of this very thing, that He which hath begun a good work in you will perform it until the day of Jesus Christ."

Philippians 1:6 (KJV)

Reflection:

Faith doesn't rush the process; it rests confidently in the promise. God is a Master Builder, and everything He initiates carries the guarantee of completion. Nothing He starts in you will ever be abandoned or forgotten. Even when you feel unfinished, He is faithfully working behind the scenes.

The seasons that feel slow or silent are not signs of neglect but evidence of His precise craftsmanship. The in-between is not delay; it is Divine development, the place where roots deepen, character forms, and understanding matures. God does some of His greatest work in the moments that feel the least productive.

When forward movement seems invisible, remember Whose hands are shaping you. The Potter never leaves the clay. He turns, presses, molds, and refines with intentional care. Every pause has purpose. Every stretch has meaning. Every moment is guided by a God Who sees the end from the beginning. Your process may not look like progress, but progress is still happening within the process. His timing ripens what your heart isn't ready to harvest yet. And His Promise remains alive even when it feels quiet. Trust the One Who started this journey in you. His work is steady, His Plan is perfect, and His finish is guaranteed.

Prayer:

Lord, thank You that Your work in me is ongoing and intentional. Help me to surrender my need for haste and rest in Your perfect timing. Teach me to rejoice in the process, knowing that every stage is filled with purpose. When I cannot see the outcome, anchor my heart in the Truth that Your Hand is still upon me. I trust Your Promise, Your pace, and Your plan. In Jesus' Name, Amen.

Every process protected by faith fulfills its promise.

Day 74
Faith That Waits Well

Scripture:

"Rest in the Lord, and wait patiently for Him."

Psalm 37:7 (KJV)

Reflection:

Faith that waits well is faith that has learned the rhythm of peace. Waiting is not wasted time it is worship wrapped in trust. When you choose stillness instead of striving, surrender instead of anxiety, you declare that God's timing is wiser than your own. The posture of patience honors Him just as much as the moment the prayer is finally answered.

The waiting room of faith is sacred ground. It's where God slows the pace so He can strengthen the foundation. In waiting, character deepens, perspective widens, and dependence grows richer. God is not withholding the answer. He is preparing your heart to carry it well.

He does not rush growth because He values the formation just as much as the fulfillment. Sometimes the answer takes time because your spirit is being shaped for the weight of what you've asked for. And sometimes the waiting itself becomes the very place where intimacy with God flourishes the most.

Waiting well does not mean waiting without feeling it means waiting without forfeiting trust. It is choosing confidence when clarity hasn't arrived yet. It is resting in the Truth that God is never late, never hurried, and never inattentive.

Your waiting is not empty; it is evidence that God is at work in ways you cannot yet see.

Prayer:

Father, teach me to wait with peace, joy, and confidence in Your perfect timing. When impatience rises or fear whispers doubt, remind me that You are never late and Your plans are always good. Let my stillness become an offering of worship, and let my waiting become a testimony of Your faithfulness. Shape my heart in this sacred space and prepare me for all You have promised. In Jesus' Name, Amen.

Faith that waits well always finishes well.

Day 75
The Vision Will Speak

Scripture:

"For the vision is yet for an appointed time, but at the end it shall speak, and not lie."

Habakkuk 2:3 (KJV)

Reflection:

Faith gives voice to the silent seasons. Even when the vision seems quiet unfinished, unseen, or delayed it is still alive. God's Promises do not wither in waiting; they wait for the moment God has ordained. What He has spoken over your life will not remain silent forever. When the appointed time arrives, the vision itself will step forward and testify that God has been faithful all along. The in-between is where trust is refined and belief is deepened. It's easy to question what we cannot yet hear, but silence is not denial. Heaven is working even when earth is still. God often prepares the vision long before He reveals its voice. So don't let the quiet steal your confidence. Don't allow delay to discourage your declaration. Keep speaking what God said, even when your circumstances say nothing. Your faith-filled words water the seed while it waits for its appointed time. The vision doesn't lie, it's simply waiting for its cue to speak. And when it does, every moment of waiting will make sense. Every silent season will echo with purpose. Every promise will stand tall, proving that God always finishes what He starts.

Prayer:

Lord, I trust the timing of every promise You have spoken. Strengthen my heart to keep believing even when the vision feels silent. Teach me to declare Your Truth with boldness until what You've spoken begins to manifest. Let my faith echo Your Word, and let my confidence remain anchored in Your faithfulness. When the appointed time arrives, let the vision speak clearly, powerfully, and undeniably. In Jesus' Name, Amen.

Every promise has a voice it speaks in God's time.

Day 76
Faith That Triumphs

Scripture:

"Nay, in all these things we are more than conquerors through Him that loved us."

Romans 8:37 (KJV)

Reflection:

Faith doesn't merely survive adversity it triumphs through it. Paul doesn't say we might conquer or that we could conquer; he declares that we are more than conquerors through Christ. This means the battle is already won before the first strike is thrown. Victory isn't dependent on how strong you feel, how perfect your response is, or how smooth the path becomes. It is anchored in the finished work of Jesus.

To be more than a conqueror is to stand in a victory you didn't earn but were gifted through Divine love. It means the outcome has already been secured, and the enemy knows it. That's why he attacks your faith because he fears what you carry. Every trial you walk through is not proof of weakness but evidence of spiritual authority. Resistance reveals strength; pressure reveals endurance; warfare reveals identity.

Your faith is not fragile, it is fortified by Christ's love. The battles you face cannot reduce you; they reveal you. They uncover the resilience God built into you by His Spirit. Victory is not something you are trying to reach, it is the position from which you fight. Even when the storm rages, you stand on a foundation that cannot be moved. Even when the warfare intensifies, your victory remains untouched. And even when you feel the weight of the struggle, you are still more than a conqueror not because of your ability, but because of His unfailing, conquering love.

Prayer:

Lord, thank You that through Your Love I stand in undeniable victory. When battles arise, help me to remember that I fight from triumph, not for it. Strengthen my heart to walk boldly in the authority You have given me through the Blood of Jesus. Let every challenge become a testimony of Your Power working in and through me. Anchor me in Your Love, steady me in Your strength, and remind me daily that I am more than a conqueror. In Jesus' Name, Amen.

Faith fights from victory, not toward it.

Day 77
The Faithful Witness

Scripture:

"Let us hold fast the profession of our faith without wavering; (for He is faithful that promised.)"

Hebrews 10:23 (KJV)

Reflection:

Faith becomes its strongest witness when it refuses to waver. Anyone can believe when the path is smooth, but steadfast faith in uncertain seasons speaks louder than a thousand sermons. Every moment you choose perseverance over panic, trust over trembling, and worship over worry, your life preaches a message the world cannot ignore. The world listens when believers keep believing. Your confidence is not anchored in your own strength, it is anchored in His Faithfulness. You can hold fast because He is holding you. God's character is the foundation beneath your confession. His Promises steady your steps even when your circumstances shake. To stand firm in faith is to declare that His Word is more trustworthy than what you see, feel, or fear.

When everything around you shifts, unwavering faith reveals a steadfast God. When life becomes uncertain, your consistency becomes evidence of His constancy. And when you choose to keep believing despite unanswered prayers, despite delays, despite battles your faith becomes a living testimony that His Promises cannot fail. Your endurance is not silent. It is a witness. It is a declaration. It is a reflection of the unshakable God you serve.

Prayer:

Lord, let my life stand as a faithful witness to Your unfailing promises. Strengthen me to hold fast even when adversity rises, and help me declare Your goodness with unwavering conviction. Let my steadfast faith reveal Your steadfast love to all who see my life. Anchor my heart in Your faithfulness, and keep my confession rooted in Your unchanging Word. In Jesus' Name, Amen.

Faith that endures becomes a living testimony.

Day 78
The LORD Will Make You the Head

Scripture:

"And the Lord shall make thee the head, and not the tail; and thou shalt be above only, and thou shalt not be beneath; if that thou hearken unto the commandments of the Lord thy God."

Deuteronomy 28:13 (KJV)

Reflection:

God never intended His Favor to be hidden or silent in your life. His Word declares that you will rise not by human striving or self-promotion but by walking in obedience to Him. To be the head and not the tail is not a statement of pride; it is a declaration of Divine positioning. It is the Lord Himself who lifts, appoints, and establishes His people in places of influence and purpose. Those who walk uprightly with God carry a distinction that cannot be manufactured His authority, His wisdom, His excellence. Being the head simply means living aligned with His will, leading with His Heart, and reflecting His character in everything you do. It is leadership marked by humility, not ambition.

Promotion in the Kingdom is never a reward for performance; it is the fruit of surrender. The world measures success by titles and platforms, but Heaven measures it by obedience and faithfulness. When you choose His Ways over your own, He positions you where your life can glorify Him most. God lifts those who bow to His will. He exalts those who remain teachable, submitted, and willing to follow His Voice. And when He places you above, it is never for dominance but for stewardship. It's not about being seen, it's about being used for His Glory. If you stay surrendered, God Himself will make you the head.

Prayer:

Lord, I thank You that Your Hand of favor is upon my life. Lift me according to Your purpose, not my pride. Position me where I can reflect Your Heart, carry Your excellence, and honor You in all I do. Help me walk in obedience that opens the door for Your Divine promotion. Let my life be shaped by Grace, not by achievement, and may every elevation point others back to You. In Jesus' Name, Amen.

Faith obeys and God elevates.

Day 79
Give Thanks to the Lord

Scripture:

"O give thanks unto the Lord; for He is good: for His Mercy endureth forever."

Psalm 107:1 (KJV)

Reflection:

Gratitude is the true voice of faith. Every time you give thanks, especially when life feels heavy you proclaim that the goodness of God outweighs the weight of your circumstance. Thanksgiving shifts your heart from focusing on what you lack to remembering Who is with you. It moves you from need to nearness, reminding you that His Mercy is your inheritance every single day.

A thankful heart never runs dry, because gratitude keeps you connected to the Source. Each word of thanksgiving draws Heaven close. It transforms the atmosphere, ushering in peace, clarity, and hope. Gratitude opens the door for God's Presence to dwell richly within you. To thank Him is to trust Him even before the answer arrives. Thanksgiving declares that God is already working, already sustaining, already faithful. It is a quiet, powerful confession that His Goodness is constant and His Mercy is unending.

When you choose gratitude, you silence the voice of complaint and magnify the greatness of your God. Thanksgiving doesn't just reflect faith, it strengthens it. It aligns your heart with Heaven's truth: He is good, and His Mercy endures forever.

Prayer:

Father, thank You for Your unfailing love, Your tender mercy, and Your goodness that never changes. Teach me to see Your Hand at work in every season of my life. Let gratitude rise in my spirit until it silences every complaint and fills my heart with peace. May my thanksgiving become worship that honors You and faith that trusts You long before the miracle comes. In Jesus' Name, Amen.

Gratitude unlocks the gates of faith.

Day 80
Bless the Lord, O My Soul

Scripture:

"Bless the Lord, O my soul: and all that is within me, bless His holy name."

Psalm 103:1 (KJV)

Reflection:

Sometimes faith must rise up and tell the soul what to do. David didn't wait for the perfect moment, the right emotion, or a peaceful day. His praise was not based on feeling it was an act of obedience, a declaration from the depths of a surrendered heart. He spoke to his own soul and commanded it to bless the Lord.

There will be days when your soul feels weary, overwhelmed, or discouraged. Those are the very moments when you must speak to yourself and say, Bless the Lord anyway. Praise is not the fruit of perfect circumstances; it is the weapon that shifts them. Praise reorders your perspective. It lifts your eyes from what hurts to the One Who heals. It turns pain into purpose, heaviness into hope, and confusion into clarity. When you bless God with all that is within you even the broken parts His Strength fills what has been emptied. His joy rises where sorrow sat. His Peace floods what worry tried to claim. Blessing the Lord is not just worship, it is warfare. It is choosing to exalt His Name above every burden, every emotion, and every battle. As you speak praise over your soul, Heaven responds, and your spirit is renewed

Prayer:

Lord, I bless You with all that I am. Even when my heart feels heavy or my soul feels tired, I choose praise. Let worship rise from deep within me until every part of my being exalts Your holy Name. Fill the empty places with Your strength and saturate my spirit with Your Presence. I bless You now and forever. In Jesus' Name, Amen.

Praise turns weakness into worship.

Day 81
The Valleys Will Be Filled

Scripture:

"Every valley shall be exalted, and every mountain and hill shall be made low: and the crooked shall be made straight, and the rough places plain."

Isaiah 40:4 (KJV)

Reflection:

God is the great equalizer and perfect Restorer. Where life has carved deep valleys of sorrow, disappointment, or fear, He promises to lift you. Where obstacles, pride, and opposition have risen like mountains before you, His Hand will bring them low. The uneven places of your journey, those seasons that felt jagged, uncertain, or overwhelming are all subject to His Divine correction. He is the God Who levels what life has distorted. The path He prepares is not for your comfort alone, it is so that His Glory can move freely through your life without hindrance. Every high thing that resisted you, every low place that tried to bury you, and every crooked path that confused you is being realigned by His Sovereignty.

Trust His Divine leveling. He does not erase your story. He redeems it. The valleys you cried through will soon stand as elevated testimonies of His Strength. The mountains that loomed large will be nothing before His Power. And the crooked roads that made no sense will reveal the straight line of His Faithfulness. What once seemed impossible will become the very places that prove His Goodness. His Grace not only evens the ground beneath your feet it prepares you to walk forward with confidence, clarity, and peace.

Prayer:

Lord, make the crooked places straight before me. Fill every valley of discouragement with Your strength, and bring down every mountain of fear, pride, or opposition. Smooth the rough places in my path and prepare my heart to walk in the beauty of Your balanced, restoring Grace. Thank You for leveling what I cannot fix and redeeming what I cannot change. In Jesus' Name, Amen.

God levels every landscape for His Glory to pass through.

Day 82
Faith That Rejoices First

Scripture:

"Rejoice in the Lord always: and again, I say, Rejoice."

Philippians 4:4 (KJV)

Reflection:

Faith doesn't wait for fulfillment; it rejoices before it comes. The deepest evidence of true belief is joy that remains steady, unshaken by delay, unanswered prayers, or unfolding circumstances. Rejoicing is not pretending everything is perfect; it is proclaiming that everything is possible with God. Joy is a declaration that the promises of God outrank the facts of the moment. It shifts the atmosphere, changes the posture of your heart, and invites Heaven's involvement. Joy keeps the door wide open for breakthrough, because a rejoicing heart is a trusting heart.

Heaven responds to those who praise through pain. Your joy is more than an emotion; it is faith's loudest amen. It tells the enemy he cannot steal what God has spoken. It tells your own soul that hope is still alive. It tells the world that your confidence is not in circumstances but in Christ. Rejoice not because every battle is easy, but because every outcome is already held in His Hands. Rejoice not because you see the full picture, but because you trust the One Who does. Rejoice because God is with you, God is for you, and God is working even before you see the answer.

Prayer:

Lord, fill me with joy that cannot be shaken or stolen by circumstance. Teach me to rejoice always in waiting, in weeping, and in winning. Let my praise rise as evidence of unshakable trust in Your goodness and power. May joy overflow from a heart anchored in Your Promises, declaring that I believe You completely. In Jesus' Name, Amen.

Rejoicing is faith's song in advance.

Day 83
O God, Enthroned in Heaven

Scripture:

"O God, enthroned in heaven, I lift my eyes toward You in worship... We look to You, our God, with passionate longing to please You and discover more of Your mercy and Grace."

Psalm 123:1 -2 (TPT)

Reflection:

The heart that looks up will never be left empty. Faith begins with adoration turning our gaze away from what burdens us and fixing it upon the One Who reigns above it all. When we lift our eyes to God, we are reminded that His throne is not distant or cold. It is the throne of Mercy, Grace, and unfailing compassion. It is always accessible to those who seek Him with sincere worship. Worship shifts the posture of the soul. It elevates us above the noise, above the pressure, above the heaviness of earth. When we look to Heaven, the storms of life lose their power to overwhelm. Worry loosens its grip, fear loses its authority, and hope rises with new strength.

Every sigh of surrender becomes a song of trust in His Presence. When the eyes of faith look upward, they do not plead from a place of defeat they worship from a place of Divine perspective. Looking up teaches us that help is not found in striving, but in beholding. Strength isn't gained in panic, but in praise. The more we gaze upon His majesty, the more our hearts hunger to please Him. And as we draw near, we discover afresh that His Mercy and Grace are not only abundant, they are unending.

Prayer:

Lord, I lift my eyes to You enthroned in majesty, surrounded by Glory, and clothed in mercy. You alone are my help and my hope. Let my worship rise before You like incense, pure and wholehearted. Fill my spirit with the peace that flows from Your throne room. Teach me to rest, to trust, and to behold You in every season. In Jesus' Name, Amen.

Faith lifts its gaze higher than fear.

Day 84
For We Are His Workmanship

Scripture:

"For we are His workmanship, created in Christ Jesus unto good works, which God hath before ordained that we should walk in them."

Ephesians 2:10 (KJV)

Reflection:

You are not an accident, you are artistry. Before you ever took a breath, the Creator shaped you with purpose. Every detail of who you are was woven with intention, meaning, and Divine foresight. Faith doesn't question worth; it walks boldly in design. You weren't created to blend in or mimic others but to uniquely reveal His Glory in the earth.

To see yourself rightly is to honor the hands that formed you. You carry the fingerprints of God evidence of His imagination, His wisdom, and His Love. Every gift He placed within you is deliberate. Every trial He carried you through has shaped depth and resilience. Every victory you've experienced is another stroke of color on Heaven's canvas. God's workmanship is not fragile. It is Divine craftsmanship strong, purposeful, and enduring. You were created in Christ Jesus with good works already prepared ahead of time. Your assignment is not something you chase; it is something you walk into. Your purpose is not something you earn; it is something you embody as you remain surrendered to the Master who crafted you. Let THIS Truth settle deeply: You are His masterpiece, and He plans to display His Goodness through your life.

Prayer:

Father, thank You for creating me with purpose, precision, and intention. Help me walk confidently in the design You ordained before I ever existed. Remove every lie that opposes my identity and replace it with Your truth. Let my life reflect Your workmanship and bring honor to the Master who shaped me. May everything, I do reveal Your Glory. In Jesus' Name, Amen.

Faith recognizes the beauty of God's design in you.

Day 85
Beloved, Do Not Be Afraid

Scripture:

"Fear thou not; for I am with thee: be not dismayed; for I am thy God: I will strengthen thee; yea, I will help thee; yea, I will uphold thee with the right hand of My righteousness."

Isaiah 41:10 (KJV)

Reflection:

God's perfect love is the antidote to fear. Fear loses its power the moment our focus shifts from what threatens us to the God Who sustains us. Peace doesn't come from understanding every detail, it comes from knowing the One Who holds every detail. When faith takes root, fear has no room to remain. Beloved, do not be afraid of what you cannot control. You are held by the Unchanging One whose strength never diminishes and whose hand never slips. The God Who walks on storms is the same God Who walks with you. He does not observe your fear from a distance. He steps into it with you.

- His Promise is personal: I am with thee.
- His identity is your confidence: I am thy God.
- His actions are your assurance: I will strengthen… I will help… I will uphold it.

The same Voice that silenced raging seas still whispers to your trembling heart, Be still. The unknown may feel intimidating, but you are not facing it alone. His righteousness supports you. His Love surrounds you. His Presence steadies you. Fear may knock, but it cannot stay where trust is rooted.

Prayer:

Lord, when fear tries to steal my peace, remind me that You are near. Strengthen my spirit and anchor my heart in Your unfailing promises. Let Your Presence quiet every anxious thought and fill me with confidence in Your Love. Help me rest secure in the Truth that I am upheld by Your righteous hand. In Jesus' Name, Amen.

Faith silences fear by remembering His Presence.

Day 86
To Everything There Is a Season

Scripture:

"To everything there is a season, and a time to every purpose under the heaven."

Ecclesiastes 3:1 (KJV)

Reflection:

Faith trusts the rhythm of God's seasons. Nothing in your life unfolds by accident; each chapter, each transition, each shift is guided by Divine appointment. God writes your story with intention, and every season carries a sacred beauty: the sowing, the waiting, the pruning, the blooming, and the harvest. When you understand God's timing, you stop resisting His process. Winter is not the end; it is the preparation of ground for new life. It is the season where roots deepen, hidden growth takes place, and strength is cultivated beneath the surface. Spring reveals what winter prepared. Summer matures what spring awakened. Autumn gathers what seasons of faithfulness have produced.

Every stage matters. Every chapter holds a purpose. Nothing is wasted in God's Hands. Seasons will change, but the God Who governs them remains the same constant, faithful, unhurried, and intentional. His timing is perfect because His wisdom is flawless. Trusting Him means embracing where you are, knowing that He is preparing you for where you are going. **Peace** comes not from understanding the season, but from knowing the One Who appointed it.

Prayer:

Lord, teach me to recognize the season I'm in and embrace it with peace and patience. Help me trust Your Timing, even when I don't understand it. Strengthen my heart to wait with hope and walk with confidence. Let every season whether sowing, growing, pruning, or harvesting draw me closer to Your purpose and deepen my dependence on You. In Jesus' Name, Amen.

Faith rests in the rhythm of Divine timing.

Day 87
Whoever Walks with the Wise

Scripture:

"He that walketh with wise men shall be wise: but a companion of fools shall be destroyed."

Proverbs 13:20 (KJV)

Reflection:

Faith flourishes in wise company. The people who surround you help shape the climate of your belief, the direction of your decisions, and the strength of your spirit. You grow in the environment you choose. Walk with those who sharpen your soul, elevate your thinking, and challenge you to live at the level of your calling.

God often imparts direction through Divine relationships. Wisdom doesn't form in isolation; it multiplies when shared among the faithful. When you walk with those who honor God, their counsel becomes guardrails for your purpose. Their faith strengthens yours. Their obedience inspires your own.

Choose companions who lift your gaze toward God, not drag your heart toward fear. Surround yourself with those who speak life, who pursue righteousness, who carry the fragrance of Christ. Wise relationships are not merely helpful, they are holy. They protect your path, nourish your faith, and position you for destiny. You become like the company you keep. Walk with the wise, and wisdom will walk with you.

Prayer:

Lord, surround me with wise and faithful people. Help me to recognize and value godly counsel, and to walk closely with those who honor You. Shape me into a vessel of wisdom for others, and let every relationship in my life glorify You. Protect my steps, guide my connections, and order my path in Your purpose. In Jesus' Name, Amen.

Faith walks wisely when it walks with the wise.

Day 88
You Have Power and Authority

Scripture:

"Behold, I give unto you power to tread on serpents and scorpions, and over all the power of the enemy: and nothing shall by any means hurt you."

Luke 10:19 (KJV)

Reflection:

Faith knows its authority. You have not been left vulnerable or powerless, you have been given Divine authority through the Blood of Jesus and the power of His Holy Name. The believer's victory is not wishful thinking; it is delegated authority, issued from the throne of Heaven and sealed by the finished work of Christ.

Authority means you don't fight for victory; you fight from victory. What Jesus conquered, you now enforce. What He defeated, you now tread on. When you speak the Word in faith, darkness has no choice but to bow. Strongholds break. Fear flees. The enemy retreats from the believer who knows who they are and Whose Name they carry.

Hell trembles not at your volume, but at your position seated with Christ in heavenly places. You are not fighting alone; you are fighting with the backing of Heaven. Stand firm. Speak boldly. Walk confidently. You carry kingdom authority everywhere you go.

Prayer:

Lord Jesus, thank You for the power and authority You've given me through Your Name. Teach me to walk boldly in that Truth and to enforce the victory You already won for me. Let faith rise until fear flees, and let every word I speak align with the authority of Heaven. Use me for Your Glory, and let Your Power be revealed through my life. In Your Holy Name, Amen.

Faith that knows its authority walks in victory.

Day 89
Expectation Shifts the Atmosphere

Scripture:

"According to your faith be it unto you."

Matthew 9:29 (KJV)

Reflection:

Expectation is the spiritual posture that welcomes God's movement into your life. It is the turning of the heart toward Heaven with confidence not in what you see, but in who God is. When you shift from worry to expectation, from fear to faith, you create room for Divine intervention. God responds to those who dare to believe Him even when circumstances offer no sign of change.

Faith is not blind optimism; it is anchored in the unwavering Truth that God is faithful to His Word. Expectation is the fruit of a heart convinced that His Promises are not only true but personal. When your focus moves from striving to trusting, from anxiety to anticipation, Heaven leans in. The atmosphere around you begins to shift not because of your effort, but because of your expectancy.

Expectation says, God, I believe You will do exactly what You said. It opens the door for miracles. It aligns your spirit with possibility. It transforms the environment of your mind, your home, and your heart. Lift your eyes today, beloved and expect Him. Expect Him to answer. Expect Him to heal. Expect Him to provide. Expect Him to move. What seems impossible is simply the next stage where God will show Himself strong on your behalf.

Prayer:

Lord, shift my heart into expectation. Remove doubt, silence fear, and lift my spirit into bold, childlike faith. I expect Your goodness, I trust Your Timing, and I rest in Your Promises. Let expectancy transform the atmosphere of my life. In Jesus' Name, Amen.

Expectation prepares the heart for Heaven's response

Day 90
Rekindle the Fire Within

Scripture:

"Wherefore I put thee in remembrance that thou stir up the gift of God, which is in thee by the putting on of My Hands."

2 Timothy 1:6 (KJV)

"Not slothful in business; fervent in spirit; serving the Lord."

Romans 12:11 (KJV)

Reflection:

There are seasons when the embers of our faith seem to dim beneath the weight of trials, distractions, or delay. Yet the fire has not gone out; it only awaits the breath of God. He is calling you to stir again the flame within, to remember His Promises, and to walk forward in the power of His Spirit. What He placed within you was never meant to be buried under fear, doubt, or fatigue.

The fire of faith must be tended. It grows through prayer, worship, and obedience through time spent in His Presence where His breath once again fills your soul. Even a small spark can become a blaze when yielded to His Wind.

Beloved, faith that once flickered can burn bright again when surrendered to the wind of His Presence. Do not let the flame grow cold; fan it into flame through renewed devotion and confident expectation.

Prayer:

Lord, breathe Your holy fire upon my heart again. Let every place that has grown cold be consumed by Your Love. Rekindle my faith, my zeal, and my devotion until I burn with a steady flame that brings You Glory. In Jesus' Name, Amen.

The flame that once flickered now burns with holy purpose.

Section Three: Identity in Christ

Day 91
You Are His Beloved

Scripture:

"Behold, what manner of love the Father hath bestowed upon us, that we should be called the sons of God..."

1 John 3:1 (KJV)

Reflection:

Your identity does not begin with what you have done. It begins with what He has declared. Before you ever lifted your voice in prayer, before you ever said yes to His call, before you even fully understood His Grace. He named you Beloved. Identity in Christ is not earned; it is bestowed. It is the overflow of the Father's love, freely given to those who abide in Him. The world may label you by your past, your mistakes, or your limitations, but Heaven calls you by your true name: child of God, redeemed, chosen, set apart. You no longer live from a place of trying to become enough. You live from the Truth that in Christ, you already are. Loved without condition. Accepted without hesitation. Secure without striving.

Let this identity settle deep within your spirit today. You are not defined by fear, failure, or the opinions of others. You are defined by the One Who formed you, called you, and sealed you with His Spirit.

Prayer:

Father, thank You for calling me Your beloved. Help me to walk in the fullness of who I am in Christ. Silence every voice that contradicts Your truth, and strengthen me to live confidently in Your Love. Let my identity be rooted in You alone. In Jesus' Name, Amen.

When you know who you are in Him, every other voice loses its power.

Day 92:
Chosen, Not Overlooked

Scripture:

"Ye have not chosen Me, but I have chosen you, and ordained you…"

John 15:16 (KJV)

Reflection:

In a world that often celebrates popularity, visibility, and status, it is easy to feel overlooked or unseen. But Heaven tells a different story. Long before anyone knew your name, Jesus chose you. Not reluctantly. Not accidentally. Not because of your perfection. But because of His Love. You were chosen with intentionality. Chosen with purpose. Chosen with destiny woven into your very existence. When Jesus said, I have chosen you, He was declaring that your life is not random, it is appointed. You are not an afterthought; you are part of His Divine design. You are selected, set apart, and ordained to bear fruit that remains.

The world may pass you by. People may overlook you. Opportunities may seem to slip through your hands. But God your Father has never once overlooked you. His eyes have been upon you from the beginning, and His Plans for your life are filled with eternal significance. Let this Truth quiet every insecurity:

You are chosen by the One whose choice never fails.

Prayer:

Jesus, thank You for choosing me before I ever chose You. Help me walk in the confidence of Your call and not in the fear of being overlooked. Align my heart with Your purpose and help me bear the fruit You have ordained for my life. In Your precious Name, Amen.

You are chosen. You are ordained. And nothing can undo God's decision over your life.

Day 93
Fully Accepted in the Beloved

Scripture:

"To the praise of the Glory of His Grace, wherein He hath made us accepted in the beloved."

Ephesians 1:6 (KJV)

Reflection:

One of the deepest wounds the human heart can carry is the fear of rejection, the ache of wondering if we are enough, worthy, or wanted. But in Christ, that fear is silenced forever. You are accepted in the Beloved not tolerated, not barely received, not conditionally welcomed but fully, joyfully, eternally embraced. Acceptance in Christ is not fragile. It does not shift with your feelings, your mistakes, or your circumstances. He does not love you more on your best days or less on your weakest ones. His acceptance is anchored in His finished work, not your performance. You no longer have to strive for approval or earn affection. You are not defined by the acceptance or rejection of people. The One whose opinion matters most has already declared you His own. Let this Truth settle deeply into the quiet places of your soul:

You are wanted. You are welcome. You belong.

Prayer:

Father, thank You that I am fully accepted in the Beloved. Remove every fear of rejection from my heart and teach me to rest in the security of Your Love. Help me walk in confidence, knowing I am chosen, cherished, and held close by You. In Jesus' Name, Amen.

The acceptance you long for is already yours in Christ.

Day 94
The Power of a Testimony

Scripture:

"A reminder that your story of redemption carries Heaven's authority to set others free. And they overcame him by the Blood of the Lamb, and by the word of their testimony; and they loved not their lives unto the death."

Revelation 12:11 (KJV)

"Come and hear, all ye that fear God, and I will declare what He hath done for my soul."

Psalm 66:16 (KJV)

Reflection:

Your testimony is more than a memory; it's a weapon. Each time you share what God has done, you remind Hell that its grip has been broken. Your story carries the fragrance of deliverance and becomes an invitation for others to believe again. Testimonies are living proof that God still moves, still heals, still restores. They tear down walls of doubt and ignite faith in those who listen. When you speak of His Goodness, Heaven bears witness; angels rejoice, and hearts are strengthened. Never underestimate what God can do through your story. It was born in battle, shaped by Grace, and sealed by victory. Your scars now shine as evidence of His Mercy and what once hurt now heals others. Speak boldly, for your voice carries the sound of breakthrough.

Prayer:

Lord, thank You for turning my story into a testimony of Your faithfulness. Give me the boldness to share it so others may find hope. Use my words to reveal Your Power and to draw many to the saving knowledge of Jesus Christ. Let my life forever proclaim You are good, and Your mercy endures forever. In Jesus' Name, Amen.

My story belongs to Him; through it others will see His Glory.

Day 95
Justice and Mercy

Scripture:

"He hath shewed thee, O man, what is good; and what doth the Lord require of thee, but to do justly, and to love mercy, and to walk humbly with thy God?"

Micah 6:8 (KJV)

"Blessed are the merciful: for they shall obtain mercy."

Matthew 5:7 (KJV)

Reflection:

Justice and mercy are not opposites; they are the heartbeat of God working in harmony. Justice upholds truth, and mercy extends Grace. Together, they reflect the balance of a holy God Who is both righteous and kind. When we walk humbly before Him, we begin to see others through His eyes through the lens of redemption rather than judgment. Justice without mercy becomes harsh; mercy without justice becomes hollow. But when both flow from a heart surrendered to Christ, lives are healed, wrongs are made right, and love fulfills the law. The Lord invites His people to become carriers of both justice and mercy in a world desperate for compassion and truth. Your actions, your words, and even your silence can echo Heaven's standard. Seek fairness. Offer forgiveness. Love deeply. Walk humbly. In doing so, you will reveal the heart of the One Who reigns in perfect balance. A reminder that God's character is revealed through how we treat others with both righteousness and compassion.

Prayer:

Father, help me to walk in Your ways with justice, mercy, and humility. Teach me to love Truth without losing tenderness and to extend mercy without compromising righteousness. May my life reflect Your Kingdom on earth as it is in Heaven. In Jesus' Name, Amen.

Justice is the weight of His Truth; mercy is the warmth of His Heart.

Day 96
Chosen and Called

Scripture:

"But ye are a chosen generation, a royal priesthood, an holy nation, a peculiar people; that ye should shew forth the praises of Him who hath called you out of darkness into His marvellous light."

1 Peter 2:9 (KJV)

Reflection:

Before the foundation of the world, God chose you. Your calling is not a coincidence; it is Divine intention woven into your very being. You were handpicked by the King of Glory to carry His Presence, declare His Goodness, and shine His marvelous light in a world growing dim with doubt and despair.

To be chosen means you are not random, overlooked, or accidental. Heaven intentionally sets you apart. And when you understand that you are chosen, insecurity loses its grip. You stop striving for approval because you begin living from acceptance. You stop questioning your worth because your identity is anchored in His declaration not in human affirmation.

God's call does not depend on perfection; it depends on willingness. He does not ask you to be flawless He asks you to be available. Every yes you give Him; echoes through eternity, becoming part of Heaven's symphony of redemption and purpose.

You were chosen to worship. Chosen to witness. Chosen to carry light. Chosen to walk in royal identity. Your calling is not small. It is sacred.

Prayer:

Father, thank You for calling me out of darkness into Your marvelous light. Help me to walk in the confidence of being chosen and to live fully from the identity You have spoken over me. Let every step reflect Your Kingdom's purpose, and let my life display Your Glory. May I honor Your call with obedience, humility, and boldness. In Jesus' Name, Amen.

Faith stands tall in the confidence of being chosen.

Day 97
Clothed in Righteousness

Scripture:

"I will greatly rejoice in the Lord, my soul shall be joyful in my God; for He hath clothed me with the garments of salvation, He hath covered me with the robe of righteousness."

Isaiah 61:10 (KJV)

Reflection:

When God clothes you in righteousness, shame loses its voice. The robe of righteousness is not stitched together by human effort, it is woven by Divine Grace. It is not earned; it is given. God Himself wraps you in a covering that hides every failure, heals every wound, and silences every accusation.

Faith wears what Grace provides. You no longer stand in your own worth but in His perfection. This robe does not merely cover your past, it redefines your present and secures your future. The garments of salvation remind you daily that you are not identified by where you've been, but by Who has redeemed you. Righteousness is not a feeling; it is a position. It restores honor where shame once lived. It replaces insecurity with identity. It reminds your soul that you are not tolerated, you are treasured. Not exposed, you are covered. Not rejected, you are accepted in the Beloved. Rejoice, beloved, your life is draped in Divine beauty. You are fully covered, fully cleansed, fully loved, and fully His.

Prayer:

Lord, thank You for clothing me in Your righteousness. Help me to walk in purity, humility, and confidence not in myself, but in the covering You have given me. Let the beauty of Your salvation shine through my life. May Your robe remind me every day of who I am in You: redeemed, restored, and made new. In Jesus' Name, Amen.

Faith wears righteousness as its royal robe.

Day 98
Renewed Mind, Redeemed Heart

Scripture:

"And be not conformed to this world: but be ye transformed by the renewing of your mind."

Romans 12:2 (KJV)

Reflection:

Transformation begins in the mind, but it flows from the heart. When the Holy Spirit renews your thinking, He reorders your living. God's Word becomes the sacred lens through which you see, reason, respond, and discern. A renewed mind recognizes lies before they take root and replaces them with Truth that liberates.

A redeemed heart, softened by Grace, learns to love Truth more than comfort and obedience more than opinion. It treasures what God treasures and rejects what once pulled it off course. Together, a renewed mind and a redeemed heart form the sanctuary where the Spirit dwells, guides, corrects, and empowers.

You are not who you used to be, you are being remade, reshaped, and restored daily into the image of Christ. Renewal is not a moment but a continual miracle. As your thoughts align with His Truth, your life aligns with His Purpose. As your heart yields to His Love, your spirit grows stronger, steadier, and more like Him. The world tries to mold you, but the Word transforms you.

Prayer:

Father, renew my mind with Your Truth and heal my heart with Your Love. Let every thought align with Your Will and every motive be shaped by Your Spirit. Transform me daily into Your likeness. Make my mind a place of purity and my heart a place of worship, that my life may reflect Your Glory. In Jesus' Name, Amen.

Faith renews the mind and redeems the heart.

Day 99
Living from Victory

Scripture:

"But thanks be to God, which giveth us the victory through our Lord Jesus Christ."

1 Corinthians 15:57 (KJV)

Reflection:

Victory is not a destination; it is a position. The cross did not make triumph possible; it made it permanent. Jesus didn't win part of the battle. He finished the whole war. Because of His resurrection, your life is anchored not in striving for victory, but in standing in it.

Every battle you face, seen or unseen is already beneath the authority of the risen Christ. Faith does not create victory; it claims it. It simply stands where Jesus has already conquered. The enemy's greatest strategy is deception, persuading believers to live defeated lives while holding a victorious inheritance. He cannot remove your victory, but he will try to make you forget it.

Living from victory means your confidence is rooted in what Jesus accomplished, not in what you feel, see, or fear. It means walking boldly, praying with authority, resisting with strength, and worshiping with certainty. The crown of triumph rests upon your Redeemer's head and because you belong to Him, that victory now rests upon you as well. You don't fight for victory. You fight from victory. You live in victory. You carry His victory.

Prayer:

Lord, thank You for giving me victory through Your Son. Help me to live from the finished work of the cross and not from striving or fear. Let Your Triumph shape my thoughts, strengthen my spirit, and guide my steps. Teach me to walk each day in the confidence of what Jesus has already conquered on my behalf. In Jesus' Name, Amen.

Faith fights from a victory already won.

Day 100
The Light Within You

Scripture:

"Ye are the light of the world. A city that is set on an hill cannot be hid."

Matthew 5:14 (KJV)

Reflection:

Identity shines, it cannot be hidden. When Christ dwells within you, His light becomes your life. You were never meant to blend into the shadows or match the temperature of the world around you. You were designed to illuminate the places others avoid and to radiate the hope many have forgotten.

The world doesn't need your perfection, it needs your presence, saturated with His Love. The light in you is not a reflection of your own strength; it is the glow of the One Who lives inside you. Faith does not shrink back, it shines. It steps into dark places with truth, compassion, and courage, carrying the brightness of Heaven into every room.

A single spark of obedience can ignite transformation in places long overshadowed. Your kindness can soften hardened hearts. Your Peace can calm anxious atmospheres. Your testimony can unlock someone else's freedom. Your life is a lamp crafted by God and lifted by Grace. Shine freely, beloved. You are not a lamp to be hidden; you are a city set on a hill. The world needs what God placed inside you.

Prayer:

Lord, thank You for filling me with Your light. Help me to shine boldly and beautifully in every sphere of influence. Let my words carry compassion, my actions reflect Your truth, and my life displays Your Love so others may see You and glorify You. In Jesus' Name, Amen.

Faith shines brightly when it carries His light into darkness.

Day 101
Adopted and Adored

Scripture:

"Having predestinated us unto the adoption of children by Jesus Christ to Himself, according to the good pleasure of His will."

Ephesians 1:5 (KJV)

Reflection:

Before you ever reached for God, He reached for you. Adoption into His family was never an afterthought, it was His desire from the beginning. He did not rescue you reluctantly; He received you joyfully. You were wanted. Chosen. Loved into belonging. Faith finds rest in this Truth: you are no longer an orphan of circumstance; you are a child of covenant. You don't stand outside hoping for a place at the table; you sit at the family feast with a seat reserved by Grace. His Name covers you. His Love keeps you. His Spirit whispers daily, You are Mine.

This is the affection that silences insecurity. This is the Truth that unmasks every lie of unworthiness. You are not tolerated, you are treasured. You are not simply accepted, you are adored. The Father delights in you with the same love He has for His Son. And nothing can undo, reverse, or diminish the adoption sealed by the Blood of Jesus. You belong and that changes everything.

Prayer:

Father, thank You for adopting me into Your family. Remind me each day that I am fully loved, deeply valued, and securely Yours. Let my life reflect the confidence and joy of One Who belongs to You forever. May Your Love shape my identity and steady my heart in every season. In Jesus' Name, Amen.

Faith rests in the assurance of adoption.

Day 102
A Heart Like His

Scripture:

"And I will give them one heart, and I will put a new spirit within you."

Ezekiel 11:19 (KJV)

Reflection:

The greatest transformation God performs is not in your circumstances but in your heart. He does not patch, mend, or modify the old heart He replaces it. He gives you a heart that beats in rhythm with His own, one shaped by Grace, softened by mercy, and strengthened by love. A heart like His Love is without condition. Forgives without hesitation. Serves without recognition. Believes without wavering.

This is the miracle of salvation not only that God saves you, but that He reshapes you from the inside out. Faith welcomes this exchange. It surrenders the hardened places, the wounded places, the fearful places, and receives a heart made new by the Spirit. When God gives you His Heart, compassion grows stronger than offense. Mercy triumphs over judgment. Kindness becomes instinct, and humility becomes strength. His Spirit gently trains your responses until your life begins to reflect His nature. A transformed heart is Heaven's greatest testimony and the world sees Christ most clearly through those who carry His Heart.

Prayer:

Lord, give me a heart like Yours pure, tender, and steadfast. Remove the hardness that life has built and fill me with love that reflects Your Character. Shape my thoughts, responses, and desires until my heart beats in sync with Heaven. In Jesus' Name, Amen.

Faith is formed in the heart that mirrors His.

Day 103
Confidence Through the Cross

Scripture:

"In whom we have boldness and access with confidence by the faith of Him."

Ephesians 3:12 (KJV)

Reflection:

The cross did more than redeem you; it restored your confidence before God. Because of Jesus, you no longer approach the Father as a beggar, hoping to be heard, but as a beloved child, welcomed with delight. Faith opens the door to Grace, and Grace gives you boldness to step into His Presence without fear or shame.

Confidence in Christ is not arrogance; it is assurance anchored in His sacrifice. You come freely not because you are flawless, but because His Blood has made the way permanently open. The veil is gone, the barrier is broken, and your access is secured by the One Who stands forever as your Advocate.

This holy confidence changes everything:

- You pray with assurance, not hesitation.
- You worship with freedom, not fear.
- You stand in identity, not insecurity.
- You draw near knowing your Father's arms are already open.

The cross did not merely forgive you, it welcomed you home.

Prayer:

Thank You, Jesus, for giving me access to the Father through Your cross. Let me live each day with holy boldness and humble gratitude. May my confidence rest entirely in Your finished work, and may I draw near to the Father with a heart full of faith. In Your Holy Name, Amen.

Faith walks boldly because the cross made the way.

Day 104
The Voice of the Shepherd

Scripture:

"My sheep hear My voice, and I know them, and they follow Me."

John 10:27 (KJV)

Reflection:

Every believer is known by name and guided by voice. Jesus, the Good Shepherd, doesn't lead from a distance He leads from nearness. He doesn't have to shout because He walks close enough to whisper. His Voice carries peace in confusion, comfort in sorrow, conviction in wandering, and clarity in decision.

Faith listens more than it speaks. It recognizes that following well requires trusting that the One leading sees farther, deeper, and clearer than we ever could. The Shepherd's direction may not always align with logic, comfort, or convenience but it will always align with safety, purpose, and love. His Voice is gentle, yet it carries authority. It does not condemn; it calls. It does not confuse; it confirms. It does not drive you with pressure; it draws you with presence. And the more you listen, the easier it becomes to recognize the familiar tone of His Heart. The Shepherd leads not just your steps but your soul.

Prayer:

Lord, attune my ears to hear Your Voice above the noise. Let Your whisper still my heart, and let Your Word guide my steps. Teach me to follow You with quiet confidence, trusting that every direction from Your Hand leads me into peace, purpose, and protection. In Jesus' Name, Amen.

Faith recognizes His Voice in every season.

Day 105
Rooted in Love

Scripture:

"That Christ may dwell in your hearts by faith; that ye, being rooted and grounded in love, may be able to comprehend... the love of Christ, which passeth knowledge."

Ephesians 3:17 -19 (KJV)

Reflection:

Roots determine endurance. A tree can withstand storms, winds, and droughts because its roots reach deep. In the same way, when you are rooted in the love of Christ, no storm can uproot your faith. The deeper your revelation of His Love grows, the stronger your peace becomes. Love is not merely something God gives; it is Who He is. And when your life is grounded in His Love, everything changes. You live from security instead of striving, from acceptance instead of anxiety, from belonging instead of fear. You stop chasing validation because you realize you already have His affection. You stop questioning your worth because His Love has settled the matter forever.

To be rooted in love is to be anchored in Truth that cannot be shaken. His Love becomes the soil where faith thrives, joy blossoms, and purpose grows. And as your roots sink deeper into Him, you begin to understand the vastness of a love that surpasses knowledge yet fills the heart to overflowing. A life rooted in love is a life unmovable.

Prayer:

Father, let my roots go deep into Your Love. Ground me in the Truth of who You are so I will not be shaken by fear or doubt. Fill my heart with the strength that comes from knowing I am fully loved. Let everything, I do flow from Your Heart and reflect the love that has transformed me. In Jesus' Name, Amen.

Faith grows where love is its soil.

Day 106
Transformed by Grace

Scripture:

"And of His fulness have all we received, and Grace for Grace."

John 1:16 (KJV)

Reflection:

Grace does not simply cover sin; it transforms identity. It doesn't just erase what was; it rewrites who you are. Every encounter with Grace becomes another chapter where God's mercy proves stronger than your memory. You are no longer defined by failure, wounds, or the shadows of your past. You are now the living reflection of His redemption. Grace meets you where you are, but it never leaves you there. It lifts, cleanses, strengthens, and reshapes. It breaks chains you thought you'd carry forever and whispers Truth into places once filled with shame. This is the miracle of Grace: it reaches every crevice of the heart and brings light where darkness lived.

Faith receives what Grace freely gives. And transformation is not a single moment; it's a continual overflow of His fullness. Day by day, Grace upon Grace builds the testimony of a life completely remade by love. As you rest in His Grace, you are steadily becoming who He always intended you to be. You are not a product of your past. You are a portrait of His Grace.

Prayer:

Lord, thank You for the abundance of Grace that renews me daily. Let me never grow familiar with the miracle of Your mercy. Transform me continually into the likeness of Christ, and let Your fullness overflow into every part of my life. In Jesus' Name, Amen.

Faith receives Grace and becomes Grace in motion.

Day 107
The Strength of Gentleness

Scripture:

"A soft answer turneth away wrath: but grievous words stir up anger."

Proverbs 15:1 (KJV)

Reflection:

Gentleness is not weakness; it is strength under the Spirit's control. True gentleness is not the absence of power but the mastery of it. It is the quiet force that can calm storms, defuse tension, and heal wounds that harshness only deepens. Jesus, the Lion and the Lamb, conquered not through cruelty but through compassion. His gentleness drew the broken, restored the fallen, and silenced the proud. When the Holy Spirit forms gentleness within you, your responses begin to mirror the nature of Christ, measured, merciful, and mighty in their restraint.

Faith expresses itself most profoundly in gentleness. Anyone can react, but it takes strength to respond with Grace. A gentle answer is a declaration that God is in control, not emotion. It shows that your identity is rooted in Christ, not in offense or anger. The meek do not lose ground; they are the very ones Jesus said will inherit the earth. Gentleness is not passive; it is powerful. It is the strength to stay calm when provoked, kind when misunderstood, and compassionate when wronged.

Prayer:

Lord, teach me the strength of gentleness. Let my words bring peace instead of division and healing instead of harm. Guard my tongue, soften my responses, and help me reflect Your calm and compassionate heart in every conversation. Shape me into One Who carries Your Peace wherever I go. In Jesus' Name, Amen.

Faith wrapped in gentleness reflects the strength of Christ.

Day 108
Living Epistles

Scripture:

"Ye are our epistle written in our hearts, known and read of all men."

2 Corinthians 3:2 (KJV)

Reflection:

You are a living letter from Heaven written not with ink, but with the Spirit of the living God. Every day, your life speaks a message that someone around you desperately needs to hear. Some will never open a Bible, but they will read your patience, your compassion, your purity, and your Grace. Faith makes your life legible. Love makes it beautiful. The world is watching, not to criticize, but to understand what God is like. Your reactions, your kindness, your humility tell a story far louder than words ever could. Every trial you endure with peace becomes a paragraph of His Faithfulness. Every forgiveness you extend becomes a sentence of His Mercy. Every sacrifice becomes a line of His Love written across the pages of your life. You are not a rough draft; you are a work in progress authored by the hand of God. The ink of His Mercy never fades. It writes redemption over regret, hope over sorrow, and Grace over every broken chapter. And the longer you walk with Him, the clearer His message becomes in you. Your life is being read. And for many, you are the only Gospel they will encounter today.

Prayer:

Lord, let my life be a letter that reveals Your Heart. Write Your Truth upon me so clearly that others see Your Love through my actions and hear Your hope through my words. Make me a faithful witness of Your goodness, a living testimony of Your Grace. In Jesus' Name, Amen.

Faith lives as a message of mercy written by Grace.

Day 109
The Image of the Son

Scripture:

"For whom He did foreknow, He also did predestinate to be conformed to the image of His Son."

Romans 8:29 (KJV)

Reflection:

Identity finds its truest shape in imitation. Before you ever lived a day on earth, God had already purposed that your life would be shaped into the likeness of Jesus. Salvation rescues you, but transformation refines you, chiseling, molding, and shaping you until His character is seen in your countenance and His nature flows through your actions.

Every trial smooths an edge. Every surrender softens a hard place. Every step of obedience adds definition to the Divine portrait He's forming in you. Christlikeness is not achieved by effort but by abiding. The more you behold Him, the more you become like Him. Faith doesn't resist the process; it welcomes it. God uses joy and sorrow, blessings and burdens, waiting and breakthrough to craft something eternal within you.

You are not being changed at random; you are being conformed on purpose. Every day, a little more of you fades, and a little more of Him emerges until your life becomes a reflection of His Humility, His Compassion, His Purity, His Strength, and His Love. The world does not need a perfect you; it needs a visible Jesus shining through you.

Prayer:

Father, continue shaping me into the image of Your Son. Transform my heart until His humility, purity, and love become my nature. Let every part of my life reflect Jesus so clearly that others are drawn to Him through me. In Jesus' Name, Amen.

Faith beholds Christ and becomes like Him.

Day 110
My Greatest Treasure Is You, O God

Scripture:

"Thy word is a lamp unto my feet, and a light unto my path."

Psalm 119:105 (KJV)

Reflection:

God's Word is the believer's greatest treasure, timeless, priceless, and overflowing with life. It is more than ink on pages; it is the very breath of God guiding, guarding, and grounding every step you take. When His Word becomes your delight, your compass, and your daily bread, you discover that no darkness can linger where His Truth shines. His Word steadies trembling hearts, lifts weary spirits, and reveals the path when everything around you feels uncertain. Scripture isn't simply instruction; it is invitation. Each verse draws you closer to the One Who knows you, loves you, and leads you.

It reminds you of Who He is, who you are, and what He has promised. To treasure His Word is to treasure His Heart. The more you meditate on His Truth, the more His Presence becomes evident in your decisions, your desires, and your daily steps. His Word becomes a hiding place in trouble, a refuge in confusion, and a wellspring of renewal for your soul. In a world filled with shifting opinions and fading voices, His Word remains your unshakable anchor. And as you hold His Word close, you realize something beautiful in every line, every promise, and every whisper of Scripture ultimately leads you to Him. The Word reveals the greatest treasure of all… God Himself.

Prayer:

Lord, thank You for the precious gift of Your Word. Let my heart value it above silver, gold, and every earthly treasure. Teach me to walk in the light it provides and to find comfort, direction, and renewal in every verse. Shape my choices through Your Truth and draw me continually into deeper fellowship with You. In Jesus' Name, Amen.

Faith treasures the Word and finds its path illuminated.

Day 111
Led by His Hand

Scripture:

"I will instruct thee and teach thee in the way which thou shalt go: I will guide thee with Mine eye."

Psalm 32:8 (KJV)

Reflection:

You are never walking blind when you walk with God. Even when the next step seems hidden, and the road ahead feels uncertain, His guidance is gentle, deliberate, and perfect. He leads not just with commands, but with care, with His Hand upon your life and His eye ever upon your path. God is taking you to places your feet have not yet known, shaping opportunities you did not expect, and preparing blessings you could not have orchestrated on your own. You may feel unsure of the process, but Heaven is not uncertain. You are not wandering; you are being led by the One Who knows every step before you take it.

There will be seasons when His leading feels subtle, more like a whisper than a shout. Yet even then, His Presence goes before you, His Peace walks beside you, and His Goodness follows behind you. Faith trusts when sight cannot. When you cannot trace His Hand, you can trust His Heart. The God Who begins a journey is the God Who completes it. His leadership is not rushed, random, or reckless; it is wise, watchful, and filled with love. Every closed door, every unexpected turn, every waiting season is woven into a path only He could design. And when you place your life in His Hands, you discover that His Hand has already been holding you all along.

Prayer:

Lord, I place my plans, desires, and steps in Your Hands. Lead me into the paths You have prepared, and steady my heart when I cannot see what comes next. When the way feels hidden, let Your Peace remind me that You are near. Guide me by Your Wisdom and keep my spirit sensitive to Your Voice. I choose to trust Your direction, knowing You are faithful to complete every journey You begin. In Jesus' Name, Amen.

Faith follows even when the path is hidden.

Day 112
Rejoice in the Refining

Scripture:

"Rejoice in the Lord always: and again, I say, Rejoice."

Philippians 4:4 (KJV)

Reflection:

Rejoicing in easy seasons is gratitude, but rejoicing in refining seasons is Glory. It is the kind of praise that shakes prisons, breaks chains, and confuses the enemy. When the fire turns up, and answers seem slow, the flesh wants to sink, but the spirit learns to soar. Joy in hardship is not pretending everything is fine; it is declaring that God is faithful even here. The refining fire is not sent to destroy you but to develop you. Gold is revealed only when the heat rises, and so is faith. Every time you choose to rejoice in the valley, you are lifting your gaze above circumstance and placing your confidence in the One Who is working all things for your good.

Rejoicing shifts the atmosphere first within you, then around you. It realigns your heart with Heaven's rhythm and silences the lies of discouragement. Heaven leans in when worship rises from wounded places, because that kind of praise is pure, costly, and powerful. Joy is not the absence of struggle; it is the presence of trust. It is the quiet confidence that the God Who is refining you is also keeping you, guiding you, and preparing you for greater Glory. So rejoice not because everything feels right, but because God is right in the middle of everything.

Prayer:

Lord, teach me to rejoice not only in triumph but in trial. Strengthen me to praise You when I do not understand what You are doing. Let my worship become a weapon that breaks discouragement and lifts my spirit into Your Presence. Refine my faith until joy flows freely from a heart anchored in You. In Jesus' Name, Amen.

Rejoicing is the song faith sings in the fire.

Day 113
You Are My Beloved

Scripture:

"And lo a voice from heaven, saying, This is My beloved Son, in whom I am well pleased."

Matthew 3:17 (KJV)

Reflection:

Before Jesus taught a sermon, healed a sickness, cast out a demon, or called a disciple, the Father declared Him beloved. His identity was affirmed before His assignment ever began. And the same is true for you. Your worth is not measured by what you do but by Whose you are. Heaven's first word over your life is beloved, deeply loved, fully known, and wholly accepted. God's pleasure is not rooted in your perfection but in your position in Christ. When He looks at you, He does not see your failures or flaws; He sees the righteousness of His Son covering you, shaping you, transforming you.

Faith begins where striving ends. You do not have to earn what has already been given, nor do you have to chase what has already been spoken. The Father's Voice still echoes over your life: You are Mine. You are loved. You are enough because I am enough in you. Let this Truth steady your heart. When insecurity whispers, His Love answers. When shame rises, His affection covers. When doubt questions your value, His declaration reminds you that you are His beloved, treasured before time, chosen before your first breath, and settled forever in His Heart.

Prayer:

Father, thank You for calling me beloved long before I ever knew You. Let Your Voice silence every lie that says I am not enough. Teach me to live from Your approval, not for it. Root my identity in Your Love, and let that love shape the way I think, live, and worship You. In Jesus' Name, Amen.

Faith rests in the identity Heaven has already declared.

Day 114
Risen with Christ

Scripture:

"He is not here: for He is risen, as He said."

Matthew 28:6 (KJV)

Reflection:

The resurrection is more than a moment in history; it is the reality that defines your identity. The empty tomb declares that the power that once held you captive has been broken forever. When Christ stepped out of the grave, every force of darkness lost its authority over your destiny. You are not bound by the failures that once buried you or the fears that tried to entomb your hope. Resurrection means you rise again, not in your own strength, but in the unstoppable life of Christ. What once seemed final is now fertile ground for God's new beginning.

The same Spirit who rolled away the stone now lives within you, lifting you from places where sorrow settled and calling forth life where dreams once died. Faith rises when you remember that resurrection is not just something Jesus did for you, it's the power He placed within you. You walk in victory because He walked out of the grave. Let this Truth settle deep: You are not defined by what ended; you are renewed by what began again when He rose in Glory. Live like one resurrected, bold, unbound, and empowered by the life of Christ.

Prayer:

Lord, thank You that through Your resurrection, I have risen into new life with You. Let the same power that raised You from the grave breathe life into every weary place within me. Remind me daily that nothing broken, buried, or lost is beyond Your restoring touch. Help me walk in resurrection victory with confidence, courage, and joy. In Jesus' Name, Amen.

Faith lives from resurrection, not remembrance.

Day 115
The Beauty of a Quiet Spirit

Scripture:

"You should clothe yourselves instead with the beauty that comes from within, the unfading beauty of a gentle and quiet spirit, which is so precious to God."

1 Peter 3:4 (NLT)

Reflection:

True beauty begins where the noise of striving ends. A quiet spirit is not silence; it is surrender. It is the inner stillness that flows from trusting God more than feelings, outcomes, or opinions. The world applauds confidence in self, but Heaven treasures confidence in Him. The gentle and quiet spirit is powerful precisely because it is anchored, not shaken. It chooses peace when provoked, softness when pressured, and humility when pride would be easier. This spirit is not weak; it is weaponized with wisdom. It is the heart that says, Lord, You fight for me, and rests while He does.

This kind of beauty never fades because it is born from the Spirit of God within you. It does not wrinkle with age or dim with disappointment. Instead, it grows deeper, richer, and more radiant as your heart yields to His shaping. The quiet spirit is not the absence of voice but the presence of virtue. It is the calm rooted in knowing that God sees, God knows, and God defends. This is beauty that attracts Heaven's attention and carries His fragrance wherever you go.

Prayer:

Lord, clothe me in the beauty that only Your Spirit can produce. Quiet the anxious places within me and replace them with Your Peace. Teach me to respond with gentleness, to stand in humility, and to reflect Your calm strength in every circumstance. Let the unfading beauty of a surrendered heart shine through me. In Jesus' Name, Amen.

Faith's quiet confidence is Heaven's kind of beauty.

Day 116
Guided by His Word

Scripture:

"Thy word is a lamp unto my feet, and a light unto my path."

Psalm 119:105 (KJV)

Reflection:

The Word of God does more than speak to your mind; it lights the way before your feet. It guides not only your direction but your decisions, your discernment, and your destiny. His Word shines with clarity when life feels clouded, reminding you that you are never navigating the unknown alone.

A lamp does not reveal the entire journey; it reveals the next step. That is where trust grows. God's Word will not always show you the whole path, but it will always show you the right path. When emotions confuse and circumstances overwhelm, Scripture becomes your unshakable compass. Every time you open His Word, light breaks into the shadows. Confusion loses its voice, and peace rises. Faith becomes steady when rooted in what God has spoken, not in what the world suggests. Walk by the light of His Word, even when the road ahead feels dim; His Truth never fails to lead you forward.

Prayer:

Lord, let Your Word be the lamp that guides my feet and the light that steadies my path. Illuminate every step, correct every direction, and anchor my heart in Your truth. Teach me to listen to Your Voice above every other and to follow Your guidance without fear. In Jesus' Name, Amen.

Faith walks where the Word lights the way.

Day 117
He Will Finish What He Began

Scripture:

"The Lord will perfect that which concerneth me: Thy mercy, O Lord, endureth for ever."

Psalm 138:8 (KJV)

Reflection:

God has never started a work He was unwilling or unable to finish. What He begins, He perfects. What He designs, He develops. Every promise He has spoken over your life carries Heaven's guarantee of completion. You are not a half-written story or an abandoned project; your life is a masterpiece under the steady hand of a faithful God.

Delays are not signs of Divine disinterest; they are evidence of Divine development. What feels unfinished to you is unfolding to Him. In the waiting, He strengthens your foundation. In the stretching, He expands your capacity. In the silence, He refines your hearing. Every season is shaping you for the fulfillment of what He promised. God's mercy is the thread that holds every piece together, weaving purpose into places you thought were wasted. Even when progress is invisible, His Hands are still working. You may feel unfinished, but you are firmly in the care of the One Who completes all things in His perfect timing.

Prayer:

Lord, thank You that You will perfect all that concerns me. When I feel unfinished or uncertain, anchor my heart in Your faithfulness. Strengthen my trust as You complete the beautiful work You began in my life. Let Your mercy cover every step and Your Hand guide every detail. In Jesus' Name, Amen.

Faith waits, knowing His work will be finished in Glory.

Day 118
Give God Your Day

Scripture:

"My voice shalt Thou hear in the morning, O Lord; in the morning will I direct my prayer unto Thee, and will look up."

Psalm 5:3 (KJV)

Reflection:

Morning is a holy threshold, an unclaimed space where your spirit can be shaped before the noise of the world begins. In those quiet first moments, your heart chooses its posture: anxiety or adoration, distraction or devotion. The first voice you speak to sets the tone for every moment that follows. When you lift your eyes early, you lift your expectations. When you give God the beginning, He orders the middle and blesses the end. The morning is not just a routine; it is an offering. A surrendered start becomes the foundation for a Spirit-led day.

Faith whispers, Before I face the world, I will face You. Looking up resets your vision, recenters your soul, and refreshes your perspective. You carry peace because you've first carried prayer. You walk with wisdom because you first walked into His Presence. The calmest days are not the ones without challenges, but the ones anchored in Him from the very start.

Prayer:

Lord, I give You my morning, and I give You my day. Set my heart in alignment with Your Will and steady my mind with Your Peace. Lead my thoughts, guide my steps, and fill my words with Grace. Let everything I do today bring Glory to Your Name. In Jesus' Name, Amen.

Faith begins each day by looking up.

Day 119
The Dream Still Lives

Scripture:

"Now Joseph had a dream…"

Genesis 37:5 (KJV)

Reflection:

The dream God placed within you is not accidental, fragile, or forgotten. It is alive, held and guarded by the One Who never fails. Like Joseph, your journey may take turns you didn't expect. The pit cannot cancel your purpose, the prison cannot silence your promise, and betrayal cannot derail what God ordained. Every season Joseph endured was shaping him for the place his dream required. What looked like setbacks were actually stepping stones, each one preparing his character, deepening his dependence, and aligning him with Divine timing.

Faith holds onto the dream even when the path feels nothing like the promise. God is the Keeper of dreams. If He planted it, He will water it. If He spoke it, He will sustain it. The dream still lives because its life source is Him. Your dream may seem delayed, but it is being developed. Heaven is arranging the details you cannot see. Trust that the God Who authored your dream is faithful to perform it. Your story is not over; the dream is simply unfolding.

Prayer:

Lord, breathe fresh life into the dreams You have placed within me. Strengthen my faith through every pit and every prison season. Give me patience to trust Your Timing and courage to keep believing. Let Your purpose rise above my plans, and bring to completion everything You have ordained. In Jesus' Name, Amen.

Faith protects the dream until destiny unfolds.

Day 120
Lifted Eyes and Anchored Faith

Scripture:

"I will lift up mine eyes unto the hills, from whence cometh my help. My help cometh from the Lord, which made heaven and earth."

Psalm 121:1 - 2 (KJV)

Reflection:

Faith begins with elevation, lifting your eyes above the valley, above the noise, above the fear. The direction of your gaze determines the condition of your heart. When you look down, circumstances overwhelm. When you look around, distractions multiply. But when you look up, faith is awakened by the reminder that your Help is higher, stronger, and greater than anything you face. The Maker of heaven and earth does not merely send help He is your help. Nothing escapes His attention, and nothing exceeds His ability. Lifting your eyes is not a posture of escape but of alignment. It shifts your focus from the instability of the natural to the unshakable faithfulness of God.

When your eyes rise, your heart steadies. Fear loses its authority. The weight you carry begins to lift. Worship lifts your vision higher than your worry. The One Who watches over you does not slumber, does not forget, and does not fail. Anchored faith is born from an upward gaze, a continual choosing to look to Him, again and again.

Prayer:

Lord, I lift my eyes to You, the source of all my strength and the anchor of my soul. Set my gaze above my circumstances and steady my heart in Your unfailing faithfulness. Keep me rooted in Your Love and unmoved by what surrounds me. Let every upward glance remind me that my help comes from You alone. In Jesus' Name, Amen.

Faith lifts its eyes and finds its footing in Grace.

Day 121
Strength for the Journey

Scripture:

"He giveth power to the faint; and to them that have no might He increaseth strength."

Isaiah 40:29 (KJV)

Reflection:

Endurance truly begins at the point where your own strength ends. God never intended for you to walk this journey relying only on what you can muster. His Power fills the places where your effort fails, and His Strength steps in where your might is exhausted. His Strength is not a supplement; it is the source. He doesn't demand resilience from you; He supplies it to you.

The weary heart finds renewal not by pushing harder, striving longer, or pretending to be strong, but by resting deeper in His Presence. Every moment of surrender becomes a Divine exchange: your weakness for His Strength, your weariness for His Renewal, your emptiness for His Abundant Grace. When you lean into Him, you discover what the journey was meant to reveal: God does not simply help the strong; He strengthens the weak. And in that sacred exchange, you rise again.

Prayer:

Lord, when my strength fades, and my spirit grows tired, remind me that You are the source of my power. Lift me above the weight of weariness and renew my heart with Your might. Teach me to draw from Your endless supply of Grace and help me rest in the strength that only You can provide. In Jesus' Name, Amen.

Faith doesn't run on willpower; it runs on His Strength.

Day 122
Endure to the End

Scripture:

"But he that shall endure unto the end, the same shall be saved."

Matthew 24:13 (KJV)

Reflection:

True endurance doesn't begin in your muscles; it begins in your spirit. God never asks you to complete the journey on your own strength. Instead, He waits for the moment when your strength runs out so His can flow in. Human effort has limits; Divine strength does not.

His Power is not a boost; it's a complete exchange. He takes the fainthearted and infuses them with supernatural might. He takes the exhausted and breathes life where weariness once lived. The places you feel weakest become the very places His Strength shines brightest.

You are not expected to carry every burden or run every mile alone. Strength for the journey comes when you lean into His Presence, when you rest in His Promises, and when you allow His Spirit to renew what life has drained. The deeper your surrender, the fuller His supply. Faith whispers, I can't, but He can. And that is where victory begins.

Prayer:

Lord, when I grow tired, remind me that You are the strength I cannot produce on my own. Lift me above the weight of weariness and renew me with Your Power. Trade my weakness for Your might, and let Your Grace carry me through every step of this journey. In Jesus' Name, Amen.

Faith finishes what fear tries to forfeit.

Day 123
The Blessing of Brokenness

Scripture:

"The Lord is nigh unto them that are of a broken heart; and saveth such as be of a contrite spirit."

Psalm 34:18 (KJV)

Reflection:

Brokenness is not the place God avoids; it is the place He rushes into. The world teaches us to hide our fractures, but Heaven calls them invitations. A broken heart is not a sign of failure; it is proof that you are human, beloved, and still in need of the One Who heals perfectly. The cracks you carry are not disqualifications; they are openings through which His Presence pours. God draws near to the contrite because humility becomes holy ground. When your strength collapses, His compassion stands tall. When your heart shatters, His Hands become the safest place for every fragment.

The beauty of brokenness is not in the breaking but in the rebuilding. God does not discard your pieces; He shapes them into something stronger, purer, and more radiant than before. The pain you bring to Him becomes the canvas where His Grace paints redemption. Your story does not end in brokenness; it begins again in His restoration. What the world calls weakness, God calls worship. What feels like ashes becomes the very material He uses to form beauty only He can create.

Prayer:

Lord, meet me in the places where I feel shattered. Gather every piece my heart cannot hold and mend them with Your healing love. Fill the empty spaces with Your Presence, and turn my surrender into strength. Make beauty from my ashes and let my brokenness become a testimony of Your Grace. In Jesus' Name, Amen.

Faith finds fullness in the hands of the Healer.

Day 124
Through the Fire

Scripture:

"When thou walkest through the fire, thou shalt not be burned; neither shall the flame kindle upon thee."

Isaiah 43:2 (KJV)

Reflection:

God never promised a life without fire. He promised His Presence within it. Trials may roar like flames, but they are never sovereign. The One Who calls you His has already declared the outcome: you will walk through, and you will not be consumed. The fire you face is not punishment; it is purification. The flames that rise against you cannot touch what God protects. They burn away fear, pride, and anything that keeps you from reflecting His Glory. Fire becomes the holy place where faith is proven, character is strengthened, and intimacy with God is deepened.

You do not walk through the flames alone. The same God Who stood with the three Hebrew men in the furnace now stands with you. His Presence becomes your shield, His Word your anchor, and His Love your protection. What should have destroyed you will instead define you, marking you as One Who has seen the fire and found God faithful in it. Endurance is not found in escaping the flames but in trusting the One Who governs them. Grace defends that what the fire cannot touch is your destiny, your purpose, your soul.

Prayer:

Lord, thank You for walking with me through every fire. Still, my fears and strengthen my faith until I trust Your Presence more than I fear the heat. Use every trial to refine me and draw me closer to Your heart. Let the flames purify, not consume, and let my life reflect Your faithfulness. In Jesus' Name, Amen.

Faith is refined, not reduced, by fire.

Day 125
The Wait That Builds Strength

Scripture:

"But they that wait upon the Lord shall renew their strength; they shall mount up with wings as eagles."

Isaiah 40:31 (KJV)

Reflection:

Waiting is not wasted time; it is sacred preparation. In the Kingdom of God, the pause is often as purposeful as the promise. The wait doesn't weaken you; it builds you. Every moment of surrender stretches your endurance, deepens your trust, and steadies your heart. Like the eagle, God is teaching you not to fight the winds of uncertainty but to rise on them. Eagles ascend not by striving but by catching the currents only available at higher altitudes. Likewise, those who wait on the Lord are lifted not by their own strength but by the strength He imparts in the stillness.

In waiting, God rewrites weariness into renewed power. In waiting, He breaks old patterns and births new perspectives. In waiting, He strengthens your spiritual muscles for the flight ahead. The waiting room of Heaven is not a holding cell; it is a workshop. It is here that God reshapes your faith, refines your desires, and equips you for the promise. What feels like a pause is actually preparation. What seems like a delay is Divine development. Don't rush what God is using to root you deeper. Let patience have its perfect work, for you are being readied to soar.

Prayer:

Father, teach me to wait well. Let my heart find renewal in stillness, and my spirit rise in Your perfect timing. Lift me above discouragement and strengthen me with hope. Help me trust that the wait is working for my good and preparing me for greater heights. In Jesus' Name, Amen.

Faith grows stronger while it waits.

Day 126
The Quiet Strength of Trust

Scripture:

"In quietness and in confidence shall be your strength."

Isaiah 30:15 (KJV)

Reflection:

Strength in the Kingdom often looks nothing like strength in the world. The world shouts, pushes, and strives. But Heaven whispers, Be still. True strength is not proven in noise; it is cultivated in quiet. It grows in the heart that refuses to panic, even when circumstances demand it.

The quiet soul is not weak; it is anchored. It rests in the confidence that God is working even when you cannot see movement. Trust transforms turmoil into peace because it shifts your focus from what you cannot control to the One Who controls all things.

Quietness is not passive; it is powerful. It is choosing surrender over stress. It is choosing worship over worry. It is choosing confidence in God's sovereignty over the chaos around you.

The still soul learns to stand when others shake. It walks through storms without fear because it knows the One Who commands the wind and waves. When your heart is calm in His Presence, no external pressure can break your peace. Quiet trust becomes a fortress strong, steady, and unwavering.

Prayer:

Lord, teach me the strength found in stillness. Quiet my mind when I long to take control, and calm my heart when fear rises. Let Your Presence be my peace and Your Sovereignty be my confidence. Anchor me deeply in trust so my soul remains steady in every storm. In Jesus' Name, Amen.

Faith's quiet trust makes the loudest statement.

Day 127
Persevering in Prayer

Scripture:

"Continue in prayer, and watch in the same with thanksgiving."

Colossians 4:2 (KJV)

Reflection:

Persevering prayer is the heartbeat of a deep and steady faith. It is the sacred rhythm that keeps your spirit aligned with Heaven, even when earthly answers seem delayed. God does not test persistence to frustrate you; He uses it to form you. Prayer that continues through silence becomes prayer that carries weight in the spirit.

Every unanswered petition is still gathered, still treasured, still working something eternal within you. Your prayers are never wasted; they are woven into God's perfect timing. As you keep praying, your heart is refined, your desires purified, and your faith strengthened. Persistence in prayer transforms your posture from outcome-driven to presence-driven. You seek not just the answer but the Answerer. You learn to pray with thanksgiving even before the blessing arrives, because gratitude creates space for faith to flourish.

The faithful do not stop praying because circumstances seem unmoved; they continue because they know God is always moving, always listening, always working behind the scenes. Prayer doesn't remind God of your need; it reminds your soul of His nearness. Every prayer shapes you. Every prayer draws you deeper. Every prayer declares trust in a God Who has never failed.

Prayer:

Lord, teach me to persevere in prayer. When answers seem distant, let gratitude carry my heart and hope steady my spirit. Keep me faithful in seeking You, not just for what I need, but for who You are. Strengthen my endurance until Your perfect timing unfolds. In Jesus' Name, Amen.

Faith keeps praying until Heaven replies.

Day 128
Grace to Continue

Scripture:

"And He said unto me, My Grace is sufficient for thee: for My strength is made perfect in weakness."

2 Corinthians 12:9 (KJV)

Reflection:

Endurance is not born from human strength; it is sustained by Divine Grace. God never asks you to push through life on your own capacity. Instead, He meets you in the exact places where your strength fails and His Power shines brightest. Weakness is not your liability; it is your landing place for Grace. Every limitation you encounter becomes an open door for God to pour out more of His sufficiency. What you cannot carry, He lifts. What you cannot endure, He sustains. What feels like a breaking point is often the breakthrough where His Strength is made perfect.

Grace doesn't always change your circumstances, but it always changes you within them. Paul's thorn remained, but the Grace that covered it turned his pain into power and his weakness into worship. The very thing that seemed to hinder him became the platform for God's Glory.

You continue not because your will is strong, but because His Grace is greater. You rise not because circumstances ease, but because His Spirit empowers. You endure not because you feel able, but because He is faithful. Grace is not merely enough, it is abundant, ever-present, and perfectly timed for every moment you need it.

Prayer:

Lord, thank You for the Grace that meets me daily and sustains me continually. When my strength reaches its end, let Your Power take over. Teach me to rejoice in weakness, knowing it is the place where Your Glory shines. Strengthen me to continue not by might, not by power, but by Your Spirit. In Jesus' Name, Amen.

Faith continues because Grace carries it.

Day 129
Beauty After the Battle

Scripture:

"To appoint unto them that mourn in Zion, to give unto them beauty for ashes."

Isaiah 61:3 (KJV)

Reflection:

God never lets a battle end without blessing. The wounds you carry, the tears you've cried, the ashes left behind from seasons of deep struggle, none of it is wasted in His Hands. What feels like the remnants of loss becomes the raw material for His masterpiece of redemption.

Beauty after the battle is not merely recovery, it is transformation. God does not hand back what was taken; He gives you something altogether greater. The ashes of heartbreak, disappointment, betrayal, or exhaustion become the very soil from which new joy is grown. What once felt like ruin becomes the foundation of renewed strength and deeper faith.

The enemy fights hardest before seasons of beauty because he fears what God will bring forth from your resilience. Scars remain, but they are no longer symbols of defeat; they are testimonies of survival, healing, and Divine intervention. They tell the world, I walked through fire, but God walked with me.

Endurance lifts your eyes beyond the smoke to see the sunrise He has already prepared. When you place your ashes in His Hands, He exchanges them for beauty every time.

Prayer:

Lord, thank You for bringing beauty out of every battle I've faced. Take the ashes of my pain and turn them into praise for Your Glory. Heal what was wounded, restore what was lost, and let every scar become a testimony of Your faithfulness. Teach me to see redemption in every chapter of my story. In Jesus' Name, Amen.

Faith finds beauty where others see only ashes.

Day 130
The Crown of Endurance

Scripture:

"Blessed is the man that endureth temptation: for when he is tried, he shall receive the crown of life."

James 1:12 (KJV)

Reflection:

Every trial carries more than pressure; it carries promise. Endurance is the sacred bridge between testing and triumph. God does not overlook the battles you've faced. He sees every moment you resisted giving up, every prayer whispered through pain, every step taken when your heart felt weak. These are the seeds of eternal reward. The crown of endurance is not made of earthly gold but of heavenly Glory. It is the evidence that your faith held firm when the winds were strong. It is Heaven's acknowledgment that you trusted God when nothing made sense and chose obedience even when it cost you comfort. This crown is not given for perfection; it is given for perseverance.

For the moments you stood when it was easier to retreat. For the tears that watered your faith. For the trials that refined your character and proved your devotion. Every tear cried in worship becomes a jewel in that crown. Every yes to God in the valley becomes part of its beauty. Endurance doesn't just get you through the trial; it transforms you for eternity.

Prayer:

Lord, help me endure every trial with joy and unwavering faith. Let perseverance shape my character and anchor my heart in Your Promises. Fix my eyes on eternity so that when the testing is over, You will find my faith still standing strong. Strengthen me to finish well and to wear the crown of life with gratitude. In Jesus' Name, Amen.

Faith that endures is crowned with eternal reward.

Day 131
Strengthened by Waiting

Scripture:

"It is good that a man should both hope and quietly wait for the salvation of the Lord."

Lamentations 3:26 (KJV)

"But they that wait upon the Lord shall renew their strength; they shall mount up with wings as eagles; they shall run, and not be weary; and they shall walk, and not faint."

Isaiah 40:31 KJV

Reflection:

Waiting is holy work. It is not wasted time; it is refining time. In seasons where nothing seems to be moving on the surface, God is doing His deepest shaping beneath it. Waiting reorders your strength, clarifies your desires, and strips away the burdens you were never meant to carry. God does not delay out of neglect but out of Divine design. He uses waiting to deepen your trust, steady your emotions, and anchor your hope in Him rather than in outcomes. What feels like a pause is often preparation. What seems like silence is actually a strategy.

Every quiet season becomes an altar where surrender is transformed into strength. When you wait well, hope doesn't wither, and it grows wings. Heaven renews what effort cannot. Patience becomes worship, trust becomes rest, and faith learns to soar far above anxiety and timelines. Waiting is not inactivity; it is the courageous choice to believe God when you cannot yet see God.

Prayer:

Lord, teach me to wait with hope, not frustration. Calm every anxious place within me and help me rest in Your Perfect Timing. Remind me that every delay is filled with Divine purpose and heavenly preparation. Renew my strength as I wait upon You. Lift my perspective like the eagle, that I may rise above discouragement and see from Heaven's view. Shape my heart in the quiet places, and let patience have its perfect work in me. Strengthen my spirit as I lean into Your Presence, trusting that You are working even when I cannot see it. In Jesus' Name, Amen.

Faith is strengthened where patience and hope embrace.

Day 132
Faith That Refuses to Quit

Scripture:

"And let us not be weary in well doing: for in due season we shall reap, if we faint not."

Galatians 6:9 (KJV)

Reflection:

Faith that refuses to quit is one of the most powerful forces in the Kingdom. It is the mark of a believer who has decided that surrender is not an option. The enemy often aims not to destroy you but to discourage you because a discouraged believer stops sowing, stops praying, stops believing. But a determined believer, One Who keeps going even when weary, becomes unstoppable. Every time you continue doing good when no one notices, Heaven notices. Every act of obedience, every prayer whispered in exhaustion, every choice to believe when doubt screams louder, these are recorded as worship. Perseverance is not the absence of struggle; it is the decision to keep moving forward in spite of it.

Due season always comes; it is Heaven's guarantee. But the harvest belongs to those who refuse to faint before the finish. Your persistence is planting seeds in soil you may not yet see. Your consistency is breaking ground where a breakthrough is about to bloom. You are closer than the enemy wants you to believe. Faith does not always roar; it often simply refuses to quit.

Prayer:

Lord, when I feel weary, remind me of the harvest You have promised. Strengthen My Hands to keep sowing, my heart to keep believing, and my spirit to remain steadfast. Let perseverance rise within me as an offering of worship. Help me endure every season with unwavering faith, trusting that You are faithful to bring the increase. In Jesus' Name, Amen.

Faith that refuses to quit reaps what others only dream.

Day 133
Joy in the Journey

Scripture:

"The joy of the Lord is your strength."

Nehemiah 8:10 (KJV)

Reflection:

Endurance was never meant to be powered by grit alone. God designed it to be fueled by joy. Joy is not an accessory to the Christian life; it is a spiritual necessity. Without joy, the journey becomes heavy. With joy, even the hardest miles gain meaning. The joy of the Lord is not an emotion; it is a Divine strength that flows from His Presence. It anchors you when weariness whispers, Quit. It lifts your spirit when circumstances try to weigh it down. Joy does not deny difficulty; it declares that God is greater than what you face.

Faith doesn't wait for the finish line to rejoice. It finds joy in the process, in the small victories, in the unseen progress, and in the constant nearness of God. Joy transforms trudging into triumph because it shifts your focus from the burden on your back to the God Who walks beside you. Heaven's joy is laughter that resurrects hope, light that pushes away heaviness, and strength that renews you from the inside out. You are not enduring on empty. God Himself is your joy, and He continually pours strength into your journey.

Prayer:

Lord, restore my joy in the journey. Let gladness rise in my spirit and become the strength that carries me forward. Teach me to rejoice not only when breakthroughs come, but while I walk toward them. May my endurance be filled with gratitude, and may joy be the song that sustains my soul. In Jesus' Name, Amen.

Faith walks farther when joy leads the way.

Day 134
The God Who Restores

Scripture:

"And I will restore to you the years that the locust hath eaten."

Joel 2:25 (KJV)

Reflection:

God is not only the Keeper of your life, He is the Restorer of your story. Nothing lost is beyond His reach. Every tear, every trial, every season that felt stolen or wasted is still under His sovereign care. In God's Kingdom, even what was devoured can be delivered. Even what was broken can be rebuilt. Restoration is deeper than returning to what once was. When God restores, He transforms. He takes the ruins and raises them into something redeemed and radiant. What you thought was the end becomes the very soil where new beginnings grow.

The enemy's intention was destruction, but God's intention is redemption. And His restoration doesn't come back empty; it comes back multiplied. Lost years become fruitful years. Empty seasons become overflowing ones. What once brought sorrow becomes the testimony that brings Him Glory. God wastes nothing. Not time, not pain, not process. The very areas where you mourned loss will become the places where you marvel at His Goodness. The God Who allowed the pruning is the same God Who brings the harvest. What once broke you will one day bless you, and the years you thought were gone will rise again, restored, renewed, and repurposed by His Hand.

Prayer:

Lord, thank You for being the God Who restores. Heal what was taken, redeem what was wasted, and breathe new life into every barren place. Turn my loss into a legacy and my pain into praise. Let my restored seasons testify to Your faithfulness and Your Power to make all things new. In Jesus' Name, Amen.

Faith believes that restoration is always on God's calendar.

Day 135
Unshaken Confidence

Scripture:

"For the Lord shall be thy confidence, and shall keep thy foot from being taken."

Proverbs 3:26 (KJV)

Reflection:

Confidence built on circumstances will always crumble, but confidence rooted in Christ stands firm in every season. The storms of life do not expose weakness in God; they expose where your trust rests. When everything around you trembles, the believer anchored in the Lord remains steady, because their foundation is unmovable.

Unshaken confidence is not loud or boastful. It is quiet assurance, deep, settled, and sure. It is the calm that whispers, God is with me, even when the winds howl. It is the strength that remains when emotions are unstable and outcomes are uncertain.

Fear tries to unseat your footing, but God Himself becomes the One Who steadies your steps. He surrounds you, upholds you, and keeps you from falling into the traps the enemy sets. True confidence comes not from what you can do, but from who He is faithful, present, unchanging, and good.

When your eyes are fixed on Christ, confidence is no longer dependent on how strong you feel, but on how strong your God is. And beloved, His Strength is everlasting. Trust transforms trembling into triumph and turns wavering hearts into steadfast ones. You don't stand because you are strong. You stand because He is.

Prayer:

Lord, be my confidence and my keeper. When fear whispers retreat, remind me who walks beside me. Steady my steps, secure my heart, and anchor my trust in Your unfailing strength. Let my confidence remain firm through every storm, resting fully in You. In Jesus' Name, Amen.

Faith stands unshaken because its footing is Divine.

Section Four:
Endurance And Resilience

Day 136
Endurance Through Worship

Scripture:

"I will bless the Lord at all times: His praise shall continually be in my mouth."

Psalm 34:1 (KJV)

Reflection:

Worship is the heartbeat of endurance. It strengthens what weariness tries to weaken and lifts your spirit when circumstances try to pull you down. When you choose to bless the Lord at all times in joy, in sorrow, in uncertainty, in waiting, you move into a realm where trials lose their power to control you.

Worship shifts your eyes from the problem to the Problem-Solver. It reminds your soul that God is still good, still sovereign, still present, and still worthy. Praise in comfort is gratitude, but praise in hardship is warfare. It is a declaration that says, My God is greater than what I feel, greater than what I face, and faithful in all things.

The strength of worship is not found in loud songs or perfect melodies; it is found in surrendered hearts. Every whispered hallelujah uttered through tears becomes a weapon that pushes back darkness. Every moment you choose praise over panic, trust over trembling, and gratitude over grief, Heaven moves on your behalf.

Worship doesn't remove the storm, but it anchors your soul until it passes. The One Who worships through adversity becomes unbreakable because their strength no longer comes from circumstance but from communion with God.

Prayer:

Lord, let my worship outlast my worry. Teach me to bless You in every season and every circumstance. Let my song be stronger than my struggle and my gratitude greater than my grief. Fill my heart with praise that endures, trusts, and triumphs. In Jesus' Name, Amen.

Faith endures longest when it worships loudest.

Day 137
Courage in the Crushing

Scripture:

"We are troubled on every side, yet not distressed; we are perplexed, but not in despair."

2 Corinthians 4:8 (KJV)

Reflection:

The crushing is not punishment, it is preparation. In the Kingdom, pressure has purpose. Just as olives release oil only when pressed and grapes release wine only when crushed, your greatest anointing often flows from your hardest seasons. God uses the weight you feel to draw out what He placed within you.

The crushing does not diminish you; it defines you. It softens what needs surrender, strengthens what needs endurance, and reveals what needs refining. Faith does not deny the pain of being pressed; it trusts that God is producing something far greater than the momentary pressure.

There is courage hidden in every crushing season. Courage to keep believing when answers are delayed. Courage to keep standing when strength feels small. Courage to keep praising when tears fall freely. Heaven sees every moment, and not one ounce of pressure is wasted in His Hands.

The crushing may bend you, but it will not break you. It will shape you into a vessel that carries Glory, not because you avoided the press, but because you endured it with trust. What feels like breaking is often the birthplace of your greatest breakthrough.

Prayer:

Lord, give me courage when I am pressed on every side. Help me to see purpose in the pressure and victory in the valley. Let the crushing produce faith, purity, and perseverance within me. Use my trials to release Your fragrance through my life, that You may be glorified. In Jesus' Name, Amen.

Faith finds courage in the crushing.

Day 138
When You've Done All to Stand

Scripture:

"Having done all, to stand."

Ephesians 6:13 (KJV)

Reflection:

Sometimes endurance looks less like movement and more like immovable faith. There are seasons when God calls you to run, seasons when He calls you to walk, and moments when the holiest thing you can do is simply stand. Standing is not inactivity; it is intentional resistance against the enemy's push to make you retreat.

When you've prayed every prayer, fought every battle, and obeyed every instruction you know, standing becomes an act of war. It declares, I will not bow to fear. I will not be moved by what I see. I will not surrender my ground. Standing is faith refusing to flinch.

Stillness before God is not weakness; it is strength wrapped in surrender. It is the posture that trusts Heaven to move even when earth feels silent. God does His greatest work in the moments when you refuse to move in unbelief. Standing says, Lord, I trust You enough to stay where You planted me.

Heaven honors the believer who holds the line when every reason says to retreat. Victory often arrives not in the running, but in the resolved stillness of a steadfast heart.

Prayer:

Lord, when I've done all I can, help me to stand in faith. Plant my feet firmly on Your Promises and steady my heart in Your truth. Let my posture of stillness become a declaration of trust, and let Your strength uphold me when mine is gone. In Jesus' Name, Amen.

Faith stands still until the winds of God move again.

Day 139
The Hidden Work of Endurance

Scripture:

"Let patience have her perfect work, that ye may be perfect and entire, wanting nothing."

James 1:4 (KJV)

Reflection:

Endurance is the holy work God performs beneath the surface, quiet, steady, unseen. While you wait, He is doing far more within you than you realize. Patience is not passive; it is spiritual construction. In the waiting, God is shaping your character, strengthening your faith, purifying your motives, and aligning your heart with His timing.

There is a perfect work underway even when nothing seems to be moving. The silence is not stagnation; it is sanctification. God hides His deepest work in seasons where your eyes see nothing, but your spirit is being sculpted for everything.

Roots grow deepest in stillness. Trees do not form strength in the storm; they form it underground, long before the wind ever arrives. So it is with you. Endurance deepens your roots until you can withstand any season. What patience builds, no trial can break.

When you let patience do its perfect work, you emerge mature, complete, and lacking nothing, fully prepared for the promise God has already written over your life.

Prayer:

Lord, let patience complete its perfect work in me. Keep me from rushing what You are refining. Strengthen my roots in this season of waiting and align my heart with Your Timing. Shape me, prepare me, and perfect me until I am ready to carry the fullness of Your Promise.

In Jesus' Name, Amen.

Faith grows strong in what seems still.

Day 140
The Anchor Holds

Scripture:

"Which hope we have as an anchor of the soul, both sure and steadfast."

Hebrews 6:19 (KJV)

Reflection:

Hope is not fragile; it is forged in the faithfulness of God. It is the anchor that holds when life feels unsteady, the unseen weight that keeps your soul from drifting into fear or despair. This anchor does not cling to circumstances; it grips the unchanging character of Christ.

Storms may shake your surroundings, but they cannot shake what is rooted in eternity. Hope fastens you to promises that cannot break, to a God Who cannot lie, and to a future He has already secured. When emotions rise, and waves roar, hope whispers, You are still held.

You do not stay steady because of your strength; you stay steady because of His. The anchor of hope reaches beyond the veil, into the very presence of God, where Christ intercedes for you. It is here, in this holy anchoring, that faith becomes unmovable and peace becomes unshakable.

Even when you cannot feel the bottom or see the shore, the anchor holds because the One Who keeps you never lets go.

Prayer:

Lord, thank You for being the anchor of my soul. When storms rise, and fears threaten to pull me away, hold me steady in Your truth. Let my hope remain rooted in Your Promises and my faith remain steadfast in Your Love. Keep me anchored to You in every season. In Jesus' Name, Amen.

Faith endures because hope holds fast.

<h1 style="text-align:center">Day 141
Still Waters, Strong Faith</h1>

Scripture:

"He maketh me to lie down in green pastures: He leadeth me beside the still waters."

Psalm 23:2 (KJV)

Reflection:

Still waters are not signs of inactivity; they are invitations to intimacy. The Shepherd leads you to quiet places not to slow your destiny, but to steady your soul. Rest is not wasted time; it is holy recovery. In the calm, faith breathes again. In the stillness, strength returns.

Sometimes God quiets the landscape around you so He can quiet the war within you. He knows when the next battle will require deeper trust, and He prepares you by bringing you into peace before sending you into purpose. What feels like a pause is actually preparation.

At the still waters, the noise of striving falls away. Anxiety loosens its grip. Worry loses its voice. It's here, in the gentle hush of His Presence, that you learn the rhythm of faith, a faith not driven by urgency, but anchored in assurance.

The Shepherd's leading is always intentional. If He brought you to still waters, it's because your soul needed restoring. Let the calm wash over you. Let His Peace settle you. Let His quiet strengthen what chaos tried to weaken.

Strong faith is not built in frenzy; it is born beside still waters.

Prayer:

Lord, thank You for leading me into places of peace. Quiet my spirit and restore my strength as I rest beside the still waters of Your Presence. Let every moment of calm draw me deeper into trust and renew my faith for what lies ahead. In Jesus' Name, Amen.

Faith grows strongest where the soul is still.

Day 142
The Pen of a Ready Writer

Scripture:

"When God fills your heart with His Word, your hand becomes His instrument. My heart is inditing a good matter: I speak of the things which I have made touching the king: my tongue is the pen of a ready writer."

Psalm 45:1 (KJV)

Reflection:

There are moments when you feel unqualified to speak, when words stumble, and fears rise, yet God whispers, Write. He doesn't ask for perfection; He asks for willingness. Your pen becomes the vessel, and His Spirit becomes the ink. Every sentence you write in faith carries the fragrance of Heaven healing the broken, strengthening the weary, and awakening hope in the discouraged. The enemy has tried to silence the voices of those who carry encouragement because he knows their words build bridges between hearts and the heart of the Father. But the Lord says, Arise, ready writer. Even when your voice trembles, your pen is steady in His Hand. You are not writing for applause; you are recording His Faithfulness for generations to come. Your stutter, your stillness, your waiting, all of it becomes worship when offered back to Him. You are proof that anointed words don't come from human eloquence but from Divine Presence.

Prayer:

Heavenly Father, thank You for trusting me with Your Words. When I feel inadequate, remind me that You are my voice and my strength. Use My Hands to write what Heaven is speaking. Let my words carry Your light into dark places and Your Peace into troubled hearts. May I remain humble, teachable, and always ready when You call me to write. In Jesus' Name, Amen.

Day 143
An Unshakable Hope

Scriptures:

"Now the God of hope fill you with all joy and peace in believing, that ye may abound in hope, through the power of the Holy Ghost."

Romans 15:13 (KJV)

"Let us hold fast the profession of our faith without wavering; (for he is faithful that promised;)."

Hebrews 10:23 (KJV)

Reflection:

Hope is not wishful thinking; it is a confident expectation rooted in the character of God. True hope stands unshaken when storms rage, because it rests not on what is seen, but on the One who has spoken. When we remember that His Word cannot return void, our hearts learn to wait with joy, not in the absence of difficulty, but in the assurance that His Promises are unfolding even now. When the world wavers, hope remains steady because its foundation is eternal. The Spirit teaches us to hope with holy expectation, to rejoice before the promise manifests, to sing while still in the hallway, to trust that the God Who began the work is faithful to complete it.

Prayer:

Father, anchor my heart in unshakable hope. Teach me to wait with joy, to trust with peace, and to expect Your promises to be fulfilled in Your Perfect Time. Strengthen my faith when I cannot yet see the outcome. Let Your hope overflow in me until it spills into the lives of others. In Jesus' mighty Name, amen.

Anchored in Expectation and Joy -- Trusting His Promises to Be Fulfilled

Day 144
My Times Are in Your Hands

Scriptures:

"My times are in Thy hand: deliver me from the hand of mine enemies, and from them that persecute me."

Psalm 31:15 (KJV)

"He hath made everything beautiful in his time."

Ecclesiastes 3:11 (KJV)

Reflection:

There are seasons when time seems suspended, prayers unanswered, dreams delayed, yet every moment is being woven by the hand of the Almighty. Nothing in your life is off schedule in the kingdom of God. What appears as waiting is often preparation, and what feels like silence is the shaping of something eternal.

God's timing is never careless. His delays are not denials but Divine alignments. The hands that hold the galaxies are the same hands that hold your days, your hopes, and your future. Rest in the assurance that the Author of time has written your story with perfect wisdom. Every season, every sigh, every victory is safe in His keeping.

Prayer:

Heavenly Father, thank You for holding my life in Your Hands. When my heart grows anxious, teach me to rest in Your Timing. Help me surrender my plans and trust that You make all things beautiful in Your time. I choose to walk in faith, knowing You have ordered every step. In Jesus' Name, Amen.

A reminder that every season of your life is safely held in God's perfect timing.

Day 145
Drink Deeply

Scripture:

"O taste and see that the Lord is good: blessed is the man that trusteth in Him."

Psalm 34:8 (KJV)

Reflection:

The Lord does not call you to sample His Goodness; He invites you to drink deeply of it. His Presence is a well that never runs dry, a table always prepared, a fountain that flows even in the desert seasons of life. To taste and see is more than a moment; it is an invitation into continual communion.

Many try to live on the sips of God while pouring themselves out in full measure to the world. But the soul cannot run on emptiness. Living water refreshes only those who linger long enough to receive it.

When you drink deeply of His Goodness, peace returns like a gentle tide. Weariness lifts. Joy awakens. Strength rises quietly within. You remember again that God is not far. He is here, offering rest to the hurried and renewal to the thirsty.

His Presence is not meant for rushed devotion but for abiding delight. Come without hurry, sit without fear, breathe without striving. Let His Goodness soak into the dry places until your heart overflows with the assurance that He is always enough.

Prayer:

Father, thank You for inviting me to draw near and drink deeply of Your goodness. Quench every thirst the world could never satisfy. Fill me with the living water of Your Spirit until my soul is refreshed, restored, and overflowing. Let my life drink deeply and dwell continually in Your Presence. In Jesus' Name, Amen.

A reminder to find refreshment for your soul in the presence of God. Selah pauses and rests in His Presence.

Day 146
The Refining of Gold

Scripture:

"The fining pot is for silver, and the furnace for gold: but the Lord trieth the hearts."

Proverbs 17:3 (KJV)

Reflection:

Refinement is the evidence of worth. God does not place worthless things in the fire, only what He treasures. The heat is not a sign of abandonment but of attentive, loving craftsmanship. The Refiner watches the flame, governs the temperature, and never steps away from the process.

In the furnace of testing, everything that cannot endure is brought to the surface. Fear rises, so faith can replace it. Pride melts so humility can shine. Impurities are exposed not to shame you, but to free you. Gold never resents the fire because it knows the flame can only reveal its brilliance.

The refining seasons of life distinguish what is eternal from what is temporary. They transform belief into conviction and devotion into purity. You are not being destroyed, you are being defined. What God sees within you is worth the fire, and what emerges from the fire will be more radiant, more refined, and more reflective of His Glory.

Trust the heat. Trust the hands that hold you. Trust that the Refiner sees the treasure long before you feel it.

Prayer:

Lord, refine my heart like gold. Burn away the impurities that cloud my devotion and hinder my purpose. Let the fire deepen my faith, purify my motives, and shape me into Your likeness. Hold me in every refining season until Your reflection shines brightly in me. In Jesus' Name, Amen.

Faith refined by fire shines with Heaven's reflection.

Day 147
When God Is Silent

Scripture:

"Be still, and know that I am God."

Psalm 46:10 (KJV)

Reflection:

Silence from God is never abandonment, it is invitation. Heaven's quiet seasons are holy classrooms where trust is deepened and dependence is refined. When God doesn't speak, He is often asking you to lean on what He already said. Silence tests whether you trust His Heart when your ears hear nothing new. Stillness is where your spirit learns to rest without striving. It is in the quiet that idols fall away, fear loses its voice, and faith becomes anchored not in feelings, but in truth. God's silence is not punishment; it is preparation. He uses the still places to strengthen your spiritual hearing, sharpen your discernment, and draw you closer than noise ever could. When you cannot trace His Hand, you learn to trust His Heart. And the heart that waits in quiet faith will always find that God was nearer in the silence than in the storm.

Prayer:

Lord, when Heaven grows quiet, steady my heart in Your unchanging faithfulness. Teach me to trust You beyond emotion and to rest in the certainty of who You are. Let stillness become sacred as I wait for Your whisper. Strengthen my faith until silence becomes a sanctuary where I know You more deeply. In Jesus' Name, Amen.

Faith hears purpose in the pauses of God.

Day 148
Strength in the Shadows

Scripture:

"Yea, though I walk through the valley of the Shadow of death, I will fear no evil: for Thou art with me."

Psalm 23:4 (KJV)

Reflection:

Shadows only appear where light is present, meaning even in your darkest valleys, God's Glory is still shining. The valley is never the final address of the believer; it is the sacred passage where trust grows muscles and intimacy deepens. The Shadow may look threatening, but it cannot harm you. It is merely the outline of something that cannot overpower the presence of the Shepherd. God does not remove every dark place, but He fills each one with Himself. In the shadows, faith stops depending on what it sees and starts relying on Who is near.

Strength is born in the places where you learn that survival is not in your stride but in His Shepherding. The same God Who restores your soul in green pastures is the God Who defends, directs, and carries you through shadowed valleys. You may tremble, but you will not fall. His rod protects. His staff pulls you close. His Presence keeps you steady until you reach the other side with a testimony you didn't have before. The Shadow is temporary. His Presence is eternal.

Prayer:

Lord, thank You for walking beside me in every valley. When fear whispers, and shadows grow long, remind me that Your Presence is my light and my protection. Strengthen my heart to trust You even in places I don't understand. Let my courage rise from Your nearness and my peace flow from knowing You will never leave me. In Jesus' Name, Amen.

Faith finds strength even where shadows fall.

Day 149
Through the Night Watch

Scripture:

"My soul waiteth for the Lord more than they that watch for the morning."

Psalm 130:6 (KJV)

Reflection:

There are seasons when the night stretches longer than expected, when answers seem slow, and the horizon shows no sign of dawn. Yet it is in these hours of the night watch that faith learns its deepest endurance. The night watch is not passive; it is the posture of a heart determined to believe that morning will come because God has promised it.

Those who watch for the morning do so with anticipation. They lean forward toward the first glimmer of light, confident that darkness cannot hold dominion forever. In the same way, your soul waits not in defeat, but in expectation. Even when you cannot see the sun rising, its arrival is certain. In the quiet hours when prayers echo softly, and tears fall unnoticed, God is closer than your breath. He works in the hours you least feel Him and speaks in the silence you least understand. His Presence guards you in the night, His Promises carry you through the shadows, and His Faithfulness ensures you will behold the dawn. The night is temporary. His nearness is eternal.

Prayer:

Lord, keep my soul awake with hope through every long night. When the darkness lingers, let my heart remain steadfast in expectation. Fill my waiting with worship and my silence with Your Presence. Bring the light of Your Comfort into every shadowed place, and strengthen me to trust You until morning breaks. In Jesus' Name, Amen.

Faith keeps watch when others fall asleep.

Day 150
The Promise Still Stands

Scripture:

"For all the promises of God in Him are yea, and in Him Amen."

2 Corinthians 1:20 (KJV)

Reflection:

God's Promises do not expire. They are not weakened by delay, diminished by discouragement, or overturned by opposition. Every word He speaks carries the weight of His character, unchanging, unfailing, unshakable. His Promises are yea and Amen, not because circumstances cooperate, but because Christ Himself guarantees them. Time may test your faith, but it never alters His Truth. The promise that feels distant is not denied; it is developing. The waiting season becomes sacred ground where trust is refined, vision is clarified, and endurance is strengthened. God is not slow; He is strategic. Every moment He withholds is pregnant with preparation.

What He whispered in the quiet remains thunderously true in the silence. His delays do not mean decline. His timing does not erase His intention. The promise still stands not because you have held onto it, but because He has held it for you. The Promise-Keeper reigns, and therefore His Word remains. Stand firm, beloved. If He said it, He will do it.

Prayer:

Lord, thank You that every promise You speak is secure in Christ. Strengthen my faith where weariness has crept in. Revive the hope that once burned bright and anchor my heart in Your unchanging truth. Let my life testify that Your Word endures and that every promise still stands. In Jesus' Name, Amen.

Faith stands tall on promises that cannot fall.

Day 151
The Shepherd's Supply

Scripture:

"The Lord is my shepherd; I shall not want."

Psalm 23:1 (KJV)

Reflection:

To say The Lord is my Shepherd is to declare that you are led, loved, protected, and provided for by the God Who owns all things. His supply is not seasonal, it is steadfast. His care does not fluctuate with circumstance; it flows from covenant. Where He guides, **Grace** abounds; where He leads, lack must flee.

The Shepherd does not respond to need He anticipates it. Before you ever recognized your deficiency, He had already prepared a pasture and poured out provision. Faith doesn't demand to understand the path ahead; it rests knowing that the Shepherd has already walked it. The One Who watches over you never slumbers, never miscalculates, and never withholds what will bless or build you.

Your confidence is not in the pasture but in the Shepherd who brings you to it. Because He is faithful, you shall not want. Because He is constant, you shall not lack. The Shepherd's supply is not determined by your surroundings; it is sustained by His sovereignty.

Prayer:

Lord, thank You for being my Shepherd, my leader, my protector, and my source. Quiet my fears and calm my striving as I rest in Your faithful provision. Lead me into the places where Your goodness overflows and Your Peace abound. Let my life reflect trust in the One Who never fails. In Jesus' Name, Amen.

Faith never fears shortage when it follows the Shepherd.

Day 152
Daily Bread

Scripture:

"Give us this day our daily bread."

Matthew 6:11 (KJV)

Reflection:

God provides portions suited for the day not too much to make you independent, and never too little to leave you lacking. Daily bread is not just food for the body; it is nourishment for the soul. It is strength for today, wisdom for today, Grace for today. Tomorrow's supply will meet you tomorrow, but today, He invites you to receive what He has prepared anew.

This rhythm of daily receiving teaches a holy dependence. It shifts your focus from stockpiling security to trusting His Faithfulness. The manna of old fell one day at a time, reminding Israel that God's presence was their portion. So it is with you. He gives fresh mercy because He desires fresh fellowship. The God Who carried you yesterday stands ready to sustain you today.

Faith breathes easier when it stops reaching into tomorrow and simply rests in the God of today. Each sunrise becomes an altar of exchange your emptiness for His fullness, your weakness for His Strength, your hunger for His heavenly bread. And as you return daily, you discover that the true gift is not the bread itself, but the One Who gives it.

Prayer:

Father, thank You for today's bread, Your Provision, Your Presence, and Your Word that nourishes my soul. Teach me to trust You one day at a time and to rest in the certainty of Your Faithfulness. May each new morning draw me closer to You as I receive all that You lovingly provide. In Jesus' Name, Amen.

Faith is fed daily by the hand of Grace.

Day 153
The God Who Goes Before You

Scripture:

"The Lord, He it is that doth go before thee; He will be with thee, He will not fail thee, neither forsake thee."

Deuteronomy 31:8 (KJV)

Reflection:

You never step into a day God has not already entered. Long before your feet touch the path, His Presence has walked its length. Every unknown you fear, He has already examined. Every obstacle you dread, He has already addressed. Every need you carry; He has already supplied in seed form waiting to be discovered in obedience.

The God Who goes before you is not scouting possibilities; He is securing outcomes. He prepares provision, aligns timing, softens hearts, arranges connections, and positions favor on the road ahead. What feels uncertain to you has already been settled in His sovereignty.

Fear thrives on the illusion of the unknown, but faith remembers: nothing is unknown to Him. You may not see around the corner, but the One Who holds all things stands there already with peace, with purpose, with protection.

And here is the mystery of trust: often, provision reveals itself only when you move. The waters' part after the step, not before. Breakthrough meets the believer already in motion. The God Who goes before you is also the God Who walks beside you ensuring you lack nothing as you follow His lead. Whatever lies ahead, He has gone ahead.

Prayer:

Lord, thank You for walking before me and preparing every step I will take. When I face the unknown, remind me that You are already there. Let each step I take be covered in Your Peace, guided by Your Presence, and secured by Your Faithfulness. Keep me moving forward in trust, knowing that the way has already been made. In Jesus' Name, Amen.

Faith follows the footsteps of a faithful God.

Day 154
Provision in the Wilderness

Scripture:

"And He humbled thee, and suffered thee to hunger, and fed thee with manna... that He might make thee know that man doth not live by bread only."

Deuteronomy 8:3 (KJV)

Reflection:

The wilderness is the classroom where dependence becomes devotion. When the familiar dries up and the predictable disappears, God reveals Himself as your only true Source. Manna does not fall in Egypt, where self-reliance thrives, it falls in the wilderness, where faith is formed.

Wilderness seasons expose the illusions of security. They strip away the false comforts that once kept you distracted and reveal the One Who keeps you sustained. When you have nothing else to lean on, you discover that God alone is enough.

Manna teaches trust. It arrives daily, not weekly. It cannot be stored, hoarded, or manipulated. It falls where obedience stands and where humility waits. In barren places, you learn that provision is not about accumulation it's about alignment. The wilderness shifts your dependence from natural bread to the Bread of Life, from external resources to eternal supply.

You may not always see overflow, but you will always see enough because God Himself stands with you in the dry places, turning scarcity into testimony and hunger into holiness. The wilderness is not a punishment; it is preparation for promised land living, where trust is not circumstantial but rooted in Him who never fails.

Prayer:

Lord, thank You for being my provision even in barren places. Teach me to recognize Your manna in moments of need and to trust You more deeply when resources seem scarce. Replace my reliance on worldly security with hunger for Your Word and dependence on Your Presence. Let every wilderness season draw me closer to Your Heart. In Jesus' Name, Amen.

Faith finds nourishment even in the wilderness.

Day 155
Streams in the Desert

Scripture:

"I will even make a way in the wilderness, and rivers in the desert."

Isaiah 43:19 (KJV)

Reflection:

God specializes in transforming the places that seem beyond hope. The desert dry, barren, and lifeless is often where His greatest miracles are born. When everything around you feels empty and the landscape of your life looks desolate, remember this: God does His finest work in impossible places.

The wilderness is not the evidence of God's absence; it is the backdrop for His breakthrough. Deserts reveal the difference between natural impossibility and supernatural intervention. When you come to the end of your own resources, He opens rivers where rain has never fallen. He creates pathways where none existed. He turns wastelands into wells of refreshing.

Faith learns to see promise where others see barrenness. It hears the sound of water beneath dry sand. It anticipates life springing up in what once felt hopeless. The desert is not a dead end, it is a Divine setup for God to display His Power, His provision, and His Faithfulness.

Beloved, do not fear the dry seasons. They are the very soil where God plants miracles. The streams He sends will not merely refresh you, they will redefine you. What once drained you will become a testimony of His living water flowing through every dry and thirsty place of your soul.

Prayer:

Lord, thank You for being my stream in every desert. When life feels barren, refresh me with the living water of Your presence. Renew my faith to believe in what I cannot yet see. Let rivers of Your Spirit flow through every dry place within me, transforming wilderness into wonder. In Jesus' Name, Amen.

Faith drinks deeply where others see only dust.

Day 156
The Door No Man Can Shut

Scripture:

"I have set before thee an open door, and no man can shut it."

Revelation 3:8 (KJV)

Reflection:

When God opens a door, it is sealed with Divine authority. No person, no opposition, no circumstance, and no spiritual force can close what His sovereignty has unlocked. His doors are not dependent on human approval, earthly qualifications, or perfect conditions; they stand on the foundation of His will alone.

Every God-ordained door carries purpose, process, and protection. It doesn't merely offer opportunity; it aligns destiny. Sometimes the door stays shut because the season isn't ready. Other times it stands open, waiting for the faith to step through. Divine doors are not entered by striving, but by surrender.

Faith doesn't pry open what God has closed, and it doesn't hesitate at what He has opened. It trusts His Hand on the handle. Your assignment is not to manipulate outcomes, it is to discern His timing and follow His leading. God's open doors always lead you into spaces your feet could never reach without His guidance and Grace.

Do not fear the doors others try to shut. Their authority ends at the threshold of God's will. What He sets before you is secure. What He ordains cannot be undone. Walk forward with confidence: the door you are meant to enter will open, and the one you are meant to leave behind will close.

Prayer:

Lord, thank You for the doors that only Your Hand can open. Close every door that is not from You, and illuminate the path to the one You have ordained. Give me discernment to recognize Your Timing and courage to walk through with unwavering faith. In Jesus' Name, Amen.

Faith walks boldly through Heaven's open doors.

Day 157
The God Who Provides Before You Ask

Scripture:

"And it shall come to pass, that before they call, I will answer."

Isaiah 65:24 (KJV)

Reflection:

When God opens a door, it carries the weight of His Divine authority. No person, no opposition, no circumstance, and no spiritual force can close what His sovereignty has unlocked. His doors are never based on human approval, earthly qualifications, or perfect conditions every opening stands firmly on the foundation of His will alone.

Every God-ordained door holds purpose, process, and protection. It doesn't simply offer opportunity; it aligns destiny. Sometimes the door remains closed because the season is still being formed. Other times it swings wide, waiting for faith to step forward. Divine doors are not forced open by striving; they are entered through surrender.

Faith does not pry open what God has shut, and it does not hesitate at what He has opened. It trusts His Hand on the handle. Your calling is not to manipulate outcomes but to discern His timing and follow His leading. Every door He opens leads you into places your own strength could never take you spaces shaped by His Grace, favor, and guidance.

So do not fear when others try to shut what God has set before you. Their authority ends at the threshold of His will. What He ordains cannot be altered, delayed, or undone. Walk forward with holy confidence: the door meant for you will open, and the one meant to close will close by His perfect hand.

Prayer:

Lord, thank You for the doors that only Your Hand can open. Close every door that is not from You, and illuminate the path to the one You have ordained. Give me discernment to recognize Your Timing and courage to walk through with unwavering faith. In Jesus' Name, Amen.

Faith finds peace in a God who's always prepared.

Day 158
Overflowing Cups

Scripture:

"My cup runneth over."

Psalm 23:5 (KJV)

Reflection:

God never pours in measure He pours in abundance. When He fills your cup, it doesn't stop at the brim; it spills into overflow. His blessings are not accidental excess; they are intentional evidence of His generous nature. The overflow is not waste, it is witness. It reveals a Shepherd whose provision is limitless and a Father whose love cannot be contained.

Overflow is the result of staying close to the Source. When your heart abides in Him, His Presence fills every empty place until joy, peace, and Grace spill into the lives around you. God's goal is never just to bless you, but to bless through you. The world is meant to taste His Goodness from the surplus of your surrender.

Faith receives freely so it can release freely. The more you pour out compassion, mercy, and kindness, the more He pours in strength, power, and refreshing. You are a vessel designed for overflow not for storage. As you give, you make room for Heaven to keep filling.

Prayer:

Lord, thank You for a cup that overflows with Your goodness. Fill me until Your Love, peace, and generosity spill into every life I touch. Let others encounter You through the abundance You pour into me. In Jesus' Name, Amen.

Faith overflows because Grace never runs dry.

Day 159
Guided by His Peace

Scripture:

"And let the peace of God rule in your hearts."

Colossians 3:15 (KJV)

Reflection:

Peace is more than a feeling; it is Divine direction. It is Heaven's compass placed within the believer, gently pointing toward the will of God. His Peace doesn't push, pressure, or confuse; it settles, assures, and aligns. When your heart is anchored in Him, peace becomes the ruler, the deciding voice that governs your steps.

God's peace is not passive; it is powerful. It protects you from wrong paths and prepares you for right ones. When your spirit feels restless or unsettled, it is not a sign of failure but a sign of the Father's guidance. He is redirecting, shielding, or slowing you because He sees what you cannot.

Every decision born from peace bears eternal fruit. God never guides through panic, fear, or haste. His will always comes wrapped in calm clarity, even if the road ahead is unfamiliar. When you follow His Peace, you follow His Presence and where His Presence goes, His provision flows.

Prayer:

Lord, let Your Peace rule in my heart and guide every step I take. Quiet every voice that brings confusion and amplify the stillness that confirms Your Will. Lead me into decisions marked by Your Presence and paths paved with Your Peace. In Jesus' Name, Amen.

Faith follows the quiet leading of peace.

Day 160
Jehovah Jireh: The God Who Provides

Scripture:

"And Abraham called the name of that place Jehovah Jireh: as it is said to this day, In the mount of the Lord it shall be seen."

Genesis 22:14 (KJV)

Reflection:

Provision is revealed where surrender is practiced. Abraham didn't see God's supply before he climbed; he saw it because he climbed. The mountain of sacrifice became the mountain of revelation. Jehovah Jireh does not simply provide things; He provides Himself His Presence, His guidance, His timing, His abundance.

God's provision is often concealed until obedience uncovers it. When Abraham raised the knife, Heaven released the ram. What looked like loss became the very place where God declared His Name. In your own mountains of trust, the same God still provides perfectly, precisely, and powerfully.

Jehovah Jireh sees your need before you speak it, prepares the answer before you seek it, and places provision exactly where your faith will find it. Every act of surrender becomes an invitation for God to display His sufficiency. What you place on the altar, He replaces with purpose.

Prayer:

Lord, thank You for being Jehovah Jireh, my faithful Provider. Give me the courage to obey even when the outcome is hidden. Teach me to trust that every step of surrender leads to a place where Your provision is revealed. Let my life testify that You always make a way. In Jesus' Name, Amen.

Faith always finds the ram in the thicket.

Day 161
Favor in the Field

Scripture:

"And when ye reap the harvest of your land, thou shalt not wholly reap the corners of thy field."

Leviticus 23:22 (KJV)

Reflection:

God hides favor in the everyday places where faithfulness is practiced. Ruth didn't discover destiny through position or prestige; she found it while gathering leftovers in a field. What looked ordinary became the very ground where God unfolded extraordinary purpose. Favor often arrives quietly, disguised as consistency.

Your field may not feel glamorous. It may feel overlooked, routine, or small. But Heaven pays attention to faithfulness. God instructs His people to leave gleaning proof that His Grace is already waiting in the places where you show up with a willing heart.

What you reap today may seem modest, but the field you're tending holds seeds of future provision, connection, and calling. Ruth's gleaning became her gateway to redemption. Your Boaz moments, your breakthroughs, open doors, Divine alignments aren't found by chasing favor, but by remaining steadfast where God has planted you.

Stay faithful. Stay present. God's favor knows exactly where to find the One Who labors with humility and trust.

Prayer:

Lord, help me to be faithful in my field, even when it feels ordinary. Let Your Favor find me where I serve, sow, and stand in obedience. Bless My Hands, my harvest, and my heart, that all I do may glorify You. In Jesus' Name, Amen.

Faith sows' obedience and reaps unexpected favor.

Day 162
God of the Details

Scripture:

"But even the very hairs of your head are all numbered."

Luke 12:7 (KJV)

Reflection:

God doesn't just oversee your life He attends to it with exquisite detail. His Love   is not distant or broad; it is precise, intentional, and deeply personal. Every moment, every emotion, every breath is known by the One Who formed you. Nothing in your life is too small for His attention or too complicated for His care.

If He counts each hair, how much more does He count every need, every concern, every step you take? You never slip His mind. You never fall outside His watch. Even the parts of your story you overlook are held securely in His Hands.

Faith finds rest not only in God's power, but in His precision. Trust grows when you realize He is not just writing the chapters He is editing every line with perfect wisdom. His attention to detail means your life will not miss what He has ordained nor lose what He has purposed. When you trust His oversight, fear loses its grip. The God Who manages galaxies also manages the details of your day.

Prayer:

Father, thank You for caring about every detail of my life. Open my eyes to see Your fingerprints in the small things and Your purpose in everything I don't yet understand. Teach me to rest in Your loving precision. In Jesus' Name, Amen.

Faith finds peace in the God Who misses nothing.

Day 163
The Path of Wisdom

Scripture:

"In all thy ways acknowledge Him, and He shall direct thy paths."

Proverbs 3:6 (KJV)

Reflection:

Wisdom is not born from intelligence it is born from intimacy. The path of wisdom begins at the feet of the One Who knows the way you should take. Acknowledging God is more than offering Him a moment; it is inviting Him into every movement. When you pause long enough to seek His counsel, the fog of uncertainty clears and the peace of direction settles.

To acknowledge Him is to say, Lord, I trust Your vision more than my own. It is surrendering the urge to rush, to assume, or to rely on your own understanding. Wisdom flows when dependence deepens. God does not simply guide the path He aligns your heart with His will so that each step becomes an extension of His Purpose.

The paths He directs are never accidental. They are ordered, intentional, and laced with Grace. When you place the weight of your decisions in His Hands, He places the weight of His wisdom in your steps. You don't walk blindly, you walk guided. You don't walk alone, you walk accompanied. And every detour becomes a Divine redirection toward destiny.

Prayer:

Lord, grant me wisdom in every step. Teach me to acknowledge You not only in the big moments but in the smallest decisions of my day. Let Your counsel steady my heart and guide my journey. Align my desires with Your Will and lead me in paths that glorify Your Name. In Jesus' Name, Amen.

Faith walks straight when wisdom lights the path.

Day 164
Grace for the Journey

Scripture:

"My Grace is sufficient for thee: for My strength is made perfect in weakness."

2 Corinthians 12:9 (KJV)

Reflection:

Grace is not a one-time gift; it is a continual supply. It does not remove the struggle; it empowers you to walk through it with Divine strength. God doesn't give you tomorrow's Grace today. He gives you exactly what you need for this moment, this step, this breath. When the road feels long and the weight feels heavy, Grace becomes the unseen hands lifting what your strength cannot. It is supernatural endurance wrapped in mercy. You don't travel the journey alone, Grace goes before you, walks beside you, and follows behind you.

Every mile reveals more of His Heart. Every weakness becomes a window for His Strength to shine through. You don't have to fear what lies ahead because the God Who called you to the journey supplies you along the way. His Grace does not expire; it renews. It does not lessen; it abounds. It does not falter; it sustains. Where your strength ends, His begins. And His is endless.

Prayer:

Lord, thank You for Grace that carries me farther than my strength ever could. Equip me for today and refresh me for tomorrow. Steady my steps with faith and fill my heart with gratitude. Let Your Grace be the wind beneath every weary moment, and Your strength the anchor of my soul. In Jesus' Name, Amen.

Faith walks far when Grace walks beside it.

Day 165
The Blessing of Boundaries

Scripture:

"The lines are fallen unto me in pleasant places; yea, I have a goodly heritage."

Psalm 16:6 (KJV)

Reflection:

Boundaries are not walls to confine you; they are fences of favor drawn by the hand of a loving Father. God places limits to guard your heart, protect your calling, and preserve your peace. The lines He draws are not random; they are measured by His wisdom and mapped by His Love.

Divine boundaries keep you where blessings flow. They shield you from distractions that drain, relationships that derail, and paths that were never meant for your feet. Many fight the limits, not realizing they are standing in the very place where Grace gathers.

Faith flourishes in order. When you submit to God's boundaries, you don't lose freedom, you gain clarity. You stop striving for what was never assigned to you. You grow stronger in what was always yours. The pleasant places are not found by pushing past His lines, but by resting within them.

Blessing is not only in what God gives but in where He places you. Trust the borders He sets… they mark the territory of your inheritance.

Prayer:

Lord, thank You for the boundaries that guard my steps and protect my peace. Help me to recognize the places You've marked for me and to honor the limits You've lovingly drawn. Keep me within the center of Your Will, where Your Presence abides and Your Favor flows. Let obedience be my joy and surrender my strength. In Jesus' Name, Amen.

Faith finds peace within Heaven's borders.

Day 166
The Still, Small Voice

Scripture:

"And after the fire a still small voice."

1 Kings 19:12 (KJV)

Reflection:

God does not need volume to reveal His will. His Voice is not found in the earthquake of chaos or the fire of crisis… It is found in the quiet. The still, small Voice is the language of intimacy. It speaks to those who draw near, those who choose stillness over striving, and surrender over noise.

Elijah expected God in the dramatic, but he found Him in the whisper. So do we. The whisper proves His closeness. You don't whisper to someone far away, you whisper to someone near enough to hear your heartbeat.

Faith grows sharper in silence. The still, small Voice doesn't command your attention through force; it invites your attention through peace. His whisper carries clarity that the world's noise can never provide. When fear is loud and emotions swirl, His Voice remains the gentle anchor that reminds you: I am here.

Quiet your soul, beloved. Lean into the whisper. He is speaking peace, guidance, reassurance, and direction just soft enough for those who listen.

Prayer:

Lord, tune my heart to hear Your still, small Voice. Quiet the noise around me and silence the distractions within me. Draw me close enough to recognize Your whisper and confident enough to follow where You lead. Let Your gentle Presence guides my steps and steady my spirit. In Jesus' Name, Amen.

Faith hears best in holy quiet.

Day 167
The Lamp of Understanding

Scripture:

"The entrance of Thy words giveth light; it giveth understanding unto the simple."

Psalm 119:130 (KJV)

Reflection:

God's Word does far more than instruct it illuminates. Each time Scripture enters your heart, it drives out confusion and ignites clarity. His Word doesn't just teach you truth; it unveils it. Revelation is the light that turns uncertainty into direction and questions into confidence.

Understanding does not come from human intellect but from holy intimacy. The more room His Word has in your heart, the brighter the inner path becomes. One whisper of Divine Truth can outshine a thousand human explanations.

Faith walks steadily where revelation shines. You may not understand everything, but when His Word breaks through, you understand enough to follow. Enough to trust. Enough to move forward without fear. Let His Word in deeply, daily, willingly and watch every Shadow lose its hold.

Prayer:

Lord, let Your Word illuminate my understanding. Chase away every Shadow of confusion and fill my spirit with the clarity that comes only from You. Give me revelation knowledge that guides my steps and anchors my faith. In Jesus' Name, Amen.

Faith walks steady in the light of revelation.

Day 168
Provision in the Path

Scripture:

"And thine ears shall hear a word behind thee, saying, This is the way, walk ye in it."

Isaiah 30:21 (KJV)

Reflection:

God never points you down a path He has not already prepared. His direction is never empty; every step He calls you to take is lined with provision, protection, and purpose. The same voice that whispers This is the way is the voice that ensures you have what you need while walking it.

Faith is not built on full visibility but on simple obedience. You do not need to see the entire road; you only need to heed the next instruction. Provision is often hidden in the step you haven't taken yet waiting to be revealed as you move forward in trust.

When you walk His path, lack becomes impossible. His guidance is your guarantee. Wherever His Voice leads, His Grace supplies. Every obedient step unlocks the next measure of strength, wisdom, and favor. You don't follow blindly; you follow One Who sees beyond the horizon.

Prayer:

Lord, help me to hear Your Voice with clarity and courage. Teach me to walk in the direction You ordain, trusting that every step holds Your provision. Confirm my path through Your Peace and sustain me with Your Grace. In Jesus' Name, Amen.

Faith never lacks when it walks where God leads.

Day 169
The God WHO Remembers

Scripture:

"And God remembered Noah."

Genesis 8:1 (KJV)

Reflection:

When it feels like you've been drifting in endless waters, unseen and uncertain, take heart God remembers. Noah floated for months with no instruction, no update, and no sign of change… yet Heaven never lost sight of him. The same is true for you.

God's remembrance is not a moment of recollection; it is a movement of restoration. When Scripture says He remembered, it means He acted. Winds shifted, waters receded, and what once drowned the world became the place where Noah's promise would land.

Your waiting is not wasted. The silence is not abandonment; it is the incubation of Divine timing. Even when clouds surround your life, God keeps a covenant. He remembers every prayer, every sacrifice, every tear. What He began in you is still alive beneath the surface.

When God remembers, seasons change. Doors open. Waters part. The ark of your obedience rests on the mountain He prepared. Faith can rest because His memory is perfect.

Prayer:

Lord, thank You that You never forget Your own. Remember me in mercy and bring forth every promise You have spoken. Let the winds of Your Timing shift my season and anchor me in Your faithfulness. In Jesus' Name, Amen.

Faith rests secure in Divine remembrance.

Day 170
The Blessing of Direction

Scripture:

"And the Lord shall guide thee continually, and satisfy thy soul in drought."

Isaiah 58:11 (KJV)

Reflection:

God's direction is not occasional, it is constant. He does not lead only in abundance; He guides just as faithfully in drought. Seasons may shift, but His shepherding never ceases. When the path feels dry, His Presence becomes your provision. When clarity seems scarce, His whisper becomes your compass.

Divine direction is one of Heaven's greatest blessings. It reminds you that you are not left to navigate life alone. Faith doesn't demand to see the entire journey; it simply follows the next step illuminated by His Mercy. And every step He reveals carries peace as its companion.

When the Lord guides you, wandering ends. Confusion quiets. Your soul becomes satisfied not by circumstance, but by His nearness. In every season, His guidance proves His Love.

Prayer:

Lord, thank You for guiding me continually. Satisfy my soul even in dry places, and lead me in the paths that glorify You. Let my life reveal the blessing of Your direction and the peace that follows Your Voice. In Jesus' Name, Amen.

Faith flourishes under continual guidance.

Day 171
The Balm of Gilead

Scripture:

"Is there no balm in Gilead; is there no physician there? why then is not the health of the daughter of my people recovered?"

Jeremiah 8:22 (KJV)

Reflection:

There is a Balm in Gilead and His Name is Jesus.

He is the cure for the wounds too deep for human hands and the Physician who treats the soul as gently as He does the body. Where grief has lingered, where trauma has tangled roots, where heartbreak has stolen breath His healing reaches without hesitation.

The balm of His Presence soothes what words cannot explain. His comfort flows into the cracks where memories ache and where the past still breathes. Healing is not always instant, but with Him, it is always inevitable.

Faith applies the balm daily through worship that softens the heart, the Word that renews the mind, and waiting that anchors the soul. Healing is not the absence of pain; it is the Presence of the Healer. And He is near… always near.

Prayer:

Lord, thank You for being the Balm of Gilead. Heal the wounds I've hidden and restore what pain has stolen. Let Your Presence bring peace, wholeness, and renewal to every part of me. In Jesus' Name, Amen.

Faith finds its cure in the hands of the Healer.

Day 172
Beauty Restored

Scripture:

"To appoint unto them that mourn in Zion, to give unto them beauty for ashes, the oil of joy for mourning."

Isaiah 61:3 (KJV)

Reflection:

God does not ask you to pretend the ashes aren't there He invites you to bring them to Him. He does not sweep away the remnants of what was lost; He transforms them into what could only be made through His redemptive love.

The very places that once felt burned, barren, or beyond repair become sacred ground in His Hands. Restoration is more than recovery, it is resurrection. It is God taking what life tried to destroy and turning it into something beautifully, undeniably marked by His Glory.

Faith releases the ashes. Faith opens its hands. Faith dares to believe that joy is still possible, that healing is still near, and that beauty can rise from what felt final. The oil of joy is poured on those who choose hope over despair. You do not rise alone He lifts you.

Prayer:

Lord, take my ashes and trade them for Your beauty. Let the oil of joy flow where mourning once lingered. Thank You for making all things new in Your perfect time. In Jesus' Name, Amen.

Faith offers ashes and receives anointed beauty.

Day 173
Healing in His Wings

Scripture:

"But unto you that fear My name shall the Sun of righteousness arise with healing in His wings."

Malachi 4:2 (KJV)

Reflection:

When Jesus rises over the broken places of your life, He does not come with partial restoration He comes with healing in His wings. His light does what darkness never could: it reveals, restores, and revives. Healing does not always come suddenly; often, it arrives like dawn.

First a glimmer, then a glow. First a warmth, then a strengthening. First a whisper of hope, then a sunrise of wholeness.

Every gentle ray of His righteousness carries power. The moment His light touches a wounded place, the process of renewal begins. What feels cold begins to warm. What felt lifeless begins to breathe again. What seemed too broken begins to find purpose.

You are not healing alone You are healing beneath His wings.

Prayer:

Lord, let the warmth of Your healing light touch every hidden wound within me. Rise over my life with righteousness and renewal. I receive the healing that flows from Your wings. In Jesus' Name, Amen.

Faith rises beneath the wings of Divine healing.

Day 174
The Gift in the Pain

Scripture:

"And we know that all things work together for good to them that love God."

Romans 8:28 (KJV)

Reflection:

Pain becomes a gift when surrendered to God. What once broke you becomes the very place He builds you. The valley that felt empty becomes the ground where compassion grows. The moments that crushed your heart become the moments that shape your calling.

Faith does not pretend the pain didn't hurt; it simply trusts that God will not waste it. Suffering sharpens vision. It softens edges. It deepens empathy. The very wounds you wished away become wells of wisdom, drawing others toward healing.

God weaves purpose through every sorrow. Your tears water seeds that will one day bloom into testimonies of Grace. What hurt you will one day help someone else. What seemed senseless becomes sacred when placed in His redeeming hands.

There is a gift hidden in the pain and God Himself is the Giver.

Prayer:

Lord, thank You for turning pain into purpose. Help me to see the beauty You are forming through what I've endured. Let every scar tell a story of Your faithfulness. In Jesus' Name, Amen.

Faith finds treasures in the soil of sorrow.

Day 175
Rest for the Weary Soul

Scripture:

"Come unto Me, all ye that labour and are heavy laden, and I will give you rest."

Matthew 11:28 (KJV)

Reflection:

Rest is not the absence of work, it is the Presence of Jesus. True rest is found not in escape, but in encounter. The Lord's invitation is tender and personal. He calls the burdened, the tired, the overwhelmed, the ones who have been carrying more than their hearts were meant to hold. When you come to Him, He doesn't simply give relief He gives Himself. He replaces strain with stillness. He trades your exhaustion for His embrace. He exchanges your pressure for His Peace. Faith rests where striving surrenders. You don't prove your worth to receive His rest, you simply come. Let your soul lean into the One Who restores, renews, and refreshes. His rest is not momentary; it is holy habitation.

This is the rest your weary soul has longed for:

Not sleep, but sanctuary. Not a break, but belonging. Not escape, but the everlasting arms.

Prayer:

Lord, I bring You my burdens and lay them down at Your feet. Quiet my heart and renew my strength in Your rest. Let my soul find peace in Your Presence. In Jesus' Name, Amen.

Faith breathes easiest in the arms of rest.

Day 176
He Restores My Soul

Scripture:

"He restoreth my soul: He leadeth me in the paths of righteousness for His name's sake."

Psalm 23:3 (KJV)

Reflection:

Restoration doesn't begin around you, it begins within you. God's healing touches the places no one else sees: the bruised emotions, the silent disappointments, the hopes that dimmed in the shadows, the strength that quietly slipped away.

The Shepherd does not patch you up; He restores you. He breathes life into the weary and revival into the broken. He reawakens what pain tried to bury and brings back to life what grief tried to silence. His restoration is personal… intentional… complete. And He leads you step by step toward righteousness, peace, and wholeness. Not because you are perfect, but because His Name is faithful. Every path He places before you is both healing and holy. Every step you take with Him rebuilds something inside you. Faith trusts the journey, because the Shepherd Himself is the one holding your heart.

Prayer:

Lord, restore my soul where it has grown weary. Heal my heart, renew my joy, and lead me in Your righteousness. Let Your Presence restore what only You can make whole. In Jesus' Name, Amen.

Faith follows the Shepherd into restoration.

Day 177
The God Who Redeems Time

Scripture:

"And I will restore to you the years that the locust hath eaten."

Joel 2:25 (KJV)

Reflection:

God does not merely give back what was taken He redeems what was lost, including the time, the tears, and opportunities you thought over. He is the only One Who can reach into yesterday and bring forth harvest from places you thought were barren. Nothing is wasted in His Hands, not the years of wandering, not the seasons of struggle, not the moments marked by regret. Redemption means He transforms loss into legacy, delay into development, and detours into Divine direction. The years you mourn, He mends. The years you question, He reclaims. The years you surrendered as gone, He resurrects with purpose. Faith lets go of regret and embraces renewal. For when God redeems time, He doesn't just restore the years He fills them with a double portion of Grace.

Prayer:

Lord, thank You for redeeming time. Heal my heart from the years I thought were lost and let Your purpose blooms in their place. In Jesus' Name, Amen.

Faith redeems time by trusting the Redeemer.

Day 178
Arise, Shield Maiden

Scripture:

"Be strong in the Lord, and in the power of His might."

Ephesians 6:10 KJV

Reflection:

There are moments when God whispers a name that stirs something inside you. Shield Maiden is not a title of war but of worship. It speaks of a woman who rises when the Spirit moves, who shields her household and her community through prayer, and who carries peace into chaos.

When the world grows sharp with complaint or fear, a Shield Maiden stands firm. She doesn't fight flesh and blood; she guards the atmosphere with praise. Her weapons are kindness, gentleness, and truth. She knows that one word of encouragement can break heaviness, one prayer can shift a room. To arise is not to strive, but to answer. The Lord is calling His daughters to stand not in their own strength, but clothed in His armor, radiant with His Love. When you walk into dark places, remember: light walks in with you.

Prayer:

Heavenly Father, teach me to rise when You call. Clothe me with Your strength and compassion. Let my words carry peace, my presence shifts the atmosphere, and my faith shields those around me. May I walk as Your daughter steadfast, gentle, and unafraid. In Jesus' Name, Amen.

Endurance and Resilience

Day 179
Rivers of Renewal

Scripture:

"For I will pour water upon him that is thirsty, and floods upon the dry ground."

Isaiah 44:3 (KJV)

Reflection:

God never sends a sprinkle where a flood is needed. His renewal does not trickle it pours. When your spirit feels cracked, thirsty, or worn thin by life, He responds not with drops but with rivers. He restores vigorously, generously, and completely. Dry ground is not a sign of God's absence; it is the place His Presence is preparing to invade. Thirst is an invitation for an encounter. Renewal begins the moment you admit your need and open your heart to receive. Faith makes room for the flood. When you stretch out your hands in surrender, His Spirit washes over grief, weariness, stagnation, and disappointment. What once felt barren becomes a garden again. What once seemed hopeless becomes fertile with promise. His Presence does not simply revive it transforms.

Prayer:

Lord, pour Your renewing Spirit upon me. Revive every dry and weary place in my heart. Let Your Presence saturates my soul until joy rises, peace overflows, and strength returns. Make rivers where there were deserts, and let my life testify of Your refreshing power. In Jesus' Name, Amen.

Faith drinks deeply from the river of renewal.

Day 180
Made Whole

Scripture:

"And He said unto her, Daughter, thy faith hath made thee whole; go in peace."

Luke 8:48 (KJV)

Reflection:

Wholeness is deeper than healing. Healing mends what was wounded, but wholeness restores what was lost, broken, or forgotten. When Jesus spoke to the woman who reached for His hem, He did more than stop her bleeding He restored her identity, dignity, and peace.

Faith not only touches Jesus; it draws virtue from Him. Her touch was desperate, but His response was tender. He called her Daughter Healed in body, seen in spirit, restored in heart.

Wholeness means the shame is gone, the fear is silenced, and the story is rewritten by Grace. It is the work of Jesus completing what no human hand could fix. When He makes you whole, every fractured place becomes a testimony of His Love.

Prayer:

Lord, thank You for making me whole. Heal every hidden place and restore every broken part of my story. Fill me with the peace that only Your Presence can bring. I receive Your Wholeness with gratitude, faith, and joy. In Jesus' Name, Amen.

Faith reaches for His hem and rises whole.

Day 181
One Body, Many Members

Scripture:

"For as we have many members in one body, and all members have not the same office."

Romans 12:4 (KJV)

Reflection:

The beauty of the Body of Christ is found in its God-designed diversity. No two believers are shaped the same, gifted the same, or called the same yet all are joined together by one Spirit and one Savior. What weakens the body is comparison, but what strengthens it is cooperation.

Every gift matters. Every calling contributes. Every member plays a part in Heaven's harmony. When we honor the unique Grace God has placed in others, envy fades and unity flourishes. Fellowship becomes fertile ground for faith to grow, because we are reminded that none of us are meant to function alone.

Unity is not sameness; it is surrender to the same Savior. It is the willingness to stand together, serve together, worship together, and love one another with the humility Christ demonstrated. When each member operates in their God-given place, the Body becomes a radiant reflection of Jesus to the world.

Prayer:

Lord, thank You for placing me within the Body of Christ. Help me serve with humility, encourage with sincerity, and honor the gifts You have given to others. Teach me to celebrate diversity within Your people and to walk in unity with those You've called alongside me. Knit our hearts together in love so that the world may see You through us. In Jesus' Name, Amen.

Faith thrives where unity lives.

Section Five:
Divine Provision and Guidance

Day 182
Love That Builds

Scripture:

"Let all your things be done with charity."

1 Corinthians 16:14 (KJV)

Reflection:

Love is the foundation upon which every Kingdom work must rest. It is the mortar that binds hearts together and strengthens what pressure tries to break. When love takes the lead, unity follows, peace grows, and the atmosphere shifts into something holy.

True love is never passive, it is purposeful. It is patience in conflict, kindness in irritation, mercy where judgment once rose. Love builds bridges where division once stood, restoring what pride and misunderstanding attempted to dismantle.

Every act done in love carries eternal weight. Love is the language of Christ, the force that transforms, and the evidence of a heart shaped by Grace. When you choose love, you choose the higher way, the way that builds, heals, and honors God.

Prayer:

Lord, let Your Love be the motive behind every word and action Teach me to build up, not tear down to lift, encourage, and restore. Make my heart a reflection of Your compassion, and let everything I do be done with love. In Jesus' Name, Amen.

Faith builds best when love holds the tools.

Day 183
The Ministry of Kindness

Scripture:

"And be ye kind one to another, tenderhearted, forgiving one another, even as God for Christ's sake hath forgiven you."

Ephesians 4:32 (KJV)

Reflection:

Kindness is one of the most powerful ministries in the Kingdom, yet it often goes unnoticed by the world. A gentle word, a soft response, or a simple act of compassion can shift the atmosphere in ways that sermons and speeches cannot. Kindness reaches where arguments fail; it steps past defenses and touches the heart.

True kindness flows from a heart softened by Grace. It is the tenderness God showed you poured back out onto others. When you extend forgiveness, patience, or compassion, you become a living reflection of His Mercy. Kindness costs little but yields eternal impact. Faith expresses itself in how you treat people, especially the ones hardest to love. Every act of kindness becomes a seed of healing, planting hope in places you may never see.

Prayer:

Lord, help me to minister through kindness every day. Let my words be gentle, my actions compassionate, and my heart tender toward others. Teach me to forgive as You forgave me and to love as You have loved me. In Jesus' Name, Amen.

Faith speaks kindness as its native tongue.

Day 184
Bearing One Another's Burdens

Scripture:

"Bear ye one another's burdens, and so fulfil the law of Christ."

Galatians 6:2 (KJV)

Reflection:

Love lightens what life loads onto weary shoulders. When you help carry someone else's burden, you step into the very heartbeat of Christ the One Who bore the weight of the world so we wouldn't have to carry ours alone. To bear a burden is to enter holy ground, where compassion becomes action and fellowship becomes ministry.

The Kingdom was never meant to be walked in isolation. God weaves strength through community, healing through shared prayers, and comfort through shared tears. Burden-bearing is not pity, it is partnership. It is choosing to stand in the gap where someone's strength feels thin and placing your shoulder beneath the weight with them.

Faith grows stronger when shared. When you bear another's burden, you turn sympathy into service and love into a living covenant. In those moments, Christ's character is seen most clearly in you.

Prayer:

Lord, teach me to bear others' burdens with Grace. Give me eyes to see needs before they're spoken and a heart willing to serve with joy. Let my compassion become an extension of Your Love and my presence is a reminder of Your Faithfulness. In Jesus' Name, Amen.

Faith walks slower so love can walk beside it.

Day 185
Restoring the Broken

Scripture:

"Brethren, if a man be overtaken in a fault, ye which are spiritual, restore such an one in the spirit of meekness."

Galatians 6:1 (KJV)

Reflection:

Restoration is sacred work. It is the gentle touch of Grace reaching into places where failure has left its mark. God never commissions His people to shame the fallen He calls them to lift, to mend, and to rebuild what has been damaged. True restoration requires a heart clothed in humility, remembering that none of us stand except by mercy.

Correction without compassion deepens wounds; but correction wrapped in meekness heals them. Those who walk closely with the Spirit know how to speak Truth without crushing, how to offer guidance without superiority, and how to extend Grace without compromise. Faith restores because it remembers. It remembers the pit God pulled you from, the patience He showed, and the kindness that transformed you.

The ministry of restoration is not about pointing out what's wrong but helping someone rise into what's right. When you restore the broken, you echo the heart of the Redeemer, who never wounds to expose He wounds to heal.

Prayer:

Lord, give me a spirit of meekness when dealing with those who have stumbled. Teach me to restore with tenderness and truth, to lift with love and not condemn with pride. Let my words carry Your mercy and my actions reflect Your compassion. In Jesus' Name, Amen.

Faith restores gently what judgment would discard.

Day 186
Unity in the Spirit

Scripture:

"Endeavoring to keep the unity of the Spirit in the bond of peace."

Ephesians 4:3 (KJV)

Reflection:

Unity is the heartbeat of the Kingdom, but it does not happen by accident it is cultivated with intention. The enemy aims for division, knowing that a divided house cannot stand. But the Spirit knits hearts together through peace, humility, and mutual surrender.

Unity doesn't require perfect agreement; it requires perfect love. It grows where Grace is extended, where pride is laid down, and where understanding is pursued instead of argument. The bond of peace is a spiritual glue strong enough to hold people together even when perspectives differ, powerful enough to silence strife when hearts choose Christ over conflict.

Faith values the relationship above being right. It seeks reconciliation before recognition. It listens more than it speaks and loves more than it demands. When believers fight for unity, Heaven fights for them. Where unity dwells, blessing flows.

Prayer:

Lord, help me to be a peacemaker in every circle You've placed me. Clothe my heart in humility, my words in gentleness, and my actions in love. Let the unity of Your Spirit bind us together with purpose and peace, that we may reflect Your Heart to the world. In Jesus' Name, Amen.

Faith defends unity because love demands it.

Day 187
The Power of Forgiveness

Scripture:

"For if ye forgive men their trespasses, your heavenly Father will also forgive you."

Matthew 6:14 (KJV)

Reflection:

Forgiveness is a Divine exchange of your pain for His Peace, your bitterness for His freedom. It is not a feeling but a choice, one that Heaven honors and hell fears. Unforgiveness chains the heart; forgiveness breaks it open for blessing.

When you release someone, you release yourself. The weight you've carried loosens, the wound begins to heal, and the atmosphere of your soul shifts. Forgiveness is not approval of the offense; it is refusal to be imprisoned by it.

Faith forgives even when memory tries to re-open the wound. Grace says, I choose peace instead. The cross stands as the ultimate reminder: Jesus offered mercy before we ever asked. When you forgive, you step into His likeness, His Love, and His liberty.

Prayer:

Lord, teach me to forgive as You have forgiven me. Release every trace of bitterness from my heart and fill me with Your Peace. Help me to extend Grace freely, letting forgiveness flow as a testimony of Your work within me. In Jesus' Name, Amen.

Faith forgives fully because it was forgiven first.

Day 188
Friendship Forged in Faith

Scripture:

"A friend loveth at all times, and a brother is born for adversity."

Proverbs 17:17 (KJV)

Reflection:

True friendship is a gift woven by the hand of God threads of loyalty, prayer, and purpose intertwined. Faith-forged friendships are not fragile; they are fortified by shared battles, whispered prayers, and seasons walked side by side. They stand firm when storms rage and remain steady when comfort is costly.

A covenant friend doesn't just speak encouragement, they embody it. They remind you of God's Promises when your own vision grows dim. They lift your arms when the weight is too heavy, and they stand guard when the enemy presses close. Faithful friends sharpen your faith, steady your steps, and strengthen your spirit.

These friendships are not built on convenience but on calling. Adversity does not weaken them, it reveals them. In the darkest valleys, covenant love shines the brightest.

Prayer:

Lord, thank You for the friends who walk with me in faith and love me with Grace. Teach me to be a faithful friend in return loyal in prayer, strong in encouragement, and tender in compassion. Bless every relationship You have ordained, and bind them with unity, purpose, and Your unfailing love. In Jesus' Name, Amen.

Faithful friendships are Heaven's gentle reinforcement.

Day 189
The Blessing of Servanthood

Scripture:

"But he that is greatest among you shall be your servant."

Matthew 23:11 (KJV)

Reflection:

In the Kingdom of God, greatness flows downward. It is found not in titles, platforms, or applause, but in hands willing to wash feet and hearts willing to stoop low in love. Servanthood is not weakness, it is Christlikeness. The One Who formed galaxies also wrapped Himself in a towel and knelt to serve.

Every quiet act of kindness, every unseen sacrifice, every time you choose humility over recognition Heaven sees it. God measures greatness by the posture of the heart, not the position in a room. True servanthood is born from revelation, not obligation. When you understand how deeply Christ has served you, serving others becomes joy, not duty.

The hands that serve become the hands through which He heals. The heart that bends low becomes the vessel He lifts high. There is no safer, sweeter, or more sacred place than the path of a servant; it is the very road Jesus walked.

Prayer:

Lord, make me a servant after Your Heart. Strip away pride and replace it with humility. Let every task, large or small, become an offering of love to You. Use My Hands to bless, my words to heal, and my life to lift others higher. May servanthood be my joy and my calling, just as it was Yours. In Jesus' Name, Amen.

Faith finds greatness in serving quietly.

Day 190
A Family of Faith

Scripture:

"Now therefore ye are no more strangers and foreigners, but fellow citizens with the saints, and of the household of God."

Ephesians 2:19 (KJV)

Reflection:

In Christ, we inherit more than salvation; we inherit a family. We are joined not by earthly lineage, but by the Blood that redeemed us. What once separated us from our backgrounds, pasts, personalities, and paths is overshadowed by the greater truth: we belong to Him, and therefore we belong to each other. The family of God is diverse yet united, imperfect yet deeply precious. We learn together, worship together, weep together, and rise together. In this household of faith, we are shaped by Grace and strengthened by shared purpose.

Community is not optional; it is God's design. Isolation weakens, but fellowship builds. Faith flourishes when surrounded by brothers and sisters who speak life, offer prayer, and walk shoulder to shoulder through every season. Together, we become a testimony of His Love, a living picture of Heaven's unity on earth.

Prayer:

Father, thank You for the beautiful family of faith You have placed around me. Teach me to love with patience, honor with sincerity, and cherish each relationship as a gift from Your Hand. Knit our hearts together in compassion, unity, and purpose. Let our fellowship bring Glory to Your Name. In Jesus' Name, Amen.

Faith feels most at home in God's family.

Day 191
Triumph Through Trials

Scripture:

"But thanks be to God, which always causeth us to triumph in Christ."

2 Corinthians 2:14 (KJV)

Reflection:

Every trial you face is not a sign of defeat, it is an opportunity for Divine triumph. God never promised a life free from battles, but He did promise that every battle would end in victory through Christ. Your struggles may feel overwhelming, but they are not the final word His triumph is.

Triumph in Christ is not determined by how circumstances look, but by who your Savior is. Victory is not something you strive for; it is something you walk in because He won it for you. Even when the path is steep, even when the nights are long, His Grace guides you from pressure to purpose, from breaking to becoming.

Trials refine your faith, deepen your dependence, and reveal His Power within you. The enemy may come to steal your confidence, but God uses the very storm to strengthen it. You don't merely survive, you rise. You overcome because He overcame. And you triumph because He leads you by the hand through every chapter, every challenge, every unseen battle.

Prayer:

Lord, thank You for causing me to triumph in every trial. When circumstances whisper defeat, remind me of the victory I already have in You. Give me eyes to see Your Hand at work even in the struggle and a heart that praises You while the battle is still underway. Strengthen my faith, steady my steps, and lead me from trial to triumph for Your Glory. In Jesus' Name, Amen.

Faith celebrates victory before it sees the outcome.

Day 192
More Than Conquerors

Scripture:

"Nay, in all these things we are more than conquerors through Him that loved us."

Romans 8:37 (KJV)

Reflection:

To conquer is to stand victorious after a battle but to be more than a conqueror is to step into battles already won. Your victory is not pending; it is permanent. Christ didn't just give you strength to fight He positioned you in triumph before the storm even began.

Every trial, every tear, every warfare moment is filtered through the love of a God Who conquered death, hell, and the grave on your behalf. His Love is not passive, it is powerful. Because of His Love, you don't fight for victory; you fight from it. The cross settled the outcome. The resurrection sealed it.

More than a conqueror means the battle may touch you, but it cannot take you. It means what was meant to break you will bless you. It means you walk through fire without the smell of smoke because His Love surrounds you like armor.

Faith becomes fearless when anchored in His Truth:

No challenge is greater than the love that already overcame it.

Prayer:

Lord, thank You that I am more than a conqueror through Your unfailing love. Remind me daily that every challenge bows to the victory of the cross. Teach me to walk boldly, confidently, and peacefully in the triumph You secured for me. Strengthen my heart to live from victory, not for it. In Jesus' Name, Amen.

Faith stands tall in a battle already won.

Day 193
Weapons of Worship

Scripture:

"Let the high praises of God be in their mouth, and a two-edged sword in their hand."

Psalm 149:6 (KJV)

Reflection:

Worship is not a soft response; it is a supernatural weapon. Praise doesn't simply rise toward Heaven; it pushes back the darkness. When you lift your voice in honor to God, you release a sound the enemy cannot stand against. Worship shifts the atmosphere, changes internal climates, and opens spiritual realms where God moves with authority.

In moments of pressure, worship turns your posture from defeated to victorious. High praise places a sword in your hand the living Word of God spoken with boldness. The same voice that exalts Jesus sends confusion into the enemy's camp and breaks chains that human strength never could. Worship disarms worry. Praise dismantles fear. Adoration invites the presence that drives out oppression.

When your heart chooses worship in warfare, you are not escaping the battle, you are engaging it with Heaven's weapons. Your song becomes a declaration, your praise becomes a proclamation, and your worship becomes the very wind that brings breakthrough.

Prayer:

Lord, teach me to fight my battles through worship. Let high praise fill my mouth and Your Word strengthen My Hands. Turn my worries into worship and my fears into faith. Let the sound of my praise scatter darkness and usher in Your Victory. In Jesus' Name, Amen.

Faith wages war through worship.

Day 194
Faith That Fights

Scripture:

"Fight the good fight of faith, lay hold on eternal life."

1 Timothy 6:12 (KJV)

Reflection:

The true battleground of the believer is not in the natural world; it is in the arena of belief. Faith's greatest opponent has never been people, circumstances, or even the enemy himself…it is doubt. Every moment you choose trust over trembling, perseverance over panic, and worship over worry, Heaven records the victory in your favor.

The fight of faith is fierce because it protects what God has spoken. Promises aren't passive; they require participation. Faith fights by holding on, even when evidence says to let go. It fights by speaking truth, even when lies shout loud. It fights by standing firm, even when strength feels small. Faith doesn't fight with fists; it fights with focus. It doesn't conquer through force it conquers through confidence in God.

The good fight is good because the outcome is guaranteed. You are not swinging at uncertainty; you are enforcing the victory already won through Christ. With every prayer, every declaration, and every step forward, you lay hold of the eternal life and destiny He prepared for you.

Prayer:

Lord, strengthen My Hands for the good fight of faith. Teach me to battle through prayer, to war through worship, and to push forward through perseverance. Anchor my heart in Your Promises and let my confidence in You remain unshakable. In Jesus' Name, Amen.

Faith doesn't fight for victory --it fights from it.

Day 195
Strength in the Battle

Scripture:

"It is God that girdeth me with strength, and maketh my way perfect."

Psalm 18:32 (KJV)

Reflection:

Strength for the battle is never drawn from your own reserves; it is poured from Heaven. The warrior who wins is the One Who leans, not the One Who lunges. Victory belongs to the surrendered, not the self-sufficient. When you depend on God, your weakness becomes the very place where His might displays itself most powerfully.

The same Spirit who empowered David to stand before Goliath now empowers you to face whatever giants rise in your path. God's strength does not merely assist it upholds, equips, and goes before you. You are not fighting for victory; you are fighting from the strength of the One Who has already secured it.

The battle may roar, but your confidence rests in the Champion who never loses. His Strength girds you like armor, fortifying your spirit, steadying your steps, and making your way perfect not because the path is smooth, but because His Presence is sure.

Prayer:

Lord, clothe me with Your strength today. Gird me for every battle I must face, and remind me that victory is found in Your Power, not mine. Make my path straight, my heart courageous, and my spirit steadfast. In Jesus' Name, Amen.

Faith finds its might in Divine strength.

Day 196
The Sound of Victory

Scripture:

"The shout of a King is among them."

Numbers 23:21 (KJV)

Reflection:

Wherever the Presence of God rests, victory resounds. The atmosphere shifts not because of human strength, but because the King Himself is in the midst. Hell does not tremble at your ability; it trembles at your agreement with Heaven. When you release praise, you release authority.

The shout of victory is more than volume, it is vision. It is the declaration of what God has already done, even when your eyes have yet to see it. Faith does not whisper in fear; it shouts in confidence. Your praise is a prophecy that declares, My God reigns! and every force of darkness recognizes that shout as the signal of its defeat.

When the King is among His people, the battle is already decided. Your worship becomes the weapon, your hallelujah the herald of triumph, and your shout the sound that shakes walls and silences the enemy.

Prayer:

Lord, fill my heart with the sound of victory. Let my praise echo Your Power and my voice declare Your reign. May the shout of triumph rise within me and testify to Your greatness. In Jesus' Name, Amen.

Faith shouts what Heaven has already settled.

Day 197
The Armor of Light

Scripture:

The night is far spent, the day is at hand: let us therefore cast off the works of darkness, and let us put on the armour of light.

Romans 13:12 (KJV)

Reflection:

Your protection is not forged in iron, it is formed in illumination. The armor of light is the covering of those who walk with Christ, a radiant shield that exposes deception and empowers discernment. Darkness can only dwell where light is absent, and every obedient step increases your brightness.

When you put on the armor of light, you are clothing yourself in purity, truth, and the brilliance of God's Presence. This armor does not merely defend its transforms. It pushes back every Shadow that once clung to your spirit and reveals the path ahead with heavenly clarity.

Faith does not fear the battlefield when wrapped in the radiance of Christ. Light wins every time. Walk boldly in the brightness He has given you, and no scheme of the enemy will prevail.

Prayer:

Lord, clothe me today in the armor of Your light. Let Truth guard my thoughts and righteousness shield my heart. Drive out every Shadow with the brilliance of Your Presence. Shine through me as a living testimony of Your Glory. In Jesus' Name, Amen.

Faith wears light as its defense.

Day 198
The Victor's Crown

Scripture:

"Be thou faithful unto death, and I will give thee a crown of life."

Revelation 2:10 (KJV)

Reflection:

Crowns in the Kingdom are not awarded for perfection they are given for perseverance. Every quiet act of obedience, every tear shed in trust, every battle fought in secret places adds unseen jewels to the reward God Himself prepares.

The Victor's crown is the promise reserved for those who refuse to give up. Faithfulness in the small, the hidden, and the hard is never forgotten in Heaven. Your endurance, your devotion, and your steadfast heart are shaping an eternal reward that reflects the Glory of the One you serve. Faith finishes strong and Heaven places the Victor's crown upon those who endure to the end.

Prayer:

Lord, keep me faithful to the end. Let perseverance be my portion and Your reward my desire. May my life bring You Glory in battle and in rest, in strength and in surrender. In Jesus' Name, Amen.

Faith finishes strong and wears The Victor's crown.

Day 199
Standing on the Promise

Scripture:

"For all the promises of God in Him are yea, and in Him Amen."

2 Corinthians 1:20 (KJV)

Reflection:

When the winds of doubt howl and circumstances shift beneath your feet, the promises of God become anchors nothing can move. His yes is not fragile; it is eternal, fixed, and fortified in Christ. No opposition, no delay, no disappointment, and no earthly obstacle can overturn what Heaven has already affirmed. Once God has spoken, His Word stands forever.

Standing on His Promises transforms uncertainty into confidence. The promises God gives you are not suggestions or hopeful possibilities; they are covenants sealed in the Blood of Jesus. Faith does not stand firm because life is easy; faith stands firm because God's Word is unshakable.

Every promise fulfilled in Christ now belongs to you. His yes is your foundation. His Amen is your assurance. Speak His Promises over your life. Believe them even when feelings waver. Stand upon them until what you have trusted Him for becomes what you see.

When everything else shifts, the promises of God remain your steady ground.

Prayer:

Lord, thank You that every promise in Christ is faithful, certain, and true. Strengthen my heart to stand on Your Word with unwavering confidence. When circumstances shake, anchor me in what You have spoken. Let my hope rest fully in Your unchanging promises, and let my faith endure until every promise becomes sight. In Jesus' Name, Amen.

Faith stands firm on unfailing promises.

Day 200
The Overcomer's Song

Scripture:

"They overcame him by the blood of the Lamb, and by the word of their testimony."

Revelation 12:11 (KJV)

Reflection:

Every overcomer carries a song not born from ease, but from endurance. It is a melody written through tears, tested in fire, and crowned in victory. Your testimony is far more than a story told; it is a declaration that darkness could not destroy you and a reminder to hell that it has already lost. It is a witness to Heaven that God's power still reigns in your life.

The blood of the Lamb is the eternal chorus of every redeemed soul, the anthem that defeats the accuser, silences shame, and declares freedom. And your testimony becomes the verses, sung through valleys and mountaintops, woven through seasons of struggle and seasons of triumph. Together, they form a song strong enough to shake darkness, push back fear, and glorify the risen King.

Your life is the overcomer's song bold, redemptive, and unstoppable. Every battle you've survived, every prayer you've prayed, every deliverance you've experienced adds another verse to the melody Heaven hears and hell fears. Sing it. Live it. Let your life echo His Victory.

Prayer:

Lord, thank You for making me an overcomer through the power of Your Blood. Let my life sing the testimony of Your Victory and reflect the strength of Your redeeming love. May my praise rise above every battle and echo Your Triumph in every season. In Jesus' Name, Amen.

Faith sings the song of the overcomer.

Day 201
Faith in the Fire

Scripture:

"When thou walkest through the fire, thou shalt not be burned; neither shall the flame kindle upon thee."

Isaiah 43:2 (KJV)

Reflection:

God never promised a fire-free life He promised a flame-proof faith. The story of Shadrach, Meshach, and Abednego reminds us that the very furnace meant to destroy them became the place where Jesus Himself appeared. Their deliverance wasn't outside the fire, it was in the fire.

Faith in the fire reveals who is truly with you. It exposes what threatens you, but it also reveals what sustains you. The flames that frighten you will not consume you; they will forge you. What looks like destruction to the world becomes refinement in the hands of God.

The fire does not destroy the faithful, it purifies them. It burns away fear, doubt, pride, and every lesser thing until what remains is stronger, purer, and more radiant. The hotter the flame, the clearer His Presence becomes. And when you come out, not even the smell of smoke will cling to you, only the shine of His likeness.

Prayer:

Lord, thank You for being with me in every fire I face. When the heat rises and the trial intensifies, let my faith burn brighter than the flames around me. Refine my heart until everything that is not of You falls away, and all that remains is Your reflection in my life. Strengthen me, sustain me, and remind me that I never walk through the fire alone. In Jesus' Name, Amen.

Faith glows brightest in the fire.

Day 202
Weapons of Peace

Scripture:

"The Lord will fight for you, and ye shall hold your peace."

Exodus 14:14 (KJV)

Reflection:

Peace is not passive; it is powerful. The enemy thrives on chaos, confusion, and emotional reaction, but peace disrupts every one of his strategies. When you choose rest over reaction, trust instead of turmoil, you step into a realm where victory is secured without you lifting a sword. Stillness is not surrender; it is spiritual positioning. It is the sanctuary where God Himself steps into the battle on your behalf. While the noise of war surrounds you, peace anchors you in the confidence that the Lord is fighting for you.

Faith's greatest weapon is the ability to remain calm when everything around you is shaking. Peace becomes a shield. Stillness becomes a stance. And when you choose to hold your peace, Heaven releases its armies. God moves where your panic ends and your trust begin. Let your peace speak louder than the war.

Prayer:

Lord, teach me to fight my battles with peace. Let Your calm be my weapon and Your stillness my strength. Quiet every fear that rises within me, and anchor my heart in trust. I release every battle into Your Hands and believe that You will defend what I cannot. In Jesus' Name, Amen.

Faith wins battles by resting, not wrestling.

Day 203
The Shield of Faith

Scripture:

"Above all, taking the shield of faith, wherewith ye shall be able to quench all the fiery darts of the wicked."

Ephesians 6:16 (KJV)

Reflection:

Faith is not merely a belief it is Divine protection. It is the invisible shield that hell cannot penetrate and the weapon the enemy cannot outwit. Every fiery dart discouragement, doubt, deception, distraction, accusation loses its flame the moment it collides with unwavering trust in God's Word. The shield of faith does not prevent the enemy from attacking; it prevents the attack from harming you. It absorbs what was meant to wound and renders it powerless. Many darts never reach your heart simply because your shield is raised.

Faith isn't passive, it is active. It must be lifted daily through Scripture, prayer, worship, and obedience. A lowered shield invites attack; a lifted shield guarantees victory. The enemy cannot defeat a believer whose faith remains raised toward Heaven.

Prayer:

Lord, strengthen my grip on the shield of faith. Help me to lift it daily with confidence in Your Word. Let every doubt, lie, and attack fall powerless when it meets Your truth. Guard my heart, steady my mind, and keep my spirit anchored in You. Teach me to stand covered, courageous, and confident in Your protection. In Jesus' Name, Amen.

Faith lifted high becomes Heaven's shield.

Day 204
The Word That Wins

Scripture:

"For the word of God is quick, and powerful, and sharper than any two edged sword."

Hebrews 4:12 (KJV)

Reflection:

Every spiritual victory begins with the Word of God. When the enemy attacked Jesus in the wilderness, He didn't reason, negotiate, or fear He declared the written Word. The sword of the Spirit never loses its edge, never misses its mark, and never returns void. The Word that wins is not the Word we merely read, it is the Word we remember, believe, and speak. Scripture becomes a weapon when it leaves your mouth with faith. The atmosphere shifts when Truth is proclaimed. Darkness retreats when promises are declared.

Speak it until fear flees.

Speak it until peace rises.

Speak it until your spirit stands strong again.

The Word in your heart brings faith. The Word in your mouth brings victory.

Prayer:

Lord, let Your Word dwell richly within me. Teach me not only to read it, but to wield it. Give me boldness to speak Your Promises with authority and confidence. Let Scripture be my defense, my strength, and my victory in every battle I face. In Jesus' Name, Amen.

Faith wins when the Word is spoken.

Day 205
Victory Over Fear

Scripture:

"For God hath not given us the spirit of fear; but of power, and of love, and of a sound mind."

2 Timothy 1:7 (KJV)

Reflection:

Fear is not just an emotion it is a spirit, and it does not come from God. Fear magnifies the size of the battle and minimizes the strength of the Savior. But perfect love God's love casts out fear with one truth-filled breath. Fear whispers, What if? Faith declares, Even if God is with me. Fear paralyzes. Faith propels. Whenever fear rises, it reveals an area where love needs to be remembered. You overcome fear not by fighting it, but by replacing it with truth, with love, with confidence in the One Who holds your life. When you remember Who walks with you, courage becomes your native language.

Prayer:

Lord, silence every fear that opposes faith. Fill my heart with Your Power, saturate my spirit with Your Love, and strengthen my mind with Your Peace. Break every chain of fear and restore boldness where timidity once lived. Let courage rise within me as I walk in the Truth of Who You are. In Jesus' Name, Amen.

Faith casts out fear by remembering God's love.

Day 206
Joy as Strength

Scripture:

"The joy of the Lord is your strength."

Nehemiah 8:10 (KJV)

Reflection:

Joy is not weakness, it is weaponry. It is the inner strength the enemy cannot steal unless you surrender it. Joy is the spiritual stamina that carries you when your steps feel heavy and the days feel long. The enemy targets your joy because he knows it fuels your endurance. But joy rooted in Jesus endures through sorrow, triumphs in trial, and shines in darkness. Joy does not depend on circumstance; it flows from communion with Christ. Faith rejoices not because of what it sees, but because of Who it knows. Protect your joy, and you protect your strength.

Prayer:

Lord, let Your joy rise within me like a fountain of renewal. Restore laughter to weary places and gladness to tired hearts. Let joy break heaviness, lift burdens, and strengthen my spirit from the inside out. Fill me with the kind of joy that only Your Presence can give. In Jesus' Name, Amen.

Faith's smile is a sign of strength.

Day 207
When the Walls Fall

Scripture:

"So the people shouted when the priests blew with the trumpets… and the wall fell down flat."

Joshua 6:20 (KJV)

Reflection:

Every wall that stands between you and God's promise has an expiration date. Jericho didn't fall because of human strength, logic, or force. It fell because obedience unlocked Divine power. God's strategies often seem unusual, marching, waiting, shouting but obedience releases what human effort never could. Praise is not noise; it is a weapon. Every shout of faith, every step of obedience, every praise in advance chips away at walls the enemy swore would never move. Faith doesn't need to understand God's methods to trust God's plan. March when He says march. Shout when He says shout. Watch walls crumble under the weight of His Power.

Prayer:

Lord, help me obey even when I don't understand. Strengthen my faith to follow Your instructions with confidence. Fill my mouth with praise that carries power and my steps with obedience that brings breakthrough. I trust You for the victory that comes through surrender. In Jesus' Name, Amen.

Faith marches until walls fall.

Day 208
The Light That Overcomes

Scripture:

"And the light shineth in darkness; and the darkness comprehended it not."

John 1:5 (KJV)

Reflection:

Light does not negotiate with darkness, light overcomes it. Even the smallest flame makes darkness retreat, for darkness has no power to resist or understand the radiance of Christ. His light exposes lie, silences fear, and shatters the shadows that once intimidated you.

You are a carrier of that light. Not a flicker created by emotion, but a flame ignited by the Spirit of God Himself. The world's darkness cannot extinguish what Heaven has ignited within you.

Faith does not waste breath cursing the darkness it lifts the lamp higher. When you shine with the character, compassion, and courage of Christ, shadows lose their influence. You don't overcome darkness by fighting it, you overcome it by being light.

Prayer:

Lord, let Your light shine through me with purity and power. Chase away every Shadow in my life and illuminate the paths You've prepared for me. Make me a mirror of Your Glory, a flame that cannot be dimmed, and a witness of Your transforming light. In Jesus' Name, Amen.

Faith shines until darkness disappears.

Day 209
Crowned with Glory

Scripture:

"What is man, that Thou art mindful of him? ... For Thou hast crowned him with Glory and honour."

Psalm 8:4 -5 (KJV)

Reflection:

From dust... to dominion. This is the miracle of Grace. God crowned humanity with Glory before we ever took a breath and long before we ever proved worthy. His honor is not earned; it is bestowed. His remembrance is not random; it is intentional. You are crowned not by human achievement but by Divine affection. God placed honor on you because you belong to Him. That crown doesn't elevate arrogance; it cultivates humility.

Humility wears the crown best, because it understands its source. When you know who you are in Him, you walk with a quiet authority that darkness cannot steal and the world cannot mimic. Heaven's dignity rests upon you live like one anointed to carry His Glory into every place your feet touch.

Prayer:

Lord, thank You for crowning me with Glory and honor. Clothe me in humility so that I wear Your Grace well. Help me walk worthy of the calling You've placed upon my life, bringing honor to Your Name in all I do. In Jesus' Name, Amen.

Faith bows low beneath the crown of Glory.

Day 210
The Unshakable Kingdom

Scripture:

'Wherefore we receiving a kingdom which cannot be moved, let us have Grace."

Hebrews 12:28 (KJV)

Reflection:

In a world that trembles under pressure, the Kingdom within you stands unshakable. Everything temporal will be shaken, plans, systems, expectations but what God has established in your spirit cannot be moved. Shaking does not come to destroy you but to reveal what is everlasting. It strips away what is unstable and strengthens what is eternal. Grace becomes your grip when the world feels unstable, anchoring you to the throne of an unchanging King.

Faith does not fear shaking; it finds security in it. For when the dust settles, only what is of God will remain and that includes you.

Prayer:

Lord, thank You for placing within me a Kingdom that cannot be shaken. Let Your Grace steady my steps, anchor my faith, and quiet my fears. Keep me rooted in what is eternal, not swayed by what is temporary. In Jesus' Name, Amen.

Faith stands firm in an unshakable Kingdom.

Day 211
Victory in Obedience

Scripture:

"If ye be willing and obedient, ye shall eat the good of the land."

Isaiah 1:19 (KJV)

Reflection:

Obedience is the soil where blessing grows. It is not a rigid demand from a distant God; it is a Divine invitation into a life aligned with His best. Every step of obedience plants a seed in Heaven waters. Every act of surrender positions your life beneath the flow of abundance God has already prepared. God does not ask for obedience to restrict you, but to release you. Breakthrough, favor, clarity, and provision often wait on the other side of simple obedience, the kind that trusts even when it does not fully understand.

Faith moves before it sees. Obedience responds because it trusts. Your Yes, Lord is never wasted. It is a key that unlocks doors no human hand can shut. It is worship expressed through action. It is love expressed through surrender. And it is the pathway to victories designed just for you. When you obey, you position yourself under the canopy of God's Promises and there, the good of the land becomes your portion.

Prayer:

Lord, cultivate in me a heart that is quick to obey. Remove hesitation, quiet every doubt, and fill me with willing surrender. Let my obedience rise as worship and my trust deepen with every step. May every yes, I offer align me with the victories, blessings, and breakthroughs You have ordained. In Jesus' Name, Amen.

Faith wins where obedience walks.

Day 212
The Captain of Our Salvation

Scripture:

"For it became Him, for whom are all things, and by whom are all things, in bringing many sons unto Glory, to make the captain of their salvation perfect through sufferings."

Hebrews 2:10 (KJV)

Reflection:

Jesus is more than Savior. He is Captain. He leads you through every battlefield with absolute authority and perfect wisdom. There is no terrain He is unfamiliar with, no enemy He fears, no circumstance He cannot command.

A captain goes first. A captain charts the way. A captain ensures victory. Jesus never asks you to face anything He has not already conquered. He leads not from behind but from before, guiding your steps into triumph that has already been secured. Faith follows the Captain with confidence, knowing every path He chooses leads ultimately to Glory.

Prayer:

Lord Jesus, Captain of my salvation, leads me into the victories You've already won. Give me courage to follow Your steps and confidence to trust Your path. Let my life march in rhythm with Your Will. In Your Holy Name, Amen.

Faith follows where the Captain leads.

Day 213
Faithful in the Fight

Scripture:

"Well done, thou good and faithful servant... enter thou into the joy of thy lord."

Matthew 25:21 (KJV)

Reflection:

Heaven does not celebrate fame it celebrates faithfulness. God's greatest rewards are reserved for those who serve Him with steady hearts, not for those who seek earthly applause. Faithfulness is proven in hidden rooms, quiet prayers, small obediences, and daily devotion. It shows up when no one is watching, stays when others walk away, and remains steady when the battle grows long. The Father's Well done is not for the perfect, but for the persistent those who keep fighting the good fight with love, humility, and unwavering commitment.

Prayer:

Lord, make me faithful in every fight. Strengthen me when weary, sustain me when unnoticed, and anchor me when the path is difficult. Let my life bring You joy through steadfast devotion. In Jesus' Name, Amen.

Faith wins battles by being faithful, not famous.

Day 214
The Power of Perseverance

Scripture:

"But let patience have her perfect work, that ye may be perfect and entire, wanting nothing."

James 1:4 (KJV)

Reflection:

Perseverance is power under pressure but it is also worship. It declares, God, I trust You enough to stay in the process. Every moment of waiting becomes an altar where faith is refined and fear is stripped away. Perseverance is not passive; it is the active surrender of your timeline to His perfect one. What God begins, He doesn't rush. He perfects. And His perfecting work often unfolds in the hidden places, where you cannot yet see progress but Heaven sees transformation. Every delay is Divine development. The longer the wait, the deeper the work. And when patience completes its assignment, you emerge lacking nothing strengthened, steadied, and shaped for the victory already prepared.

Prayer:

Lord, strengthen me to endure with joy. Teach me to embrace Your process, even when it stretches me. Let patience finish what faith began, and make my heart steadfast in every season. Help me to trust Your Timing more than my own understanding, knowing You perfect everything that concerns me. In Jesus' Name, Amen.

Faith waits well and wins fully.

Day 215
The Triumph of Trust

Scripture:

"Blessed is the man that trusteth in the Lord, and whose hope the Lord is."

Jeremiah 17:7 (KJV)

Reflection:

Trust turns trials into triumphs because trust shifts the weight of the outcome from your shoulders to God's. It is not the absence of uncertainty, but the presence of confidence in a faithful and unfailing Father. True trust does not require full clarity, only full surrender.

When you choose to trust in the middle of what you don't understand, Heaven counts it as victory before the answer ever arrives. Trust silences the lies of fear and steadies you in the storms of life. Faith does not demand an explanation; it rests in expectation knowing that the God Who is your hope will never fail to be your help.

Prayer:

Lord, teach me to trust You deeply and depend on You daily. Anchor my hope in who You are, not in what I see. Let Your goodness steady my heart, and let my confidence remain rooted in Your Character, not my circumstances. May trust rise in me until it becomes triumph in every area of my life. In Jesus' Name, Amen.

Faith triumphs when trust takes root.

Day 216
The God Who Wins

Scripture:

"The Lord your God is He that goeth with you, to fight for you against your enemies, to save you."

Deuteronomy 20:4 (KJV)

Reflection:

God never enters a battle He hasn't already won. Before the conflict appears in your life, the victory is already written in His sovereignty. He does not observe your battles from a distance He steps into them with warrior power and Fatherly protection. When you surrender the fight to Him, victory becomes inevitable. Your strength may run out, but His never does. Faith's greatest weapon is not striving; it is surrender. When you let the Almighty Warrior take His rightful place, you stand still, and He secures the victory that brings Him Glory.

Prayer:

Lord, thank You that You fight for me. Help me to release every battle into Your Hands. Teach me to stand still, trust deeply, and watch as You bring salvation, deliverance, and victory. Let every conflict become a canvas where Your Power is made known and Your Name is exalted. In Jesus' Name, Amen.

Faith stands while God wins.

Day 217
Endurance Unto Glory

Scripture:

"For our light affliction, which is but for a moment, worketh for us a far more exceeding and eternal weight of Glory."

2 Corinthians 4:17 (KJV)

Reflection:

Every hardship carries hidden Glory. Heaven measures weight differently not by the heaviness of suffering but by the substance it produces. What feels difficult today is creating eternal strength, refining character, and preparing you for a depth of Glory you cannot yet imagine. Suffering is temporary, but the Glory it builds is eternal. The fire that pains you is the fire that purifies you. Faith keeps its eyes on eternity. It refuses to interpret life through the lens of momentary struggle, choosing instead to see the unseen work of God. Endurance today becomes the seed of Glory tomorrow.

Prayer:

Lord, help me endure every trial with eternal vision. Let my present struggles produce lasting strength and eternal Glory for Your Name. Strengthen my spirit to persevere, and remind me that every moment of pain has purpose in Your Hands. Help me to finish strong. In Jesus' Name, Amen.

Faith endures what Glory will explain.

Day 218
The Promise of Peace

Scripture:

"The Lord will give strength unto His people; the Lord will bless His people with peace."

Psalm 29:11 (KJV)

Reflection:

Peace is not the reward at the end of the battle; it is the strength that carries you through the middle of it. God's peace doesn't wait for circumstances to calm; it calms you while circumstances rage. The Prince of Peace reigns even in storms, speaking stillness into the soul long before He speaks stillness to the waves. Faith walks in serenity while the world shakes, not because the path is easy, but because God Himself is the anchor. His Peace is both shield and shelter, holding you steady in every season.

Prayer:

Lord, bless me with Your Peace that surpasses understanding. Let Your calm governs my thoughts and Your Presence rule my emotions. Strengthen me with supernatural serenity, and let Your Peace flow into every fearful or anxious place within me. In Jesus' Name, Amen.

Faith finds victory in peace, not panic.

Day 219
The Watchman's Reward

Scripture:

"I will stand upon my watch, and set me upon the tower, and will watch to see what He will say unto me."

Habakkuk 2:1 (KJV)

Reflection:

The watchman's role is not glamorous; it is grounded, humble, and hidden. Yet it is in the hidden places that Heaven releases revelation. Those who stay awake in prayer guard the gates others forget. When you remain faithful on your spiritual watch, God entrusts you with insight, direction, and Divine strategy. Breakthrough often comes to those who refuse to slumber in the Spirit. Faith stays alert while others rest, interceding until the first light of victory breaks through the horizon.

Prayer:

Lord, make me a faithful watchman in prayer. Sharpen my discernment, strengthen my vigilance, and let my intercession carry weight in the Spirit. Let my watch protect, my prayers prevail, and my patience bear fruit in Your perfect timing. In Jesus' Name, Amen.

Faith watches until victory arrives.

Day 220
Victory Through Vision

Scripture:

"Write the vision, and make it plain upon tables, that he may run that readeth it."

Habakkuk 2:2 (KJV)

Reflection:

Vision sustains victory. When God gives vision, He also gives sight the ability to see beyond your current situation into what He has promised. Vision turns confusion into clarity and hesitation into momentum. When you can see beyond what surrounds you, you walk by faith instead of frustration. You stop reacting to the present and begin responding to the promise. Faith runs with what it sees in the Spirit, even when the path ahead is still forming in the natural. Where vision leads, victory follows.

Prayer:

Lord, renew my vision for what You've called me to. Make it clear, ordered, and full of faith. Restore what has grown dim, revive what has been delayed, and align my steps with Your Divine direction. Help me to run with endurance, courage, and holy expectation. In Jesus' Name, Amen.

Faith runs where vision leads.

Day 221
The Strength to Stand

Scripture:

"Having done all, to stand."

Ephesians 6:13 (KJV)

Reflection:

When the fight feels long and the outcome remains unseen, standing is victory enough. Standing says, I will not surrender ground God has given me. Heaven honors those who refuse to retreat, because standing is the posture of unwavering trust. Sometimes the greatest act of faith is not marching forward but refusing to fall back. Every moment you stand in faith, you testify that the battle belongs to God and not to you. Standing doesn't mean you feel strong; it means you refuse to bow to fear. Faith's greatest posture is perseverance, a quiet, steady resolve rooted in the assurance that God finishes what He starts. You don't have to win today... just don't walk away. Stand until strength rises. Stand until peace settles. Stand until breakthrough dawns.

Prayer:

Lord, strengthen me to stand when I feel weak. Let Your Spirit uphold me when my strength fails. Let my stillness declare Your Power and my endurance reveal Your Glory. Help me trust that when I stand in faith, You move in victory. In Jesus' Name, Amen.

Faith stands when sight cannot.

Day 222
The Song of the Redeemed

Scripture:

"Sing unto the Lord a new song: sing unto the Lord, all the earth."

Psalm 96:1 (KJV)

Reflection:

Victory births a new song, one shaped not by ease but by encounter. Every redeemed life carries a melody that suffering helped compose and Grace alone could complete. Your song changes because you have changed. The redeemed sing differently because they've seen the faithfulness of God in the valleys and the goodness of God on the mountaintops. Their worship is not performance, it is testimony. Faith keeps singing when others stop, because redemption rewrites every refrain. When the Lord becomes your salvation, your sorrow gives way to praise, and your pain becomes a verse in a song only Heaven could teach you to sing.

Prayer:

Lord, put a new song in my mouth, one that declares Your Victory over my life and my gratitude for Your mercy. Let my worship speak louder than worry, and let my praise tell the world that You reign. In Jesus' Name, Amen.

Faith keeps its song through every season.

Day 223
The Triumph of Truth

Scripture:

"And ye shall know the truth, and the Truth shall make you free."

John 8:32 (KJV)

Reflection:

Truth is Heaven's key to freedom. Lies bind, confuse, distort, and imprison but revelation breaks chains. Every time the Word of God exposes deception, the fog lifts and the chains of confusion fall away. God does not reveal Truth to shame you; He reveals Truth to free you.

Truth does more than inform it transforms. It realigns your identity with God's design, renews your thinking, and restores the clarity the enemy tried to steal. It brings light into places where darkness once whispered, and it restores the steady ground beneath your feet.

Faith clings to Truth even when it is uncomfortable, because the cost of deception is always greater than the price of obedience. Truth may confront you, but it will never condemn you. It leads you into healing, wholeness, and holy confidence. When Truth enters, freedom follows. And every step you take in Truth is a step into the life God intended for you, a life marked by clarity, joy, and spiritual authority.

Prayer:

Lord, fill me with Truth that transforms. Expose every lie I've believed, every fear I've embraced, and every thought that rises against Your Word. Replace them with revelation that brings freedom, clarity, and peace. Let Your Truth steady my steps and shape my life until I walk boldly in the freedom You have purchased for me. In Jesus' Name, Amen.

Faith stands on Truth and walks in freedom.

Day 224
Endurance of the Elect

Scripture:

"But he that shall endure unto the end, the same shall be saved."

Matthew 24:13 (KJV)

Reflection:

Endurance is not glamorous, it is glorious. Those whom God has chosen do not endure by human resolve but by Divine Grace. The elect of God do not quit because their strength is supernatural. Endurance is the evidence of the Spirit's work within you. It is the quiet, steady faithfulness that refuses to bow, break, or back away even when the pressure is great. Grace gives perseverance a face, and faith gives it a voice that says, God is worthy, even here. Enduring faith reveals the reality of eternal life already alive in your spirit. You endure because Heaven lives in you.

Prayer:

Lord, grant me endurance to finish my race with joy. Strengthen my faith, steady my heart, and keep my hope unwavering until the end. Let my perseverance honor You and reveal Your Grace at work in me. In Jesus' Name, Amen.

Faith endures because Grace empowers.

Day 225
The Victor's Rest

Scripture:

"There remaineth therefore a rest to the people of God."

Hebrews 4:9 (KJV)

Reflection:

True victory does not end in exhaustion it ends in rest. Rest is not laziness; it is spiritual confidence. It is the stillness that comes when **faith** has completed its assignment and God receives the Glory. It is the posture of a heart that knows the battle is already won, even before the outcome is seen.

The rest God offers is holy. It is a deep, settled assurance that the burden is lifted, the striving is finished, and the outcome is secure in His Hands. This rest does not come from circumstances; it comes from surrender. It comes from trusting that God finishes what He starts, perfects what He begins, and sustains what He establishes.

Faith does not live in panic, it settles. It steps out of fear and into peace. It refuses to fight battles that belong to God and refuses to carry weights that Grace has already lifted. This is the Victor's Rest: the quiet place of confidence where you stop wrestling and start resting, knowing the victory is already sealed in Christ.

The Victor's Rest is not the end of the battle; it is the beginning of peace. It is the invitation to breathe, to believe, and to rest in the finished work of God.

Prayer:

Lord, thank You for the rest reserved for Your people. Teach me to enter it fully, leaving behind striving, fear, and self-reliance. Quiet every anxious thought within me and steady my heart in Your Promises. Let Your Peace reign over every part of my life and settle my spirit in Your finished work. In Jesus' Name, Amen.

Faith's finish line is rest.

Day 226
The Hands That Heal

Scripture:

"And He laid His Hands on every one of them, and healed them."

Luke 4:40 (KJV)

Reflection:

The hands of Jesus never turned away a soul in need. His touch reached the sick, the broken, the rejected, and the forgotten and His touch still reaches today. Every person who came to Him found compassion, and not a single one was denied His healing presence.

His healing is not limited to the body. His touch reaches deeper into the heart, the memory, the mind, and the silent places no one else has access to. Jesus heals what pain has fractured, restores what trauma has scarred, and revives what disappointment has buried. His Hands not only mend what is broken, they make new what was lost.

Faith draws near to His healing hands not out of desperation alone, but out of devotion a deep trust that one touch from Jesus can shift everything. The wounds we carry become holy places where His compassion is revealed and His Power is made perfect.

No pain is too deep. No scar is too old. No burden is too heavy. His Hands still heal completely, gently, and gloriously.

Prayer:

Lord, lay Your healing Hands upon me. Touch every place that hurts, every burden I carry, and every wound time has not healed. Restore what pain tried to steal and breathe life into every place that has grown weary. Make me whole by the power of Your Presence and the tenderness of Your Touch. In Jesus' Name, Amen.

Faith reaches for the hands that never fail.

Section Six:
Healing & Restoration

Day 227
Rest in His Renewal

Scripture:

"They that wait upon the Lord shall renew their strength."

Isaiah 40:31 (KJV)

Reflection:

Renewal is born in stillness, not striving. The strength God gives is not gained through pushing harder, performing more, or carrying everything alone; it comes through pausing longer in His Presence. Waiting on God is never wasted time; it is sacred preparation. In the quiet places, He rebuilds what life has drained, restores what stress has scattered, and breathes life back into weary places.

Those who wait on Him do not grow weaker, they grow deeper. The weary find wings. The fainthearted find fire. The burdened find breath. Strength rises not from self-effort but from surrender. Renewal comes when you choose to rest in His Presence instead of wrestling in your own power.

Faith renews itself through intimacy, not activity. Renewal flows through nearness, not noise. The moment you stop running and lean into Him, Grace begins to restore what striving could never fix. In the stillness, your soul remembers Who sustains you, and your spirit rises with a strength only Heaven can supply. The deeper the rest, the stronger the rise.

Prayer:

Lord, I wait on You in quiet trust. Renew my strength where I am weak and restore my soul where I am tired. Let Your Peace refills my heart and Your Presence revive what weariness has diminished. Lift me up on wings like eagles and carry me into renewed strength, renewed hope, and renewed purpose. In Jesus' Name, Amen.

Faith rests to rise again.

Day 228
The Oil of Joy

Scripture:

"Thou hast loved righteousness, and hated wickedness: therefore God… hath anointed thee with the oil of gladness above thy fellows."

Psalm 45:7 (KJV)

Reflection:

Joy is the fragrance of Divine healing. It is not the result of perfect circumstances, but the evidence of God's touch upon a surrendered heart. When God anoints you with His oil, mourning loses its grip. This joy isn't shallow laughter, it's deep assurance. It declares, God still reigns even when life feels fragile. Where sorrow once lingered, His oil softens the hardened places and heals what disappointment once wounded. Faith doesn't fake joy; it receives it. The oil of gladness flows where surrender replaces sorrow and where trust replaces trembling. Joy restored by God becomes a testimony that no season of suffering is final.

Prayer:

Lord, anoint me with the oil of joy. Let gladness rise from the ashes and hope bloom in every weary place within me. Replace heaviness with praise and sorrow with Divine strength. Let joy mark my life as evidence of Your healing. In Jesus' Name, Amen.

Faith smiles through tears and calls it worship.

Day 229
He Calls You Daughter

Scripture:

"And He said unto her, Daughter, be of good comfort: thy faith hath made thee whole; go in peace."

Luke 8:48 (KJV)

Reflection:

When Jesus called her Daughter, He restored more than her health He restored her identity. She came trembling, broken, and hidden, but He spoke belonging, acceptance, and dignity over her. Healing begins the moment you realize you are fully known and deeply loved. The world may label you by your past, your pain, or your mistakes but Jesus names you according to your future. You are not just healed, you are His. Every name the world tried to give you falls silent beneath the one He speaks over you: Daughter. Beloved. Whole. Faith doesn't just receive healing; it receives identity.

Prayer:

Lord, thank You for calling me Your daughter. Heal every wound of rejection, silence every lie of unworthiness, and let my soul rest in Your embrace. Make me whole in Your Love, and let my identity be rooted in who You say I am. In Jesus' Name, Amen.

Faith finds healing in belonging.

Day 230
Wounds That Worship

Scripture:

"My Grace is sufficient for thee: for My strength is made perfect in weakness."

2 Corinthians 12:9 (KJV)

Reflection:

Your scars can sing if you let them. The places where life wounded you, the deep breaks, the hidden fractures, the silent hurts can become altars of Grace when surrendered to God. What once brought pain becomes a platform for His Power. What once felt like loss becomes the very place His Glory rests.

Worship that rises from weakness carries a fragrance Heaven cannot resist. It is worship unfiltered, unpolished, and honest born from truth, surrender, and complete dependency on God. It is the song of a heart that has walked through fire and discovered that Grace was waiting there. Faith does not hide its wounds; it hands them to The Healer. And as His Hands touch those tender places, your wounds become instruments of praise. Your scars begin to testify. Your history becomes hope. And every place of brokenness becomes a canvas for His redemption.

God's power shines brightest where your strength runs out. Nothing you've endured is wasted. Every tear, every ache, every valley becomes sacred when laid at His Feet. In His Hands, wounds become worship and your weakness becomes a spotlight for His Strength.

Prayer:

 Lord, take my wounds and turn them into worship. Let every scar tell the story of Your strength, Your mercy, and my surrender. Use what once broke me to reveal Your Glory. Heal every hidden place, redeem every painful memory, and remind me always that Your Grace is more than enough. In Jesus' Name, Amen.

Faith's deepest praise often comes from broken places.

Day 231
Restored by His Word

Scripture:

"He sent His Word, and healed them, and delivered them from their destructions."

Psalm 107:20 (KJV)

Reflection:

The Word of God is more than language, it is life. Every verse carries Divine power to realign what pain has distorted and restore what sin, sorrow, or seasons have damaged. His Word heals by revealing truth, breaking lies, and rebuilding the places of fear once fractured. It reaches deeper than emotions, deeper than memories, deeper than the wounds no one else can see.

When His Word is spoken, it creates. When His Word is believed, it restores. Healing flows wherever Scripture is received with faith. You do not heal by trying harder, you heal by opening your heart to the Truth that sets you free. His Word becomes the lamp that guides you, the anchor that steadies you, and the sword that defends you.

Faith feeds on Scripture the way the body feeds on bread. In every promise, there is strength. In every command, there is wisdom. In every verse, there is the breath of God renewing, reviving, and rebuilding.

His Word does not merely speak, it sustains. It lifts the weary, restores the broken, and breathes life into places where hope once faded. When you cling to His Word, restoration begins from the inside out.

Prayer:

Lord, send Your Word and heal me. Let it wash away doubt, correct my thinking, renew my mind, and restore every weary place in my heart. Fill me with the power, purity, and peace of Your truth. I receive the healing, freedom, and strength that comes from Your Word alone. In Jesus' Name, Amen.

Faith listens and lives again.

Day 232
The Potter's Hands

Scripture:

"As the clay is in the potter's hand, so are ye in Mine hand."

Jeremiah 18:6 (KJV)

Reflection:

The Potter never discards the clay. He reshapes it. What looks ruined to us is raw material in His Hands. Brokenness is not the end of your story; it is the beginning of refinement. The pieces you fear are useless become the very places where His Glory is formed. When life feels shattered, the Potter's hands draw near not to discard you, but to lovingly remake you. The pressure you feel is not punishment; it is precision. The shaping you sense is not rejection; it is redemption. Every press of His fingers is purposeful. Every turn of the wheel is intentional.

Faith trusts the process of Divine craftsmanship. The hands that break are the same hands that bless. The hands that press are the same hands that protect. The hands that reshape are the same hands that hold you with unwavering love. Every turn of the wheel, every touch of His fingers, every uncomfortable moment of reshaping is guided by a perfect love forming you into something more beautiful, more usable, more surrendered, and more reflective of His Heart than ever before. You are never safer than you are in the Potter's hands.

Prayer:

Lord, mold me into what pleases You most. Where I am cracked, restore me. Where I am hardened, soften me. Shape my life according to Your Will and form in me a heart that fully reflects Your beauty and purpose. In Jesus' Name, Amen.

Faith rests in the Potter's process.

Day 233
When Hope Breathes Again

Scripture:

"This I recall to my mind, therefore have I hope. It is of the Lord's mercies that we are not consumed."

Lamentations 3:21 -22 (KJV)

Reflection:

Hope doesn't die, it simply becomes buried beneath the rubble of pain, disappointment, and delay. But the mercy of God breathes life where despair once whispered defeat. You don't regain hope by pretending the struggle isn't real; you regain hope by remembering the God Who has never failed you.

Every sunrise declares that Grace is still alive. Every breath you take is proof that mercy is still working. Every moment you stand is evidence that God has held you.Faith remembers what mercy refuses to forget: God is faithful still. When you recall His kindness, His provision, His rescues, His Promises, hope rises like a flame rekindled. Memories of His Goodness ignite fresh courage. What once seemed lost begins to stir again. The discouraged places begin to breathe. Because God's mercy never abandons what it saves, it restores, renews, and revives. Where mercy is present, hope is never gone. It only awaits your remembrance.

Prayer:

Lord, breathe new hope into me today. Awaken dreams I thought were gone and revive the places in me that have grown weary. Let Your mercy strengthens my heart and fill me again with courage to believe. In Jesus' Name, Amen.

Faith inhales mercy and exhales hope.

Day 234
Streams in the Desert

Scripture:

"I will even make a way in the wilderness, and rivers in the desert."

Isaiah 43:19 (KJV)

Reflection:

God specializes in impossible landscapes. The very places that feel barren, dry, and lifeless become the canvas for His miraculous provision. Where you see a desert, He sees the perfect setting for streams of Grace. Where you see emptiness, He sees the birthplace of renewal. He often brings water to the places you thought were beyond recovery, beyond redemption, or beyond hope.

Your desert is not a dead end; it is a stage for His Power. Healing sometimes arrives like a sudden flood, overwhelming and undeniable. Other times it comes as a gentle trickle, slow but steady, restoring you drop by drop. But in every season, His Timing is perfect, His Provision precise, and His Presence unchanging. Faith does not curse the desert; it looks for the river. It chooses to believe that even when everything appears dry, God is still carving out unseen channels beneath the surface. When you trust Him in the wilderness, your eyes shift from what is lacking to what is forming. Even in dry seasons, He is preparing refreshing, breakthrough, and new beginnings. There is no desert so desolate that God cannot send a river through it.

Prayer:

Lord, make a way in my wilderness. Let Your living water flow through every dry place within me. Refresh my soul, revive my hope, and restore what has felt barren. Let life bloom again by Your Power and Your Presence. In Jesus' Name, Amen.

Faith sees rivers where others see dust.

Day 235
The God Who Remembers

Scripture:

"And God remembered Rachel."

Genesis 30:22 (KJV)

Reflection:

When God remembers, restoration begins. His remembrance is not the recovery of a forgotten thought; it is Divine activation. It means God moves, God intervenes, God breathes life into what has waited long. His remembrance signals that the season you've prayed for is shifting. The promises that seemed dormant are never forgotten by the One Who spoke them. God does not misplace His Words. He does not overlook your prayers. Every tear you've cried has been counted, and every longing of your heart has been heard. What feels like silence is often sacred preparation. What seems delayed is being perfected behind the scenes.

When God remembers, the impossible becomes possible, the barren becomes fruitful, and the long-awaited breakthrough finally arrives. His remembrance turns waiting into birthing, sorrow into singing, and endurance into testimony. Faith waits with worship, trusting that Heaven's clock never runs late. What feels forgotten on earth is fully remembered in Heaven, and what you call delayed, God calls being prepared. His timing may stretch you, but it will never fail you.

Prayer:

Lord, thank You for remembering me. Breathe life into every promise that has waited and bring forth the fruit of what You planted long ago. Let Your remembrance become my renewal, my strength, and my testimony. In Jesus' Name, Amen.

Faith rests in Divine remembrance.

Day 236
The Sound of Healing

Scripture:

"For the joy of the Lord is your strength."

Nehemiah 8:10 (KJV)

Reflection:

Joy has a sound of laughter redeemed by Grace, hope reborn in a weary soul, praise rising where pain once settled. Before healing is seen, it is often heard. It echoes in quiet gratitude, in whispered worship, in sighs replaced with songs. Healing doesn't always begin with a miracle; sometimes it begins with a melody, a heart choosing joy even while the wound is still tender. The sound of healing is not silence, but praise reborn. It is the declaration that the Healer is near, long before the circumstances fully shift. Faith rejoices before the report changes, not because denial is present, but because God is. Joy becomes strength, and strength becomes healing.

Prayer:

Lord, restore my song. Let joy overflow until my spirit sings louder than my sorrow. Replace every sigh with sacred praise. Heal me through the sound of worship, and let Your joy become my strength. In Jesus' Name, Amen.

Faith sings where pain once sighed.

Day 237
Beauty Restored

Scripture:

"He hath made everything beautiful in His time."

Ecclesiastes 3:11 (KJV)

Reflection:

God doesn't rush restoration. His timing is never hurried, because the beauty He forms lasts beyond every season of loss, waiting, or weariness. Beauty in God's Hands is not surface-deep; it is soul-deep. It is shaped slowly, carefully, and intentionally through seasons of pruning, healing, stretching, and quiet growth. Waiting is not wasted; it is the sacred place where beauty begins to form beneath the surface. Faith doesn't demand immediate; it delights in eternal. It trusts the unseen work of the Master Artist who makes all things beautiful not by chance, but by design.

Prayer:

Lord, make all things beautiful in Your time. Help me trust the quiet work of Your Hands even when I cannot see the progress. Let patience polish the beauty You're creating in me, and let Your Timing perfect all things. In Jesus' Name, Amen.

Faith waits while beauty unfolds.

Day 238
Restoring the Ruins

Scripture:

"And they shall build the old wastes; they shall raise up the former desolations."

Isaiah 61:4 (KJV)

Reflection:

Restoration is not about returning to what once was, it is about rebuilding into something stronger, steadier, and more glorious than before. God does not simply patch broken places; He transforms ruins into testimonies of resilience and redemption. What once symbolized defeat becomes a monument of His Mercy. What others dismissed as hopeless becomes the place where His Grace proves its unmatched power. The ruins of your life, the shattered moments, the painful chapters, the seasons of loss are not wasted. In God's Hands, they become the foundation of something new and breathtaking. Faith does not hide the ruins it rebuilds upon them. It sees rubble and remembers that God forms beauty out of dust. Every broken stone becomes a reminder that your story is not over.

The rubble becomes revelation:

God brings beauty out of devastation, strength out of weakness, and purpose out of pain.

He restores not to what was, but to what can be when touched by His Hands. His restoration does not merely recover it elevates. It reveals His Goodness, His Faithfulness, and the power of a God Who rebuilds lives from the inside out.

Prayer:

Lord, rebuild what life has torn down. Strengthen my foundations in faith. Restore joy to every broken wall and raise up hope in every place that once felt desolate. In Your Power, make the ruins radiant again and shape my life into a testimony of Your Grace. In Jesus' Name, Amen.

Faith rebuilds on ground redeemed by Grace.

Day 239
Healing Beneath the Surface

Scripture:

"He healeth the broken in heart, and bindeth up their wounds."

Psalm 147:3 (KJV)

Reflection:

Some wounds are invisible, but none are ignored. God specializes in soul surgery healing what no one else can see, touching what lies beneath the surface of strength, smiles, or silence. His Love goes deeper than pain's reach and mends from the inside out. He knows every hidden bruise, every quiet ache, every buried memory, and every unspoken fear.

Faith invites the Healer beneath the surface into the fragile places where trust is hard, where tears have dried, and where pain has been tucked away. There, in the secret chambers of the heart, restoration becomes real.

Prayer:

Lord, heal the hidden places of my heart. Bind up every unseen wound, soothe every silent hurt, and make me whole from within. Restore what has been buried under years of pain and bring healing that only Your touch can give. In Jesus' Name, Amen.

Faith trusts the Healer with hidden pain.

Day 240
The Balm of Forgiveness

Scripture:

"Forgive, and ye shall be forgiven."

Luke 6:37 (KJV)

Reflection:

Forgiveness is the balm that soothes both the giver and the receiver. It is not a feeling it is a choice; a holy act of surrender that frees the heart and releases the weight you were never meant to carry. Unforgiveness keeps wounds open; Grace closes them gently and completely. Forgiveness is not denying that the pain mattered, it is declaring that God matters more. It acknowledges the hurt but refuses to let bitterness take root. It is choosing healing over hostility, restoration over resentment, and peace over poison. Faith forgives because it remembers mercy. It recalls how deeply God has forgiven us and allows that same mercy to flow outward. Forgiveness is not weakness; it is spiritual strength. It is the doorway to freedom, the pathway to healing, and the evidence of a heart aligned with God's own. When you forgive, you do not excuse the wrong, you release the burden. And in that release, your soul breathes again.

Prayer:

Lord, help me to forgive freely as You have forgiven me. Pour Your healing balm over old hurts and touch the places where bitterness once tried to grow. Heal my heart, soften my spirit, and teach me to walk in the freedom that forgiveness brings. In Jesus' Name, Amen.

Faith heals by forgiving.

Day 241
The Breath of Renewal

Scripture:

"And He breathed on them, and saith unto them, Receive ye the Holy Ghost."

John 20:22 (KJV)

Reflection:

When God breathes, new life begins. His breath is not merely air it is impartation, transformation, and holy awakening. One breath from God can revive what weariness has silenced, restore what sorrow has drained, and awaken what disappointment tried to suffocate. Renewal doesn't come by force; it comes by yielding, inhaling His Presence again and again until your spirit rises. Just as the first breath in Eden gave life to dust, the breath of the Spirit revives hearts that feel tired, empty, or undone.

Faith breathes deeply of Grace and exhales gratitude. It learns to live on the rhythm of His Presence receiving strength with every breath He gives and releasing worship with every breath you return.

Prayer:

Lord, breathe Your Spirit upon me anew. Revive what has grown weary and awaken fresh passion in my heart. Restore my joy, renew my strength, and let Your breath fill every place that feels depleted. Let new life rise within me as I receive Your Holy Spirit. In Jesus' Name, Amen.

Faith lives on Divine breath.

Day 242
The Gift in the Pain

Scripture:

"And we know that all things work together for the good to them that love God."

Romans 8:28 (KJV)

Reflection:

Pain becomes a gift when placed in God's Hands. It may not feel like a gift at first, it may feel sharp, unfair, or overwhelming but in the hands of the Master Redeemer, even suffering becomes sacred. What once felt cruel becomes a classroom of compassion. Pain teaches you to see with softer eyes, love with deeper empathy, and lean on God with greater dependence.

Suffering refines your sight until you can see Grace even in grief. You begin to recognize the fingerprints of God shaping you, strengthening you, and preparing you for purposes you never imagined. Faith doesn't deny pain; it discovers purpose within it. Every tear becomes a seed of tenderness. Every trial becomes a testimony waiting to bloom. And every scar becomes a reminder that God brings beauty out of ashes and purpose out of sorrow.

Prayer:

Lord, thank You for turning pain into purpose. Help me see the beauty You are forming through what I've endured. Turn every wound into wisdom, every tear into strength, and every scar into a story of Your faithfulness. Let nothing I have walked through be wasted in Your Hands. In Jesus' Name, Amen.

Faith finds treasures in the soil of sorrow.

Day 243
My Times Are in Your Hands

Scripture:

"My times are in Thy hand."

Psalm 31:15 (KJV)

Reflection:

There comes a sacred peace when the soul finally releases its hold on what it cannot control. To know that your times are in His Hands is to rest in the assurance that every chapter of your story both the waiting and the fulfillment is woven with Divine intention. So often we struggle against delay, fearing we have been forgotten, yet the Father's timing is never random. He ordains every pause as purpose, every still moment as preparation. In the silence, He is strengthening you for the season that will unfold in His perfect rhythm.

The same hands that carved the mountains and measured the seas hold your future with care. Nothing is wasted. Nothing is missed. Every promise will bloom in its appointed time. And when you surrender your anxious striving, peace takes its rightful place in your heart. Trust that what He begins, He completes and that your timeline, though hidden, is holy in His sight.

Prayer:

Father, I surrender the timeline of my life into Your keeping. Teach me to rest when I cannot see and to rejoice when You reveal the next step. Help me trust Your Timing above my own understanding. Let my waiting become worship, and my surrender become strength. I know that my times are safely in Your Hands. In Jesus' Name, Amen.

Peace is found where trust replaces striving.

Day 244
He Restores My Soul

Scripture:

"He restoreth my soul: He leadeth me in the paths of righteousness for His name's sake."

Psalm 23:3 (KJV)

Reflection:

When the journey has worn you thin and your strength seems spent, the Shepherd steps near--not to demand, but to restore. He does not rush your recovery or rebuke your weariness.

Instead, He gently leads you beside still waters, reminding you that healing is not found in striving, but in His Presence. Restoration is not a return to what was, but a renewal into what is being made new. The Lord restores your soul by reminding you who you are in Him beloved, chosen, and whole. Every weary sigh becomes a prayer He understands. Every quiet tear becomes a seed of renewal planted in His Grace. Even when the path feels uncertain, His Purpose remains unshaken. He leads you not for Your name's sake, but for His. And in that Truth is peace: you are never lost to the One Who restores, guides, and upholds you with everlasting love.

Prayer:

Lord, thank You for restoring my soul. When I am tired, remind me to rest in Your Arms. When I am uncertain, lead me by Your Peace. Heal the places within me that have grown weary from the journey, and breathe new life into the spaces I thought were beyond repair. I trust You to make me whole again   for Your Name's sake. In Jesus' Name, Amen.

True restoration begins where stillness meets His Presence.

Day 245
The Balm of Gilead

Scripture:

"Is there no balm in Gilead; is there no physician there?"

Jeremiah 8:22 (KJV)

Reflection:

There are wounds the world cannot see   hidden tears, silent aches, memories you carry quietly beneath a steady smile. Some pain is too deep for human understanding, too sacred to speak aloud. Yet there is One Who sees, One Who knows, One Who heals with a tenderness no earthly hand can offer.

Jesus is the Balm of Gilead the Divine Healer Who touches the broken places not to expose shame, but to pour in oil and wine. His healing is not hurried. It flows through compassion, mercy, and presence. He is not shocked by your pain nor weary of your prayers. He meets you in the very place you feel most fragile and whispers, Peace, be still.

Healing in Christ is not merely recovery, it is redemption. What once brought sorrow becomes a testimony of Grace. What once felt unbearable becomes a doorway into deeper intimacy with the One Who binds up the brokenhearted. Lay every wound at His feet. There is no sorrow so heavy that His Love cannot lift it, no scar so deep that His Hands cannot restore it.

Prayer:

Jesus, my Balm of Gilead, I bring to You every wound   spoken and unspoken. Apply Your healing to the places that ache within me. Let Your Love mend the broken pieces of my heart and restore what pain has tried to steal. Thank You for being gentle with my fragility and strong in my weakness. Heal me in a way only Heaven can. In Your holy Name, Amen.

Healing flows where His Presence touches our deepest pain.

Day 246
You Make All Things New

Scripture:

"And He that sat upon the throne said, Behold, I make all things new."

Revelation 21:5 (KJV)

Reflection:

There comes a moment when the ache that once defined you begins to fade, and in its place blooms something holy and new. God never restores things to their former state   He renews them to reflect His Glory. The broken places become testimonies, the deserts bloom again, and what was once lost is transformed by Grace into something far greater. The beauty of Divine renewal is that it does not erase the past; it redeems it. Every tear, every trial, every waiting season becomes a brushstroke in the masterpiece of His Mercy. His new is not merely repair   it is resurrection. The same power that raised Christ from the grave is at work within you, bringing life where there was once sorrow, and peace where there was once despair. Let hope rise again. The old has passed away, and in His Presence, all things are made new. Trust the process of transformation. What feels unfamiliar is simply the unfolding of His promise, a new beginning born from His Faithfulness.

Prayer:

Lord, thank You for making all things new in my life. Where I have seen endings, You bring fresh beginnings. Where there was pain, You plant peace. Let the beauty of Your renewal shine through me as a testimony of Your redeeming love. I choose to release the old and embrace the new You are creating within me. In Jesus' Name, Amen.

New life begins where surrender meets His resurrection power.

Day 247
Beauty for Ashes

Scripture:

"To appoint unto them that mourn in Zion, to give unto them beauty for ashes, the oil of joy for mourning, the garment of praise for the spirit of heaviness; that they might be called trees of righteousness, the planting of the Lord, that He might be glorified."

Isaiah 61:3 (KJV)

Reflection:

God never leaves His children in the ruins. What feels like an ending in your hands becomes the beginning of restoration in His. The ashes of what was your loss, your grief, your disappointments are the very soil from which He grows something beautiful. He doesn't sweep away the ashes as if they never existed; He transforms them into the foundation of new joy.

The oil of joy is not the absence of pain, but the Presence of His comfort. The garment of praise is not stitched in moments of ease, but woven through worship in the midst of sorrow. Every exchange He offers is born out of His tender mercy ashes for beauty, mourning for joy, heaviness for praise. You are the planting of the Lord. Your roots run deep in His Faithfulness, and your life bears the evidence of His transforming power. When others see your joy rise from the ashes, they will know that God alone is your Restorer.

Prayer:

Father, thank You for the Divine exchange You offer   beauty for ashes, joy for mourning, praise for heaviness. Teach me to lay down my sorrow and receive Your Peace. May my life bloom with evidence of Your faithfulness and bring Glory to Your Name. I trust You to make all things beautiful in Your time. In Jesus' Name, Amen.

Joy blossoms where surrender meets Divine exchange.

Day 248
The Oil of Joy

Scripture:

"Thou lovest righteousness, and hatest wickedness: therefore God, Thy God, hath anointed Thee with the oil of gladness above Thy fellows."

Psalm 45:7 (KJV)

Reflection:

The oil of joy is not found in moments untouched by sorrow; it is born from the pressing. Just as olive oil is drawn from the crushing of the fruit, joy often emerges from seasons that have pressed us deeply. Yet in the hands of the Master, that pressing becomes the purpose. It refines the heart, teaching us to depend wholly on Him. This joy is not a fleeting emotion; it is a holy anointing. It flows from intimacy with the One Who endured the cross and conquered death with rejoicing. The same oil that anointed Jesus to fulfill His Purpose is poured over those who choose to love righteousness, forgive freely, and walk in peace. The oil of joy marks you as One Who has endured and been renewed. It speaks of endurance refined by faith and worship born of trust. You carry the fragrance of Grace   proof that mourning has met mercy. And where His anointing flows, heaviness must lift, and beauty must bloom again.

Prayer:

Lord, thank You for anointing me with the oil of joy. Let Your Presence fill every weary place and overflow into the lives of others. May this anointing remind me that I am chosen, called, and covered by Your Love. Let my life shine with the gladness that comes only from You. In Jesus' Name, Amen.

Joy flows where hearts once broken now overflow with His anointing.

Day 249
The Garment of Praise

Scripture:

"Put on the garment of praise for the spirit of heaviness; that they might be called trees of righteousness, the planting of the Lord, that He might be glorified."

Isaiah 61:3 (KJV)

Reflection:

Praise is not merely a response to joy; it is often the doorway that leads us to it. When the weight of sorrow tries to settle upon the soul, God invites us to put on praise as a covering. It is not denial of pain, but a declaration of faith that His Goodness is greater than our grief.

The garment of praise is a choice, woven from gratitude and trust. It is what the weary soul wraps around itself when heaviness whispers that hope is gone. And as you lift your voice whether through a whisper or a shout heaven breathes life into your worship. The spirit of heaviness cannot remain where praise abides. Each word of worship becomes a thread of strength. Each song is a shield against despair. In time, praise becomes more than a response; it becomes your rhythm, your restoration, your renewal. You are the planting of the Lord rooted, steadfast, radiant in His Glory.

Prayer:

Father, I choose to put on the garment of praise. Even when my heart feels heavy, I will bless Your Name. Clothe me with gratitude and cover me with joy until praise becomes the rhythm of my soul. Let my life reflect Your strength and testify of Your faithfulness. In Jesus' Name, Amen.

Praise rises where heaviness once lived, and Glory takes its place.

Day 250
The Fragrance of Grace

Scripture:

"Now thanks be unto God, which always causeth us to triumph in Christ, and maketh manifest the savour of His knowledge by us in every place."

2 Corinthians 2:14 (KJV)

Reflection:

There is a fragrance that follows those who have been healed by Grace. It cannot be manufactured or imitated it flows from the overflow of a heart that has known both brokenness and restoration. Like the lingering scent of costly perfume, Grace leaves a trace wherever it has been poured. When you have walked through the fire and found peace on the other side, others can sense it. There is gentleness in your words, compassion in your eyes, and patience in your spirit. What once pain has become perfume, rising as worship before the Lord. You no longer carry the scent of ashes, but the aroma of redemption.

God causes you to triumph not through striving, but through surrender. And through that triumph, His Presence is made known His Goodness revealed through your life. Everywhere you go, you carry the fragrance of Grace, a living reminder that mercy rewrites every story it touches.

Prayer:

Lord, thank You for the fragrance of Your Grace upon my life. May it remind me that every victory belongs to You. Let my words, actions, and presence release the aroma of Your Love wherever I go. Use my story to draw others closer to Your Heart. In Jesus' Name, Amen.

Grace lingers where mercy has rewritten the story.

Day 251
The Touch of His Hand

Scripture:

"And Jesus put forth His Hand, and touched him, saying, I will; be thou clean. And immediately his leprosy was cleansed."

Matthew 8:3 (KJV)

Reflection:

One touch from the Master changes everything. When others withdrew, Jesus reached out. When the world saw impurity, He saw possibility. His touch was never hurried, never hesitant

it was holy, intentional, and filled with compassion. The man with leprosy came to Jesus not only in need of healing but longing to be seen, to be restored to belonging. And Jesus answered with both power and tenderness. His Words declared healing, but His touch restored dignity.

That same hand still reaches for you today. When life has left scars unseen, His Hand brings comfort and cleansing. When isolation has silenced your joy, His Hand draws you near. The touch of His Hand does not simply remove affliction it restores connection. You are no longer an outcast of circumstance, but a beloved child held close by Grace. Let His touch remind you that He is not afraid of what you've been through. He meets you in the brokenness, declaring over every wound: I will; be thou clean.

Prayer:

Jesus, thank You for Your healing touch upon my life. When I felt unworthy, You reached for me. When I felt unseen, You called me beloved. Touch the hidden places within my heart that still need Your restoration, and let Your Power and Presence make me whole. I am forever grateful for the touch of Your Hand. In Your holy Name, Amen.

Wholeness begins where His Hand meets the heart in love.

Day 252
The Sound of Healing

Scripture:

"And immediately his mouth was opened, and his tongue loosed, and he spake, and praised God."

Luke 1:64 (KJV)

Reflection:

When God heals, He doesn't just restore what was lost; He gives voice to what was silenced. Zechariah's silence was not punishment; it was preparation. In the stillness, faith was refined, and when the promise was fulfilled, praise was the first sound to rise. Healing has a sound. It's the laughter that returns after grief, the worship that flows after waiting, the quiet thank You whispered through tears. When God restores the heart, He restores the song within it. And that song, born from both sorrow and surrender, carries a depth that only Grace can compose.

Your voice matters to Heaven. It is the evidence that what once was broken now breathes again. So let your praise rise freely. Let it echo through the places where silence once reigned. Every word of gratitude becomes a testimony. He healed me, and I cannot stay silent.

Prayer:

Father, thank You for giving me back my song. Where silence once lived, let praise overflow. Teach me to use my voice to glorify You to declare Your goodness, Your mercy, and Your Power to heal. May the sound of my worship testify to Your unfailing love. In Jesus' Name, Amen.

Healing is complete when the heart finds its voice in praise.

Day 253
The River of Peace

Scripture:

"For thus saith the Lord, Behold, I will extend peace to her like a river, and the Glory of the Gentiles like a flowing stream."

Isaiah 66:12 (KJV)

Reflection:

Peace is not the absence of trouble; it is the Presence of God flowing steadily through every circumstance. Like a river, His Peace moves quietly, yet with power. It carves through the hardened places of the heart, smoothing what was jagged, refreshing what was dry, and carrying away what no longer belongs. The river of peace does not begin in external calm; it begins in inward trust. It flows from the assurance that the One Who healed you will also sustain you. When anxiety tries to return, remember the waters that once cleansed you still cover you. His Peace is continual, not conditional. Sit beside the banks of His Promises and listen to the steady rhythm of His Presence. The river is still flowing. It's current carries rest, renewal, and quiet strength. Allow it to wash over you until your spirit settles into the still confidence that everything is held in His Hands.

Prayer:

Lord, thank You for the river of peace that flows from Your Presence. When my heart feels restless, draw me to still waters. Let Your Peace guard my thoughts and quiet every storm within me. May it flow through me to others, bringing calm where there has been chaos and hope where there has been fear. In Jesus' Name, Amen.

Peace flows endlessly where trust abides in His Presence.

Day 254
The Silence of His Presence

Scripture:

"But the Lord is in His holy temple: let all the earth keep silence before Him."

Habakkuk 2:20 (KJV)

Reflection:

There is a depth of healing that can only be found in silence. It is in the quiet that the heart finally exhales, and the soul begins to hear the gentle rhythm of God's nearness. When words fail, when prayers become tears, His Presence speaks in stillness more powerfully than in sound. The silence of His Presence is not emptiness; it is fullness unspoken. It is where striving ceases and peace takes root. Here, burdens lift not because you've solved them, but because He holds them. The same God Who thundered on Sinai also whispers in secret places. And it is often in that hush where your weary spirit recognizes His steady love once more. Do not fear the quiet. It is holy ground. The noise of the world fades, but His Voice endures as a soft reminder that you are seen, known, and safe. In silence, He restores what words could never reach.

Prayer:

Lord, teach me to rest in the silence of Your Presence. When I cannot find the words, let my stillness be worship. Quiet every storm within me until Your Peace reigns completely. I welcome Your Whisper, Your Comfort, and Your Calm. Thank You for meeting me in the silence and renewing my soul. In Jesus' Name, Amen.

In the silence, His Presence speaks louder than words.

Day 255
The Secret Place

Scripture:

"He that dwelleth in the secret place of the most High shall abide under the Shadow of the Almighty."

Psalm 91:1 (KJV)

Reflection:

There is a place the world cannot enter, and the noise cannot reach a hidden dwelling known only to those who seek the Lord with their whole heart. The secret place is not found by distance but by devotion. It is the quiet within the soul where fear loses its grip, and faith finds its anchor.

In the secret place, you are not striving to be seen; you are simply resting in being known. Here, His Presence covers you like a shield. Wounds that once bled quietly begin to heal under His shadow. The storms may rage beyond your walls, but inside, peace reigns. You learn that safety is not found in control but in communion, knowing that the Almighty shelters you Himself.

To dwell is to remain. Not a visit, but a habitation. Healing deepens when you choose to stay, returning again and again until your heart learns the rhythm of rest in Him. From this hidden sanctuary, strength rises, faith matures, and love overflows.

Prayer:

Father, thank You for the refuge of the secret place. Teach me to dwell there daily, not just to visit in moments of need. Let Your Presence be my home and Your Shadow my shelter. In that quiet communion, heal my heart, renew my mind, and strengthen my faith. I rest safely under the wings of the Almighty. In Jesus' Name, Amen.

Healing endures where the soul learns to dwell in His shadow.

Day 256
Under His Wings

Scripture:

"He shall cover thee with His feathers, and under His wings shalt thou trust: His Truth shall be thy shield and buckler."

Psalm 91:4 (KJV)

Reflection:

There is no safer place than under His wings. Like a mother bird guarding her young from the storm, the Lord covers you with a love that shields, comforts, and restores. The winds may blow and the night may fall, but beneath His covering, you are secure. His wings speak of both tenderness and strength, the nearness of compassion and the might of protection. When you feel exposed or uncertain, remember: you are not forgotten in the open; you are hidden in the Shadow of His Presence. Every fear that whispers you are alone is silenced by the warmth of His embrace. Under His wings, healing takes root. The trembling heart grows still. The weary mind finds rest. His Truth becomes your guard, His Faithfulness your shelter. You are held not by circumstance, but by covenant. So remain close, beloved. Rest where love covers and peace abides. The same wings that shelter you will also lift you when it is time to soar again.

Prayer:

Father, thank You for the covering of Your wings. When fear rises, draw me near. Let Your Truth be my shield and Your faithfulness my refuge. Help me to stay beneath Your care and trust in the strength of Your Love. Under Your wings, I am safe, I am seen, and I am whole. In Jesus' Name, Amen.

Safety is found where trust rests beneath His wings.

Day 257
The Shadow of the Almighty

Scripture:

"He that dwelleth in the secret place of the most High shall abide under the Shadow of the Almighty."

Psalm 91:1 (KJV)

Reflection:

There is a sacred stillness that exists beneath the Shadow of the Almighty. It is the quiet confidence of those who have learned that protection is not merely a promise, it is a presence.

To dwell under His Shadow is to live continually aware that your life is hidden in His Strength, your days ordered by His Hand, and your heart surrounded by His Peace. The Shadow of the Almighty is not darkness; it is covering. It is the gentle proof of nearness, the soft reminder that where His Shadow falls, His Glory rests. Even when the sun of understanding fades, and you cannot see what lies ahead, His Shadow keeps you close. It is here that fear loses its voice. Here, striving ceases. Here faith breathes freely again. The Almighty casts no Shadow apart from His light, so if you are standing beneath it, you are nearer to Him than you realize. Abide there. Let your spirit learn the rhythm of trust that comes from resting in His Strength. For every moment spent in His Shadow becomes a testimony of peace to the watching world.

Prayer:

Lord, thank You for the safety of Your shadow. When uncertainty surrounds me, remind me that I dwell beneath Your covering. Let Your strength be my rest and Your Presence my assurance. Teach me to live every day aware that I am sheltered by the Almighty. In Jesus' Name, Amen.

Peace endures where the soul abides in His shadow.

Day 258
The Still Waters

Scripture:

"He maketh me to lie down in green pastures: He leadeth me beside the still waters."

Psalm 23:2 (KJV)

Reflection:

In a world that constantly rushes and demands, the Shepherd calls you to stillness. He does not drive you with force but leads you with love. His still waters are not stagnant; they are peaceful, pure, and life-giving. They reflect the calm of His character and the steadiness of His care. It is here, beside the still waters, that your soul remembers what peace feels like. The noise of the past begins to fade, the burdens of yesterday lose their grip, and your heart beats in rhythm with Him again. Healing deepens in the quiet places where He teaches you to rest rather than strive to drink deeply from His Presence rather than run dry from self-effort. Sometimes, He makes you lie down, not as discipline, but as mercy. For in the stillness, He restores perspective and reminds you that you are sustained by His Grace, not by your own strength. Let the waters of His Spirit wash over you today. Let His Peace settle every anxious thought until your soul mirrors the calm of His leading.

Prayer:

Lord, thank You for leading me beside the still waters. Teach me to rest in the quiet of Your presence and to drink deeply from Your Word. Let Your Peace refresh my heart and steady my spirit. When life grows loud, draw me back to this place of stillness where Your Voice is clear and Your Love is near. In Jesus' Name, Amen.

Rest is restored where the Shepherd leads beside still waters.

Day 259
The Table He Prepares

Scripture:

"Thou preparest a table before me in the presence of mine enemies: Thou anointest my head with oil; my cup runneth over."

Psalm 23:5 (KJV)

Reflection:

Even in the midst of opposition, the Lord spreads a feast of peace and provision. The table He prepares is not set in the absence of conflict but in the assurance of His authority. Surrounded by what once intimidated you, He invites you to sit and rest, to eat, to drink, to be renewed in His Presence.

This is the table of Grace. Here, your soul is nourished not by striving but by surrender. The same oil that anoints your head also heals your wounds. The cup that once felt empty now runs over with mercy and joy. Every seat at this table speaks of victory, not because of your power, but because of His Presence.

Healing becomes a celebration here. The One Who led you through the valley now feeds you in abundance. What the enemy meant for harm, He turns into honor. You no longer dine in survival, you feast in fellowship with the Shepherd who never left your side. Take your place at His table, beloved. Every promise on it was prepared for you.

Prayer:

Lord, thank You for the table You have prepared before me. Even in the midst of trials, You nourish my soul and anoint me with Your Peace. Teach me to sit and receive without fear, to eat of Your goodness, and to overflow with gratitude. May my life be a continual feast of praise to You. In Jesus' Name, Amen.

Abundance begins where the soul learns to rest at His table.

Day 260
My Cup Runneth Over

Scripture:

"My cup runneth over."

Psalm 23:5 (KJV)

Reflection:

When the Shepherd fills your cup, it is never halfway. His blessings overflow, not because of what you have done, but because of who He is: abundant, generous, and faithful. The overflow is not excess; it is evidence of His Presence. It is the joy that spills from a heart so filled with Grace that it cannot contain it.

There was a time when your cup felt empty when loss, waiting, or weariness left you dry. But through the journey, He has poured in mercy, one drop at a time, until sorrow gave way to song. Now, what was lacking has become overflowing. Healing does that it transforms emptiness into abundance, pain into purpose, and despair into praise.

Your overflowing cup is meant to refresh others. The love He's poured into you is not meant to be hoarded but shared. When kindness flows through you, when compassion becomes your response, when gratitude fills your words, that is the overflow of a healed heart. Lift your cup today, beloved, and let it spill with joy. For every drop that overflows bears witness to a Shepherd who never stopped pouring.

Prayer:

Lord, thank You for filling my cup until it overflows. Let the abundance of Your Love within me spill into every place I go. Teach me to pour out Grace as freely as You have poured it into me.

May my life be a reflection of Your generosity and my heart a vessel of Your joy. In Jesus' Name, Amen.

Overflow begins where gratitude meets Grace.

Day 261
Surely Goodness and Mercy

Scripture:

"Surely goodness and mercy shall follow me all the days of my life: and I will dwell in the house of the Lord for ever."

Psalm 23:6 (KJV)

Reflection:

When the Shepherd restores the soul, He doesn't send you forward alone. He appoints goodness and mercy to follow close behind. They are not visitors that come and go; they are lifelong companions, tracing every step with Divine purpose. Goodness provides, and mercy redeems. Together, they mark your path with the fingerprints of Grace.

Every day of your life is held within their reach. When you look back, you will find that even in seasons of pain, they were there, goodness sustaining you, mercy covering you. The valley was not your end; it was the passageway to greater revelation of His Faithfulness.

To dwell in the house of the Lord forever is not merely a promise for eternity; it is the present reality of abiding in His Presence here and now. Healing leads to habitation. Restoration leads to a relationship. You no longer wander; you belong. And in that belonging, peace reigns.

So walk confidently, beloved. You are never without His Goodness, never beyond His Mercy, and never outside His care.

Prayer:

Father, thank You for the promise that Your goodness and mercy will follow me all the days of my life. When I cannot see the way ahead, let me trust the Grace that walks behind me. Teach me to live each day aware of Your Presence, secure in Your Love, and confident in Your Faithfulness. I will dwell with You forever. In Jesus' Name, Amen.

Healing is complete when the soul walks daily in goodness and mercy.

Day 262
The House of the Lord

Scripture:

"I will dwell in the house of the Lord for ever."

Psalm 23:6 (KJV)

Reflection:

To dwell in the house of the Lord is more than a promise of eternity; it is an invitation to abiding fellowship even now. His house is not made only of stone and light; it is built upon His Presence, filled with His Glory, and open to all who seek Him in spirit and truth.

After every valley, every tear, every season of waiting, this is where the Shepherd leads you to His home, to His Heart. The place of healing becomes the place of habitation. No longer wandering, no longer weary, you find rest in the certainty that you belong.

To dwell with Him is to live in continual awareness of His Love to breathe His Peace, to walk in His light, and to rest under His covering. This is the fulfillment of every longing, the answer to every ache. The Lord Himself is your dwelling place, and in Him, you are forever whole. The house of the Lord is not a destination; it is a daily dwelling; a life lived within the embrace of unending presence.

Prayer:

Father, thank You for preparing a dwelling place for me in Your Presence. Teach me to live every day aware that I already abide in the house of the Lord. Let my heart be a sanctuary of praise, my mind a garden of peace, and my life a reflection of Your Glory. I am home with You now and forever. In Jesus' Name, Amen.

The journey ends where it began, dwelling in the Presence of the Shepherd.

Day 263
The Healer's Heart

Scripture:

"When He saw the multitudes, He was moved with compassion on them, because they fainted, and were scattered abroad, as sheep having no shepherd."

Matthew 9:36 (KJV)

Reflection:

The heart of Jesus is not distant from your pain; it beats with compassion for you. Every time He looked upon the broken, the weary, or the forgotten, His response was not judgment but mercy. His healing flowed from a love so deep it could not look away. The Healer's heart is tender toward weakness. He understands the hidden exhaustion that no one else sees, the tears that fall in silence, the longing to be made whole. Yet He does not rush your restoration. He sits with you in the ache, speaks peace into your confusion, and waits with patience as faith takes root again. To know His healing is to experience His Heart. He does not simply fix what is broken. He restores with affection. His touch is gentle because His Love is endless. Every scar you bear is seen, every sorrow known, every prayer treasured. And in His timing, every wound will meet His wholeness. Let His compassion be the medicine for your soul. The same hands that reached for the leper still reach for you, saying, I will; be thou clean.

Prayer:

Jesus, thank You for Your Heart that still heals with compassion. Teach me to see myself through the eyes of Your mercy. Let the tenderness of Your Love touch every place that still aches within me. Heal me not only in body, but in spirit and mind, until I reflect the gentleness of Your Heart to others. In Your holy Name, Amen.

Healing begins where the wounded heart encounters His compassion.

Day 264
The Hands That Heal

Scripture:

"And He laid His Hands on every one of them, and healed them."

Luke 4:40 (KJV)

Reflection:

The hands of Jesus were never idle. They touched the blind, lifted the fallen, blessed the children, and broke the bread that would feed the multitudes. Every movement of His Hands revealed the heart of the Father's compassion in action, love made visible. When He touches, He does not merely comfort; He transforms. His Hands do not flinch at weakness nor withdraw from brokenness. They reach through shame, sickness, and fear to restore what life has wounded. The same hands that formed the heavens now shape healing in your life. He lays His Hands upon you, still not physically, but through His Spirit, through the prayers of others, through moments of worship and quiet surrender. In every gentle stirring of His Presence, His Hands are near, applying mercy like balm to your soul. Let His touch define you, not your pain. For the hands that once bore nails now carry healing for every wound. In them is safety, strength, and renewal.

Prayer:

Jesus, thank You for the healing touch of Your Hands. Reach into every corner of my heart that still aches and bring Your wholeness there. Let Your touch remind me that I am never beyond Your reach. Use My Hands, too, as instruments of kindness and healing to others. In Your holy Name, Amen.

Wholeness flows where His Hands meet a willing heart.

Day 265
The Word That Heals

Scripture:

"He sent His Word, and healed them, and delivered them from their destructions."

Psalm 107:20 (KJV)

Reflection:

Before His Hand ever touched, His Word went forth. Every miracle began with a command spoken in love: Be healed, Rise up and walk, Peace, be still. The Word of the Lord carries creative power, breaking through despair and calling life from what once seemed lifeless.

When God speaks, healing happens. His Word does not return void; it accomplishes what it was sent to do. Sometimes that healing comes in a moment, other times it unfolds layer by layer as His Truth rewrites every lie you once believed about who you are. Let His Word dwell richly within you. Read it until it becomes your heartbeat, speak it until it shapes your perspective, and trust it until it transforms your pain into peace. Scripture is not merely ink on a page; it is living breath, carrying the same authority that spoke the world into being. There is no wound His Word cannot reach. There is no soul too far gone for its light to penetrate. The same voice that calmed the sea still whispers to your heart: Be whole.

Prayer:

Father, thank You for sending Your Word to heal and deliver me. Let Your Promises take root in my heart and bring renewal to every weary place within me. Teach me to speak Your Truth with faith and to believe that what You have spoken will surely come to pass. In Jesus' Name, Amen.

Healing flows wherever His Word is received in faith.

Day 266
The Breath of Life

Scripture:

"And the Lord God formed man of the dust of the ground, and breathed into his nostrils the breath of life; and man became a living soul."

Genesis 2:7 (KJV)

Reflection:

From the beginning, life began with His breath. The same breath that formed Adam in the garden still flows through every heart that yields to His Spirit. When you feel empty, faint, or worn, it is His breath that revives you, gentle, steady, and full of power.

The Breath of Life is not only what gives existence; it sustains it. Every sigh of surrender becomes an invitation for the Holy Spirit to move again. When you whisper prayers too soft for words, His breath carries them to the throne. When you cannot find the strength to speak, His Presence breathes peace where striving once lived. You are not sustained by circumstance, but by communion. Each inhale is a reminder of His nearness; each exhale, a release of every burden you were never meant to carry. The Spirit renews the weary, restores the broken, and revives what seemed lost. So breathe deeply, beloved. The same God Who breathed life into dust is breathing life into you even now.

Prayer:

Lord, breathe Your life into me again. Fill the empty places with Your Spirit and revive what has grown weary within me. Let every breath I take remind me that I live because You sustain me. May Your Presence flow through me, bringing renewal, strength, and peace. In Jesus' Name, Amen.

Life begins again where His Spirit breathes upon the soul.

Day 267
The Winds of Renewal

Scripture:

"And suddenly there came a sound from heaven as of a rushing mighty wind, and it filled all the house where they were sitting."

Acts 2:2 (KJV)

Reflection:

When the wind of God moves, nothing remains the same. The same Spirit that hovered over creation and filled the upper room still moves upon hearts today, reviving what was dormant, awakening what was silent, and renewing what was weary. The winds of renewal are not always gentle; sometimes they come suddenly, shifting what you thought was settled. But every Divine wind carries purpose. It clears away the debris of yesterday and breathes direction into the next chapter. What may feel like disruption is often preparation. God makes room for new growth, deeper dependence, and fresh anointing. Healing brings peace, but renewal brings purpose. The Spirit doesn't only comfort; He commissions. When His Wind fills the house of your heart, He doesn't just restore you, but begins to move again, speak again, believe again. Do not fear the wind, beloved. Let it fill the places that have grown still. Lift your sails of faith, and allow the Spirit to carry you where His Grace is leading.

Prayer:

Holy Spirit, thank You for the winds of renewal that move through my life. Sweep away the dust of yesterday and breathe fresh direction into my soul. Fill me anew with power, peace, and purpose. Let Your Presence move freely through me, reviving my heart to follow wherever You lead. In Jesus' Name, Amen.

Renewal begins when the Spirit's wind fills the heart once again.

Day 268
The Fire That Refines

Scripture:

"For our God is a consuming fire."

Hebrews 12:29 (KJV)

Reflection:

The same Spirit Who comforts also refines. His fire is not meant to destroy but to purify, to burn away what hinders love and to strengthen what is eternal. When God sends His refining fire, it comes wrapped in mercy, consuming only what cannot remain while revealing the pure gold of your faith beneath the ashes.

Fire in Scripture is both presence and process. It is the warmth of His Glory and the purging of His holiness. In the wilderness, it led Israel by night; in the upper room, it fell as tongues of flame. And today, it still burns not around you, but within you. His Spirit refines the heart until every trace of fear, pride, and doubt gives way to surrender.

Do not resist the refining, beloved. The flames that test you are the same ones that anoint you. The fire may feel fierce, but it is forming Christ within you, turning pain into power and endurance into praise. When the fire passes, you will not smell of smoke; you will shine with Glory. For those who trust the Refiner's hands, every flame becomes a forge of faith.

Prayer:

Lord, let Your holy fire refine my heart. Burn away all that is not of You, and purify my motives, thoughts, and desires. Teach me to see Your refining as love, not punishment, and let my life reflect the beauty that remains after the fire. Make me steadfast, pure, and yielded to Your purpose. In Jesus' Name, Amen.

Refinement is the fire that reveals the beauty of surrender.

Day 269
The Gold of His Glory

Scripture:

"That the trial of your faith, being much more precious than of gold that perisheth, though it be tried with fire, might be found unto praise and honour and Glory at the appearing of Jesus."

Christ. 1 Peter 1:7 (KJV)

Reflection:

The Refiner's fire does not consume, it reveals. What once felt like loss is often the unveiling of treasure long hidden within you. Every test, every trial, every tear that met His Presence has been purifying your faith, making it shine with Heaven's reflection. Gold is not made valuable by avoiding the fire but by enduring it. Likewise, your faith becomes radiant through surrender, patience, and trust. The flames that once frightened you have shaped you into One Who carries His Glory, not the kind that fades, but the kind that glows quietly from within. When others see you now, they may not know the battles you've faced or the fires you've walked through, but they will sense His Presence. That is the gold of His Glory-the evidence of Grace refined by trial and sealed by love. You are no longer defined by the fire, but by the faith it produced. Beloved, let the gold of His Glory shine through you. The world needs the light that comes from a soul refined by His Hands.

Prayer:

Father, thank You for the refining that brings forth the gold of Your Glory in my life. Help me to see every trial as an invitation to deeper faith. Let the radiance of Your Presence be seen in me -not as pride, but as proof of Your Mercy. May my life reflect the beauty of what You have refined. In Jesus' Name, Amen.

Glory shines brightest in the soul refined by His Love.

Day 270
The Beauty of Completion

Scripture:

"Being confident of this very thing, that He which hath begun a good work in you will perform it until the day of Jesus Christ."

Philippians 1:6 (KJV)

Reflection:

There is a sacred beauty in the moment when you realize He has finished what He began. The tears, the waiting, the refining, and the surrender were all threads in the tapestry of His design. What once felt like breaking was the careful shaping of His masterpiece. Completion in Christ is not the end of the journey; it is the fulfillment of purpose. Healing becomes wholeness, and what was once a wound becomes a well of testimony. The God Who began your restoration has not missed a detail. Every delay, every detour, every silent season was part of His perfect timing, weaving strength into your spirit and Grace into your story.

Wholeness does not mean perfection; it means peace. You are complete because His Presence fills every place that was once empty. You are whole because His Love has reached what was once broken. Lift your eyes, beloved. The work He has done in you is beautiful, and it is only the beginning of Glory yet to come.

Prayer:

Father, thank You for the beauty of completion. I rest in the confidence that You finish what You start. Let the work You've done in me reflect Your faithfulness to the world around me. Help me to walk in wholeness, peace, and gratitude, trusting that every season served its purpose in Your plan. In Jesus' Name, Amen.

Wholeness is the quiet beauty of His completed work within the soul.

Day 271
The Fellowship of Believers

Scripture:

"And they continued steadfastly in the apostles' doctrine and fellowship, and in breaking of bread, and in prayers."

Acts 2:42 (KJV)

Reflection:

When God restores a heart, He rarely leaves it standing alone. Healing draws us toward others to share, to serve, to strengthen, and to love. The early believers understood His Truth well: faith flourished in fellowship. In their gathering, there was unity, prayer, and shared Grace, each heart knit together by the Spirit of Christ.

True fellowship is more than conversation; it is communion. It is where burdens are shared, encouragement flows freely, and Christ is the center of every bond. In a world quick to isolate, the body of Christ reminds us that we are not meant to heal or grow alone. The Spirit who comforts also connects you to others who are walking the same road of faith.

In fellowship, we find balance and strength when we are weak, joy multiplied through gratitude, and the comfort of knowing we are seen and understood. Every meal shared, every prayer whispered together, every act of kindness extended in love all become sacred expressions of God's Presence among His people.

Prayer:

Father, thank You for the gift of fellowship and the family of faith. Help me to walk in love and unity with others, sharing Your goodness freely. Knit my heart with those who pursue Your truth, and let our fellowship reflect the beauty of Your Kingdom. Teach me to encourage, forgive, and build others up in love. In Jesus' Name, Amen.

Fellowship is the overflow of healed hearts joining in His Love.

Section Seven:
Community And Relationships

Day 272
One Body, Many Members

Scripture:

For as the body is one, and hath many members, and all the members of that one body, being many, are one body: so also is Christ.

1 Corinthians 12:12 (KJV)

Reflection:

In the wisdom of God, we were never designed to live or serve alone. Just as the human body is made of many parts, each with its own purpose, so is the body of Christ. Every believer is a vital member, and they are different in function but equal in value. The beauty of the Church is found not in sameness, but in unity, born of love. When one rejoices, all rejoice. When one suffers, all feel the pain. The strength of the body depends not on the prominence of a single part, but on the harmony of all working together. A hand cannot say to the foot, I have no need of you, nor can the eye dismiss the ear. We were created to connect each gift, each calling, woven together to reveal the fullness of Christ on earth. Comparison is the enemy of community, but gratitude is its safeguard. When you honor the unique Grace upon another's life, you strengthen the whole. When you offer your gift in humility, you glorify the Giver. Beloved, you are needed. Your Voice, your Heart, and Your Presence each carry something sacred that completes the body of Christ.

Prayer:

Lord, thank You for making me part of Your body. Teach me to value the gifts You've placed in others as much as my own. Help me to walk in unity, humility, and love, contributing what You have entrusted to me for the good of all. Let our diversity bring harmony, and let Christ be glorified through our unity. In Jesus' Name, Amen.

Unity is the song Heaven hears when every member plays their part in love.

Day 273
The Bond of Peace

Scripture:

"Endeavoring to keep the unity of the Spirit in the bond of peace."

Ephesians 4:3 (KJV)

Reflection:

Peace is the thread that holds unity together. It is not the absence of conflict but the Presence of Christ reigning within hearts that choose love over pride and **Grace** over grievance. The bond of peace is what makes fellowship last; it is the commitment to honor one another even when differences arise, to listen before speaking, and to forgive before resentment takes root.

Unity in the Spirit is not effortless; it must be kept. That word reminds us that peace requires stewardship, a willingness to guard what God has built between His people. We do this through humility, patience, and gentleness, remembering that we are all recipients of the same mercy.

The enemy cannot destroy a unified Church, so he seeks to divide it. But when believers walk in peace, their unity becomes an unbreakable bond, a reflection of Heaven's harmony. Each act of kindness, each word of Grace, each prayer lifted for another weaves another strand into the fabric of peace. Beloved, peace is powerful. It is the atmosphere where healing continues and where love grows strong enough to hold a community together through every season.

Prayer:

Lord, help me to be a keeper of peace in every relationship You have entrusted to me. Teach me to respond with gentleness, to speak with Grace, and to love with patience. Let Your Spirit rule my heart so that I may walk in unity with others, reflecting Your Love to the world. In Jesus' Name, Amen.

Peace is the bond that keeps hearts united in His Love.

Day 274
Bearing One Another's Burdens

Scripture:

"Bear ye one another's burdens, and so fulfil the law of Christ."

Galatians 6:2 (KJV)

Reflection:

Love becomes real when it bears weight. To bear one another's burdens is to step into the sacred space of empathy to feel what another feels, to pray when they cannot, to stand when they are too weary to walk. This is not pity; it is partnership. It is the reflection of Christ's own compassion, who bore the heaviest burden of all on the cross, so that we might walk free.

In a community, no one is meant to carry their load alone. God calls us to be His Hands and heart to lift, comfort, encourage, and intercede. Sometimes it means offering words of hope; other times, it means a silent presence that simply says, You are not alone. Each act of love, no matter how small, is a weight lifted, light shared, healing extended.

To bear burdens is to walk in the rhythm of Grace where mercy flows freely between hearts. And as we carry one another, we find that our own burdens grow lighter, for the same Spirit who strengthens us to help others also sustains us in our weakness. Beloved, when you lift another's load, you mirror the love of Christ, and in that moment, Heaven draws near.

Prayer:

Lord, thank You for bearing my burdens and teaching me to bear those of others. Give me eyes to see those who are struggling and a heart willing to help. Let my compassion be sincere and my love steadfast. Strengthen me to lift others in prayer, in kindness, and in faith. May Your Grace flow through me as I fulfill the law of Christ. In Jesus' Name, Amen.

Love grows stronger where hearts carry one another's burdens.

Day 275
The Ministry of Encouragement

Scripture:

"Wherefore comfort yourselves together, and edify one another, even as also ye do."

1 Thessalonians 5:11 (KJV)

Reflection:

Encouragement is not just a kind gesture; it is a ministry of Grace. Every word spoken in love carries power to heal, restore, and awaken courage in weary hearts. God often sends His comfort not through thunder or vision, but through people, through the voice of a friend who reminds you that hope still lives and God is still faithful. To encourage is to breathe life into another's spirit, to see beyond their struggle and speak to their strength. It is noticing the quiet battles others fight and offering the gentle assurance: You are not forgotten. God is not finished. Encouragement costs little but yields eternal fruit; it strengthens faith, renews joy, and weaves the bonds of fellowship tighter.

The world speaks words that wound, but the Church must speak words that heal. Every believer is called to this ministry. Sometimes encouragement is a bold declaration of truth; other times, it is soft--a whisper of empathy. Both are sacred. Beloved, your words carry weight in Heaven when they lift the hearts of others. Speak them freely, for encouragement plants seeds of hope that eternity will water and bloom.

Prayer:

Lord, thank You for those who have spoken encouragement into my life. Help me to do the same for others. Let my words bring strength where there is weakness, peace where there is worry, and faith where there is fear. Teach me to listen with compassion and to speak with **Grace**. May my voice echo the comfort of Your Love. In Jesus' Name, Amen.

Encouragement is the language of love spoken through a healed heart.

Day 276
Forgiving One Another

Scripture:

And be ye kind one to another, tenderhearted, forgiving one another, even as God for Christ's sake hath forgiven you.

Ephesians 4:32 (KJV)

Reflection:

Forgiveness is the fragrance of Grace released when the heart chooses mercy over memory. It is not the denial of pain but the decision to surrender it to place what was unjust into the hands of a just God. True forgiveness sets both the giver and the receiver free, restoring the flow of peace where bitterness once lived. In every relationship, offense will come, but love is proven through forgiveness. The enemy seeks division; forgiveness builds bridges. It is not a weakness to forgive; it is the reflection of Divine strength. When we forgive, we echo the heart of Jesus, who, while wounded, prayed for those who hurt him. To forgive does not always mean forgetting, but it does mean releasing the right to revenge, the need to be understood, the burden of resentment. It is choosing to let Grace have the final word. And in that moment of release, healing begins to bloom again. Forgiveness is not only obedience, but it is restoration. It allows the light of God's love to flow unhindered through our hearts, binding wounds and restoring unity. Beloved, you are never more like Jesus than when you forgive.

Prayer:

Lord, thank You for forgiving me completely and without condition. Teach me to extend that same Grace to others. Heal the places in my heart where pain has taken root and help me to release every offense into Your care. Let forgiveness flow through me until love becomes my only response. In Jesus' Name, Amen.

Forgiveness is the doorway where mercy enters and healing abides.

Day 277
Love Covers All

Scripture:

"And above all things have fervent charity among yourselves: for charity shall cover the multitude of sins."

1 Peter 4:8 (KJV)

Reflection:

Love does not ignore wrong; it redeems it. The love that flows from God's heart is not shallow emotion but a steadfast decision to protect, believe, and forgive. When Scripture says that love covers a multitude of sins, it does not mean hiding them in denial; it means healing them through Grace. When love covers, it builds shelter instead of walls. It creates a space where mercy can breathe, where Truth is spoken in gentleness, and where relationships can mend without fear of condemnation. This kind of love does not expose weakness to shame others; it protects hearts so that repentance and reconciliation can flourish.

The world is quick to judge, but the Kingdom calls us to cover. It is the same covering Christ provided for you when you were still broken, still learning, still growing. His Love did not overlook your sin; it overcame it. And when His Love fills your heart, it empowers you to extend that same Grace to others. Beloved, love is the highest ministry, the greatest healing, and the purest reflection of Jesus. When you choose to love, you invite Heaven into every relationship around you.

Prayer:

Father, thank You for Your Love that covered my sin and clothed me in Grace. Teach me to love others with that same steadfast compassion. Let my heart be a refuge for those who need mercy, and my words a balm of healing and truth. Above all, let love be the mark of my life and the bond of every relationship You've entrusted to me. In Jesus' Name, Amen.

Love heals deepest when it is covered in Grace and truth.

Day 278
The Gift of Friendship

Scripture:

"A friend loveth at all times, and a brother is born for adversity."

Proverbs 17:17 (KJV)

Reflection:

Friendship is one of God's most tender expressions of love toward us. It is His way of reminding the soul that we are not meant to walk alone. A true friend doesn't just stand beside you in the sunlight; they remain when the clouds gather, holding faith steady when your own feels faint.

Friendship is sacred because it mirrors the heart of Jesus, the Friend who calls us His own, who loves without condition, who stays when others walk away. Through friends, God speaks encouragement, brings laughter, and strengthens hearts that might otherwise grow weary.

The gift of friendship is not measured by proximity but by presence. It's the phone call that comes just in time, the prayer whispered in secret, the hand that lifts you when you've stumbled. In those moments, friendship becomes a ministry, a living reminder that God sees you and sends help wrapped in human kindness. Cherish the friends God has placed in your life. Be to them what Christ has been to you, faithful, forgiving, and full of Grace. Every friendship grounded in Him becomes a garden where joy, healing, and hope continually bloom.

Prayer:

Lord, thank You for the gift of friendship. Bless the friends who have encouraged, prayed, and walked beside me through every season. Help me to be that same kind of friend, faithful, patient, and full of Your Love. Let every friendship in my life honor You and reflect Your Heart of compassion and loyalty. In Jesus' Name, Amen.

Friendship is love made visible through faithfulness and Grace.

Day 279
Iron Sharpens Iron

Scripture:

"Iron sharpeneth iron; so a man sharpeneth the countenance of his friend."

Proverbs 27:17 (KJV)

Reflection:

True friendship does more than comfort; it shapes. God places certain people in our lives not only to walk beside us but to refine us, to challenge us toward righteousness, and to call forth the best within us. Like iron meeting iron, their words may sometimes strike sparks, but those sparks are holy; they bring clarity, strength, and growth. The sharpening of friendship is a sacred exchange. It is the courage to speak Truth in love and the humility to receive it. When done through Grace, this kind of honesty builds rather than breaks, corrects without condemning, and strengthens without shaming. Such relationships require trust, patience, and a shared desire to honor God above comfort.

In a world where flattery is common, sharpening friendships is rare, but they are priceless. They remind us that accountability is not criticism; it is care. A true friend will pray for you through your pain, celebrate your victories, and lovingly hold you to God's standard when you begin to drift. Beloved, do not resist the friends who sharpen you. They are Heaven's gift to your growth, forging your faith until you reflect Christ more clearly with every strike of love and truth.

Prayer:

Lord, thank You for the friends who sharpen my faith and speak Truth with Grace. Help me to receive corrections with humility and offer them with compassion. Let my friendships be rooted in love, strengthened by honesty, and guided by Your Spirit. May we refine one another until Your image shines through us both. In Jesus' Name, Amen.

Sharpening friendships is where love refines and Truth restores.

Day 280
Walking Together in Unity

Scripture:

"Behold, how good and how pleasant it is for brethren to dwell together in unity!"

Psalm 133:1 (KJV)

Reflection:

Unity is Heaven's harmony expressed on earth. It is not mere agreement, but alignment, a shared surrender to the will of God. When believers walk together in unity, their lives form a melody that delights the Father's heart. There is strength in that harmony, beauty in that peace, and blessing in that bond. Walking in unity requires humility. It means choosing relationship over rivalry, understanding over offense, and purpose over pride. The enemy thrives in division, but the Spirit dwells where unity abides. It is there that the anointing flows freely like oil poured over Aaron's head, running down to cover the whole body.

Unity does not erase individuality; it celebrates diversity surrendered to Divine order. Each person brings a unique tone to the song of the Kingdom. When hearts beat in rhythm with love, unity becomes a testimony, a visible reflection of the invisible God Who binds us together.

Beloved, walk in unity with those God has placed beside you. Let your steps be guided by peace, your words seasoned with Grace, and your love wide enough to embrace imperfection. Where unity dwells, the Lord commands a blessing.

Prayer:

Father, thank You for the beauty of unity among Your people. Help me to walk in peace with others, to listen more than I speak, and to love more than I judge. Let my life contribute to the harmony of Your Kingdom. Teach me to pursue unity without compromise and to reflect Your Love in all I do. In Jesus' Name, Amen.

Unity is the melody of love played in harmony by hearts surrendered to God.

Day 281
The Ties That Bind

Scripture:

"And above all these things put on charity, which is the bond of perfectness."

Colossians 3:14 (KJV)

Reflection:

There are threads Heaven weaves between hearts that no distance or trial can sever. These are the ties that bind relationships strengthened not by convenience, but by covenant; not by circumstance, but by Christ. Such bonds are formed in prayer, sealed in Grace, and held together by love that endures beyond emotion. The bond of perfectness is love that chooses commitment over comfort. It is loyalty born from compassion, patience that outlasts misunderstanding, and Grace that covers imperfection. These ties are evidence of Christ at work within His people, knitting lives together in His likeness. In a world quick to let go, God calls His children to hold fast to bear with one another, to believe the best, to forgive quickly, and to love deeply. These relationships become sacred cords of strength, reminding us that we belong not only to Him but also to each other. Cherish the bonds He has given you. Nurture them through prayer, protect them through forgiveness, and anchor them in love. For in these ties, Heaven's harmony is made visible on earth.

Prayer:

Lord, thank You for the precious bonds of love and faith You have woven into my life. Teach me to honor these relationships with humility, Grace, and steadfast affection. Help me to love others as You have loved me with patience, forgiveness, and truth. Let every tie be strengthened by Your Spirit and glorify Your Name. In Jesus' Name, Amen.

Love is the thread that binds hearts together in the fabric of His Grace.

Day 282
Kindness in Action

Scripture:

"And be ye kind one to another, tenderhearted, forgiving one another, even as God for Christ's sake hath forgiven you."

Ephesians 4:32 (KJV)

Reflection:

Kindness is love in motion. It is the quiet language that all hearts understand: the soft word, the patient ear, the helping hand extended without expectation. In a world often hardened by hurry and self-interest, kindness becomes a sacred act of resistance--a reflection of Heaven's gentleness on earth.

To be kind is not merely to be polite; it is to see with compassion. It means noticing the unseen, listening beyond words, and offering Grace where judgment might feel easier. Every kind act carries the fragrance of Christ, for He Himself was kindness incarnate, welcoming the weary, feeding the hungry, and forgiving the undeserving. Kindness transforms communities. It bridges divides, heals misunderstandings, and reminds us that every person we meet bears the image of God. A simple gesture, an encouraging word, a prayer, a smile may seem small, but in the Kingdom, it is a seed sown in eternal soil. Beloved, let your kindness be intentional and abundant. When you act in love, Heaven draws near, and hearts are softened by the touch of God through you.

Prayer:

Lord, fill me with Your compassion so that kindness becomes my natural response. Help me to see others as You see them and to love with sincerity and gentleness. Let my actions reflect Your Heart and bring comfort, joy, and hope wherever I go. In Jesus' Name, Amen.

Kindness is the echo of His Love heard through the actions of His people.

Day 283
The Power of Words

Scripture:

Death and life are in the power of the tongue: and they that love it shall eat the fruit thereof.

Proverbs 18:21 (KJV)

Reflection:

Words are seeds; once spoken, they take root in the soil of another's heart. They can either nurture or wound, build up or tear down. Every word you speak carries weight because it bears the reflection of the One Who spoke creation into being. In His image, your words, too, have creative power. The power of words is holy stewardship. When guided by love and truth, words bring light where darkness lingers. They heal what silence once held captive and water the dry places of the soul.

But when driven by anger or pride, they can cut deeply, leaving scars unseen. This is why Scripture calls us to let our speech be seasoned with Grace. The healed heart learns to speak healing. Those who have been restored by mercy find it easier to offer mercy through their mouths. To speak life is to partner with God's purpose to declare His Promises, to bless rather than curse, to remind others of who they are in His eyes. Beloved, may your words be living wells of Grace, flowing from a heart touched by Heaven. Speak with kindness, listen with care, and let your tongue be an instrument of peace.

Prayer:

Father, set a guard over my lips and fill my heart with Grace so that my words bring life and light. Let what I say reflect Your truth, and may every conversation be marked by love, patience, and wisdom. Use my voice to encourage and heal those around me. In Jesus' Name, Amen.

Words become miracles when spoken with love and truth.

Day 284
Listening with Grace

Scripture:

"Wherefore, my beloved brethren, let every man be swift to hear, slow to speak, slow to wrath."

James 1:19 (KJV)

Reflection:

Listening is one of the purest forms of love. It requires stillness, humility, and compassion, the willingness to set aside our need to respond so that another may be truly seen and heard. In a world that is quick to speak and slow to understand, a listening heart becomes a sanctuary of peace.

To listen with Grace is to hear beyond words to discern the ache behind the silence, the hope hidden in hesitation, and the Truth woven between the lines. Jesus modeled this perfectly. He listened to the heart of the woman at the well, to the cries of the blind, to the unspoken pain of the broken. His listening was healing. Grace-filled listening builds trust and restores connection. It turns conversations into communion and misunderstandings into moments of mercy. When we listen through the lens of love, we make room for the Holy Spirit to move, softening hearts and knitting relationships back together. Beloved, ask God to teach you the holy art of listening. In your stillness, His compassion will flow through you, and in your gentleness, others will encounter His Peace.

Prayer:

Lord, teach me to listen with Grace. Quiet my thoughts so I can hear with understanding and love without judgment. Help me to offer my presence as a gift, creating space where others feel safe and valued. Let my listening reflect Your Heart, full of patience, wisdom, and compassion. In Jesus' Name, Amen.

Listening is love in stillness where Grace makes space for the heart to speak.

Day 285
Servants of One Another

Scripture:

"For, brethren, ye have been called unto liberty; only use not liberty for an occasion to the flesh, but by love serve one another."

Galatians 5:13 (KJV)

Reflection:

True freedom in Christ is not the right to do as we please, but the Grace to love as He loves. Service is not the posture of the lesser; it is the position of the Christlike. When Jesus knelt to wash His disciples' feet, He revealed that greatness in the Kingdom is found not on thrones, but on knees.

To serve one another is to love with action. It is noticing a need and meeting it without fanfare. It is offering time, compassion, or prayer even when no one sees. Every act of service, however small, becomes a seed of Grace planted in humility and watered by love. The beauty of serving is that it mirrors the heart of God. He, who has all authority, chooses daily to serve His creation through mercy, provision, and patience. When we serve, we step into His rhythm, we become His Hands extended, His Love embodied. Beloved, never underestimate the quiet power of a humble heart. Service is not a loss; it is a gain. For in lifting others, you rise nearer to the likeness of Christ Himself.

Prayer:

Lord, thank You for calling me to serve in love. Teach me to serve others with joy, humility, and compassion. Let my actions reflect Your Heart, and My Hands carry Your kindness. Help me to see service not as an obligation, but as worship unto You. In Jesus' Name, Amen.

Love grows strongest in hearts that serve one another.

Day 286
Bearing with One Another in Love

Scripture:

"With all lowliness and meekness, with longsuffering, forbearing one another in love."

Ephesians 4:2 (KJV)

Reflection:

To bear with one another is to love beyond convenience, to choose patience where frustration could take root, and Grace where judgment could grow. It is one of the purest forms of Christlike love: the quiet strength that endures misunderstanding, overlooks offense, and remains faithful when relationships are tested. Forbearance is love stretched wide. It is humility in motion, a decision to see others through the eyes of mercy rather than through the lens of imperfection. In doing so, we imitate the heart of Jesus, who bears with us daily in our weakness, never withdrawing His Love but drawing us gently toward His Truth.

Every relationship will face moments of friction, but the love that endures is the love that matures. It refines our hearts, teaching us that community is not built on perfection, but on patience. As we bear with one another, we become living testimonies of Grace, proving that love is stronger than offense and peace greater than pride. Beloved, let your heart be soft where others are hard, gentle where others are sharp, and steadfast where others waver. The love that bears will always build what impatience tears down.

Prayer:

Lord, thank You for bearing with me in endless Grace. Teach me to extend that same patience to others. Help me to love through discomfort, to forgive without keeping record, and to walk humbly in all my relationships. Let my heart reflect Your gentleness, and may Your Love be my example in every interaction. In Jesus' Name, Amen.

Enduring love builds the bridge that keeps hearts connected through Grace.

Day 287
Harmony in the Spirit

Scripture:

"Now the God of patience and consolation grant you to be like-minded one toward another according to Christ Jesus: That ye may with one mind and one mouth glorify God, even the Father of our Lord Jesus."

Christ. Romans 15:5   6 (KJV)

Reflection:

Harmony in the Spirit is the melody of Heaven played through surrendered hearts. It cannot be manufactured by effort or agreement alone; it is birthed in the Presence of God, where pride yields to humility and love becomes the common language. When the Holy Spirit fills a community, self fades, and Christ shines. Unity then becomes more than cooperation; it becomes communion.

Every voice blends into one song of praise, every heart beats in rhythm with His Peace, and every difference finds its place in Divine balance. Harmony does not mean sameness; it means shared surrender. Just as each instrument in an orchestra contributes its unique sound, each believer brings a distinct Grace that, under the Spirit's direction, creates beauty greater than any could alone. In this harmony, healing flows freely. Division melts away, and joy takes root where strife once lived. The Spirit Himself conducts this symphony--drawing from each life a note of Grace, until the whole body glorifies Christ in perfect love.

Prayer:

Holy Spirit, make me an instrument of Your harmony. Quiet my pride, soften my words, and align my heart with Yours. Let Your Peace rule in my relationships and Your Presence guide every connection. May my life blend beautifully into the song of Your people, glorifying Christ with one heart and one voice. In Jesus' Name, Amen.

Harmony is Heaven's song heard where hearts live in surrender and love.

Day 288
The Strength of Unity

Scripture:

"Two are better than one, because they have a good reward for their labour. For if they fall, the one will lift up his fellow: but woe to him that is alone when he falleth; for he hath not another to help him up."

Ecclesiastes 4:9 -10 (KJV)

Reflection:

Unity is more than harmony; it is strength forged in shared faith. When hearts walk together under the banner of love, the Power of God multiplies among them. Alone, we may stand for a moment; together, we endure every storm. The strength of unity is not found in numbers but in agreement. When two or more gather in His Name, Heaven leans in. The prayers of one can move mountains, but the prayers of many can shift nations. Unity joins faith to faith, courage to courage, until the impossible becomes possible. In the Kingdom, strength is never about control; it is about connection. The body of Christ grows stronger when its members choose compassion over competition, forgiveness over pride, and understanding over offense. Unity disarms the enemy and amplifies the voice of praise, drawing others toward the love that binds us. Beloved, never underestimate the power of walking in one accord. You were not made to strive alone. There is blessing in togetherness, power in agreement, and victory in unity.

Prayer:

Lord, thank You for the strength that comes from walking in unity with others. Teach me to build bridges, not walls. Help me to value the gifts of others and to pursue peace where division once lived. Let our shared faith become a testimony of Your Power and love in this world. In Jesus' Name, Amen.

Unity turns ordinary faith into extraordinary strength.

Day 289
The Circle of Compassion

Scripture:

"Rejoice with them that do rejoice, and weep with them that weep."

Romans 12:15 (KJV)

Reflection:

Compassion is the heartbeat of community. It is love made visible in the willingness to enter another's joy or sorrow, not to fix, but to feel. To rejoice with those who rejoice is to celebrate selflessly; to weep with those who weep is to love sacrificially. Both are reflections of Christ, who rejoices over His people and weeps for their pain. The circle of compassion is where burdens become lighter, and blessings grow larger. In that sacred exchange, joy is multiplied and sorrow divided. Compassion does not require perfect words; it simply requires the presence of a heart willing to stand beside another and say, You are not alone.

When compassion flows freely, healing spreads quietly through the body of Christ. It bridges divides, restores broken trust, and makes community a refuge for the weary. Compassion is the language Heaven speaks fluently, and every act of kindness echoes that holy dialect.

Beloved, let your life complete the circle, receiving compassion when you need it, and offering it when others do. For in that continual exchange of mercy, Christ Himself is revealed.

Prayer:

Father, thank You for surrounding me with Your compassion and for teaching me to extend it to others. Give me eyes that see the needs around me and a heart that responds with gentleness and love. Let my presence bring comfort to the hurting and joy to the rejoicing. May Your mercy flow through me, completing the circle of Your Love. In Jesus' Name, Amen.

Compassion completes the circle of love where hearts meet in mercy.

Day 290
The Beauty of Fellowship

Scripture:

"For where two or three are gathered together in My Name, there am I in the midst of them."

Matthew 18:20 (KJV)

Reflection:

There is a beauty in fellowship that cannot be found in solitude, a Divine nearness that manifests when hearts gather in the Name of Jesus. In those moments, the Presence of God fills the space between souls, turning a simple connection into sacred communion.

Fellowship is more than shared time; it is shared presence, believers coming together to worship, pray, laugh, cry, and grow as one body. It is a living expression of Grace, where burdens are lifted, joy is renewed, and hope is rekindled. The Holy Spirit weaves unseen threads of strength between those who gather, making each heart more resilient and every bond more tender.

When believers unite, Heaven smiles. The Father delights in the sound of His children joined in praise, not because of perfection, but because of love. In such gatherings, isolation loses its hold, and loneliness gives way to belonging. Beloved, cherish the beauty of fellowship. Seek out moments to gather, to pray, to share your heart, and to listen deeply. For where love abides, and faith unites, Jesus Himself is there walking among His people, healing, strengthening, and dwelling in their midst.

Prayer:

Lord, thank You for the beauty of fellowship and the blessing of community. Let every gathering in Your Name be filled with Your Presence. Teach me to bring encouragement, faith, and joy wherever I gather with others. Knit our hearts together in love, and let our unity draw others to You. In Jesus' Name, Amen.

Fellowship is the garden where love blooms and Christ walks among His people.

Day 291
Shared Joy

Scripture:

"O magnify the Lord with me, and let us exalt His Name together."

Psalm 34:3 (KJV)

Reflection:

Joy is magnified when shared. The laughter that rings through a room of thankful hearts is worship in motion, a living hallelujah echoing Heaven's gladness. When one rejoices, and another joins in, God's goodness becomes even greater in the telling. Joy shared is joy multiplied, and praise shared is praise intensified.

The people of God were never meant to celebrate in silence. Every testimony, every answered prayer, every moment of breakthrough is an invitation for others to join in thanksgiving. This shared joy builds faith within the community; it reminds weary hearts that if God did it for one,

He can do it for all. Joy also heals. It loosens the grip of sorrow and revives the spirit that once felt heavy. As believers rejoice together, unity deepens, and hope rises. This is why the psalmist cries, Let us exalt His Name together. For when voices lift in harmony, the sound becomes a song that Heaven recognizes as worship. Beloved, never hold your praise in solitude. Let your joy ripple outward, encouraging others to see the goodness of God through your life. In shared joy, His Presence abides, and His Glory is revealed.

Prayer:

Father, thank You for the joy that overflows when Your people praise You together. Teach me to celebrate the victories of others with sincerity and gladness. Let my gratitude inspire faith, and may our shared praise bring delight to Your Heart. You are worthy of all joy and every song of thanksgiving. In Jesus' Name, Amen.

Joy multiplies where hearts rejoice together in His Goodness.

Day 292
The Strength of Togetherness

Scripture:

"Again I say unto you, That if two of you shall agree on earth as touching anything that they shall ask, it shall be done for them of My Father which is in heaven."

Matthew 18:19 (KJV)

Reflection:

Togetherness is not just comfort; it is power. When hearts agree in faith, Heaven listens. Agreement in the Spirit unlocks authority in prayer, drawing Divine strength into human weakness. The strength of togetherness lies in the unity of belief in the simple yet profound act of saying, We trust Him together. God designed community so that when one grows weary, another stands in faith beside them. When one voice falters, another carries the song. This is the mystery of His Mercy that no child of God ever walks alone, for His Spirit moves through the prayers and love of His people. Togetherness does not erase individuality; it amplifies it through harmony. It joins hearts in a shared rhythm of purpose and perseverance. The early church knew this well; they prayed together, served together, and endured together. Their unity became their testimony, and their strength their song. Beloved, lean into the strength found in togetherness. When you link your faith with another's, you build a bridge between your need and Heaven's answer. For where two agree in His Name, His Power moves, His Presence dwells, and His Promises unfold.

Prayer:

Father, thank You for the gift of togetherness and the power of agreement. Teach me to stand in unity with others to pray with faith, love with sincerity, and serve with joy. Strengthen the bonds of fellowship in my life, and let our shared faith move mountains for Your Glory. In Jesus' Name, Amen.

Togetherness is strength multiplied by faith and sealed in love.

Day 293
The Blessing of Shared Faith

Scripture:

"That I may be comforted together with you by the mutual faith both of you and me."

Romans 1:12 (KJV)

Reflection:

Faith was never meant to flourish in isolation. God designed it to grow in the garden of fellowship, watered by encouragement and strengthened through shared testimony. When two hearts believe together, something holy happens. Their faith intertwines, becoming a lifeline of hope that neither could hold alone. Shared faith brings comfort in suffering, courage in uncertainty, and joy in victory. It is the strength found in a whispered prayer between friends, the assurance that someone else believes when your own heart trembles. Even the apostle Paul, mighty in faith, longed to be encouraged by the faith of others, reminding us that no believer outgrows the need for community. The blessing of shared faith is found in its exchange: your hope lifts another's spirit, and their praise renews your strength. This Divine reciprocity sustains the Church through generations. It is the quiet miracle that happens every time believers pray together, speak life to one another, or join hearts in worship. Beloved, never underestimate the blessing of your faith, it was given not only for you, but for those around you. When your light joins with theirs, the darkness trembles, and the Glory of God shines brighter through you both.

Prayer:

Lord, thank You for the gift of shared faith. Surround me with people who strengthen my spirit and help me to strengthen theirs. Let my faith bring comfort, hope, and courage to others, and may our unity in You be a living testimony of Your Power and love. In Jesus' Name, Amen.

Faith grows stronger where hearts believe together.

Day 294
A Cord of Three Strands

Scripture:

"And if one prevail against him, two shall withstand him; and a threefold cord is not quickly broken."

Ecclesiastes 4:12 (KJV)

Reflection:

The beauty of God's design for relationship is found in His Truth: love and unity are strongest when intertwined with Him. A cord of three strands, two hearts joined by the presence of Christ, cannot be easily broken. His Spirit becomes the third strand, weaving strength, protection, and Grace through every bond. Without Him, even the closest relationships fray under pressure. But when Christ is central, what once was fragile becomes fortified by Divine strength. His Love becomes the anchor through conflict, His Peace the thread through misunderstanding, and His faithfulness the tie that holds when feelings fade. In friendship, marriage, family, or ministry, the threefold cord symbolizes covenant. It reminds us that love built on God endures storms and seasons. It is not dependent on perfection, but on His Presence, steady and sure. Beloved, let every relationship in your life be bound by that sacred third strand. Pray Christ into the center of your connections. Invite Him to be the strength that holds, the peace that restores, and the love that endures. For when He binds hearts together, no force can unravel what Heaven has woven.

Prayer:

Lord, be the center strand of every relationship You have placed in my life. Weave Your Love through my friendships, my family, and every bond of fellowship. Strengthen what is weak, mend what is frayed, and let Your Presence be the tie that holds us together. May our unity reflect Your Glory and endure through every season. In Jesus' Name, Amen.

Relationships endure when Christ becomes the strand that binds them in love.

Day 295
The Fruit of Fellowship

Scripture:

"I am the vine, ye are the branches: He that abideth in Me, and I in him, the same bringeth forth much fruit: for without Me ye can do nothing."

John 15:5 (KJV)

Reflection:

Fellowship grounded in Christ is not fleeting; it is fruitful. When believers remain connected to the Vine and to one another, their relationships bear evidence of His Presence: peace, joy, patience, kindness, and love that endures. These fruits are not self-grown; they are Spirit-given, cultivated through abiding and shared devotion. Every godly relationship becomes a branch in the garden of His Kingdom. As we abide in Him, His life flows through us, nourishing the bonds we share. Words become gentler, forgiveness comes easier, and joy flows freely. The fruit of fellowship is seen not only in laughter and prayer but in quiet faithfulness, the steadfast love that remains through seasons of growth and pruning alike. Healthy fellowship always multiplies. The fruit of love you offer today may feed someone else's soul tomorrow. A word of encouragement, a prayer spoken in faith, or an act of Grace may take root in another heart and bear fruit that you may never see, but Heaven does. Beloved, stay connected to the Vine and cherish the branches around you. For when hearts abide in Jesus together, the harvest is abundant, and the Glory belongs to Him alone.

Prayer:

Lord, thank You for the gift of fellowship that bears fruit through Your Spirit. Keep me rooted in Your Love and teach me to nurture the relationships You've entrusted to me. Let the fruit of my life bring nourishment to others and Glory to Your Name. May every bond I share in You reflect the sweetness of Your Presence. In Jesus' Name, Amen.

True fellowship bears fruit that nourishes hearts and glorifies God.

Day 296
The Blessing of Belonging

Scripture:

"Now therefore ye are no more strangers and foreigners, but fellow citizens with the saints, and of the household of God."

Ephesians 2:19 (KJV)

Reflection:

Belonging is one of the soul's deepest needs and one of God's greatest gifts. In Christ, we are no longer wandering hearts searching for home. We are found, known, and welcomed into the family of God, where Grace builds the walls, and love keeps the doors open wide.

To belong in His household is to rest in identity not earned, but given. It means you have a place at His table, a name written on His Heart, and a purpose within His Kingdom. The family of God is vast and diverse, yet united by the same Spirit, bound by the same Blood, and anchored in the same hope.

In this Divine fellowship, loneliness meets love, and rejection gives way to acceptance. Every believer becomes both guest and host welcomed by God, and called to welcome others in turn. For the heart that truly knows it belongs in Him will always make room for others to belong too. Beloved, let this Truth settle deep within you: you are not an outsider. You are part of His family, woven into His story and cherished in His home. You belong.

Prayer:

Father, thank You for welcoming me into Your family and calling me Your own. Heal every place in me that has felt unwanted or unseen. Help me to live from the security of belonging to You, and extend that same love and acceptance to others. May my life reflect the warmth of Your household. In Jesus' Name, Amen.

Belonging is the blessing of being known, loved, and welcomed by God.

Day 297
The Family of Faith

Scripture:

"As we have therefore opportunity, let us do good unto all men, especially unto them who are of the household of faith."

Galatians 6:10 (KJV)

Reflection:

In every generation, God knits together a family not limited by heritage or nation, but united by faith in His Son. This family of faith is a living testimony of Grace: many stories, one Savior; many hearts, One Spirit; many members, one body. It is through this sacred fellowship that the love of God is both received and revealed. To belong to the household of faith is to share life on holy ground. It means rejoicing with those who rejoice, standing with those who struggle, and praying for one another through every season.

Within this family, there is no rank or rivalry, only the shared identity of sons and daughters redeemed by mercy. The beauty of God's family is found in its diversity. Each believer carries a different reflection of His image, and together we form the portrait of His Love. Our differences were never meant to divide us, but to display the richness of His Grace. Beloved, cherish the family of faith around you. Encourage, forgive, and love freely within it. For the world will know we belong to Jesus not by the walls we build, but by the love we share.

Prayer:

Father, thank You for the family of faith You've placed around me. Help me to love deeply, serve joyfully, and forgive quickly within Your household. Unite us by Your Spirit and let our fellowship be a light to those still searching for home. May our unity bring Glory to Your Name. In Jesus' Name, Amen.

The family of faith is Heaven's reflection of love on earth.

Day 298
Brothers and Sisters in Christ

Scripture:

"Love one another with brotherly affection. Outdo one another in showing honor."

Romans 12:10 (ESV)

Reflection:

In Christ, family extends beyond Bloodline. Every believer you meet is a brother or sister born of the same Spirit, redeemed by the same sacrifice, and held by the same Father's hand. The Kingdom of God is not built on status, but on relationship, and its foundation is love. Brotherly and sisterly affection is more than friendliness; it is genuine care that chooses to honor, protect, and uplift. It means rejoicing in one another's victories and offering Grace in one another's weakness. It is loyalty rooted not in convenience but in covenant. The beauty of this spiritual family is that love is its language and humility its posture. When we honor one another, we reflect the heart of Christ, Who, though Lord of all, became servant of all. The Church becomes strongest when it remembers this Truth: we are siblings in Grace, not competitors in calling. Beloved, let your relationships within the family of God be marked by warmth, patience, and respect. When love leads, unity follows, and together, we mirror the Father's heart to a watching world.

Prayer:

Father, thank You for the brothers and sisters You've placed in my life. Teach me to love them as You have loved me with sincerity, gentleness, and Grace. Help me to honor others above myself and to seek peace in every relationship. May our love reflect Your family's beauty and draw others to Your Kingdom. In Jesus' Name, Amen.

Brotherly love is the thread that weaves Heaven's family together in Grace.

Day 299
Building One Another Up

Scripture:

"Wherefore comfort yourselves together, and edify one another, even as also ye do."

1 Thessalonians 5:11 (KJV)

Reflection:

To edify is to build to strengthen what is weak, to restore what is weary, and to help another stand taller in faith. God calls His children to be builders, not breakers; encouragers, not critics. Every word of Grace spoken, every act of love extended, lays another brick in the house of hope that is the body of Christ. Building one another up is not always grand or public. Often, it happens in quiet moments, a message of encouragement, a whispered prayer, a gentle reminder that someone is not alone. These small acts, though unseen by the world, resound loudly in Heaven. When we build others, we become co-laborers with Christ. His Spirit flows through our kindness, shaping hearts and strengthening faith. The more we lift others, the stronger we become as one. The Church grows not by competition but by compassion, each believer adding strength to the next until love becomes the foundation of all things. Beloved, look for opportunities to build today. Your words can heal, your prayers can steady, and your presence can remind another heart of God's Faithfulness. Be the builder that Heaven delights in.

Prayer:

Lord, thank You for the gift of encouragement. Use my words and actions to strengthen the hearts of those around me. Help me to see where I can lift another's **faith** and to build with gentleness, truth, and love. Let my life add to the beauty and unity of Your Church. In Jesus' Name, Amen.

When we build one another up, we raise the walls of love where God's Presence dwells.

Day 300
The Gift of Accountability

Scripture:

"Faithful are the wounds of a friend; but the kisses of an enemy are deceitful."

Proverbs 27:6 (KJV)

Reflection:

True friendship does not flatter, it refines. Accountability, when wrapped in love, is a sacred gift. It is the willingness to speak Truth even when it stings, and the humility to receive correction even when pride resists. It is love brave enough to care more about your growth than your comfort. The faithful wounds of a friend are not meant to harm but to heal. God places people in our lives who can see what we cannot, hear what we ignore, and speak what we need to face. Their honesty, when Spirit led, becomes a mirror reflecting both our need for Grace and our potential for greater holiness.

Accountability is not control; it is care. It says, I'm standing with you, not above you. It strengthens integrity, guards against deception, and calls us to maturity in Christ. In a culture that celebrates independence, accountability is the quiet courage of humility, it keeps our hearts aligned with Truth and our steps guided by love. Beloved, treasure those who challenge you with Grace and correct you with compassion. For they are instruments of God's mercy, helping you become more like Jesus day by day.

Prayer:

Lord, thank You for the friends who love me enough to speak the truth. Give me a teachable spirit and a heart that welcomes correction. Help me to offer the same accountability to others with gentleness and Grace. Let every word exchanged be seasoned with love and lead us closer to You. In Jesus' Name, Amen.

Accountability is love refined by Truth and anchored in Grace.

Day 301
The Joy of Serving Together

Scripture:

"Serve the Lord with gladness: come before His Presence with singing."

Psalm 100:2 (KJV)

Reflection:

There is a unique joy found in serving God not alone, but together. When believers labor side by side in love, their service becomes more than duty; it becomes worship. Each act, whether great or small, joins a holy symphony of Grace, echoing Heaven's harmony on earth.

Serving together builds unity, not through sameness, but through shared surrender. Every task offered in love, every prayer whispered, every hand extended becomes a thread in the fabric of God's work. In the weaving, hearts are knit together, and purpose takes root in fellowship.

The joy of serving is not in recognition, but in the quiet satisfaction of seeing Christ's heart mirrored in your own. He, the Servant King, invites His people to partner with Him in bringing comfort, hope, and redemption to the world. And when His children serve side by side,

His Presence fills the room with joy unspeakable. Beloved, serving with others refines the soul and refreshes the spirit. It turns labor into love and work into worship. Together, we shine brighter, love deeper, and accomplish more for His Glory than we ever could alone.

Prayer:

Lord, thank You for the joy of serving alongside others in Your Kingdom. Unite our hearts in purpose and let our service flow from love, not obligation. May our teamwork reflect Your Humility and bring Glory to Your Name. Fill our efforts with joy, and let Your Presence dwell among us as we serve. In Jesus' Name, Amen.

When hearts serve together, Heaven smiles and joy overflows.

Day 302
The Blessing of Shared Purpose

Scripture:

"Fulfil ye my joy, that ye be likeminded, having the same love, being of one accord, of one mind."

Philippians 2:2 (KJV)

Reflection:

Shared purpose is the heartbeat of Kingdom work. When God joins lives together for His Glory, it is never accidental; it is intentional alignment. Each heart brings a different rhythm, each hand a unique strength, yet under His direction, they move in perfect harmony toward one holy goal: to make Him known. The blessing of shared purpose is not found in ambition but in unity. It transforms ordinary work into a sacred partnership. When believers labor together with one mind and one love, the Presence of God multiplies their impact. Their unity becomes testimony proof that love can overcome division and that humility can accomplish what pride never could. Shared purpose also refines character. It teaches patience, humility, and dependence. It reminds us that success in the Kingdom is never measured by personal achievement, but by collective obedience. The truest joy comes when hearts are so united in love that individual agendas fade, and only His will remains.

Beloved, cherish those who share your calling and vision. Pray for one another, encourage one another, and keep Christ at the center of every effort. For when your purposes align with His and with one another, the blessing flows like oil, anointing everything you do.

Prayer:

Lord, thank You for the blessing of shared purpose. Unite my heart with others who love and serve You. Let our work together reflect Your humility, our words reflect Your Grace, and our vision reflect Your Kingdom. Keep us of one mind and one heart, bringing Glory to Your Name in all we do. In Jesus' Name, Amen.

Shared purpose turns labor into worship and unity into blessing.

Day 303
Strength in Prayerful Agreement

Scripture:

"For where two or three are gathered together in My Name, there am I in the midst of them."

Matthew 18:20 (KJV)

Reflection:

Prayer becomes even more powerful when it is shared. When believers join hands and hearts in agreement, their petitions rise like a symphony before the throne of God. Agreement in prayer is not merely about matching words; it is about aligning hearts with Heaven's will and with one another in faith. When two or more gather in Jesus' Name, His Presence fills the space between them. Doubt begins to fade, strength begins to grow, and peace settles in like holy stillness. There is a mystery in this kind of unity, one that multiplies faith and amplifies Heaven's response. The strength of prayerful agreement comes not from numbers, but from the oneness of spirit.

The early Church was born in such unity that believers prayed with one accord, and Heaven responded with fire, power, and purpose. That same Spirit still moves today wherever hearts unite in faith. Prayer binds us together, not only to God but to one another, weaving threads of Grace through every need and every praise. Beloved, never underestimate the power of praying with others. Agreement is not just participation, it is a partnership with Heaven. And when two or more believe together, the impossible bows to the authority of His Name.

Prayer:

Lord, thank You for the gift of agreement in prayer. Teach me to stand in faith with others, believing that where we gather in Your Name, You are present. Unite our hearts in purpose, align our prayers with Your Will, and let Your Glory be revealed through our agreement. In Jesus' Name, Amen.

When hearts unite in prayer, Heaven draws near with power and peace.

Day 304
United in Spirit and Truth

Scripture:

"But the hour cometh, and now is, when the true worshippers shall worship the Father in spirit and in truth: for the Father seeketh such to worship Him."

John 4:23 (KJV)

Reflection:

Worship unites what the world divides. When hearts gather to lift the Name of Jesus, differences fade, distractions fall away, and only love remains. In that holy moment, believers become one body, one voice, and one offering joined together in spirit and Truth before the Father.

To worship in spirit is to come with sincerity, from the depths of the heart. To worship in Truth is to come with reverence, grounded in the Word. When these two meet, Heaven leans close. True unity in worship is not about music, place, or form; it is about shared surrender. It is the sound of hearts beating in rhythm with Grace.

In such unity, God's Presence fills the atmosphere. Chains break, burdens lift, and healing flows quietly from His throne. When the people of God worship together in harmony, it becomes a glimpse of eternity, every tribe, tongue, and nation exalting one Name in unbroken love. Beloved, let your worship unite with others in spirit and truth. For where His children gather in sincerity, His Glory rests, and every heart becomes a dwelling place of peace.

Prayer:

Father, thank You for calling me into worship that unites hearts and glorifies You. Let my spirit join with others in pure devotion, and may our unity in Truth reveal Your beauty to the world. Fill our gatherings with Your Presence and teach us to worship with one heart, one voice, and one purpose to honor You. In Jesus' Name, Amen.

Unity in worship is Heaven touching earth through hearts joined in Truth and love.

Day 305
Carriers of His Presence

Scripture:

"Know ye not that ye are the temple of God, and that the Spirit of God dwelleth in you?"

1 Corinthians 3:16 (KJV)

Reflection:

Every child of God carries something sacred, the very Presence of the Holy Spirit. His Glory no longer resides in stone temples, but within hearts surrendered and lives consecrated to Him. When believers walk together in unity, the presence they each carry becomes a radiant flame, igniting faith and spreading light wherever they go. To be a carrier of His Presence is to walk in awareness of His nearness. It means realizing that you bring the atmosphere of Heaven into every conversation, every workplace, every home. The same Spirit that raised Christ from the dead dwells within you, not to be contained, but to be released through love, peace, and kindness. When the people of God unite, their collective presence becomes a sanctuary. The Spirit moves freely among them, comforting, convicting, and healing. Through unity, the Church becomes not just a gathering place but a living temple, each heart a flame, together forming a fire that cannot be quenched. Beloved, never forget that you carry His Presence. Walk with reverence and confidence, knowing that every step you take can shift the atmosphere around you, not by your strength, but by His Spirit within you.

Prayer:

Lord, thank You for the precious gift of Your Presence within me. Help me to walk with awareness, humility, and joy as a vessel of Your Spirit. Let Your Presence flow through me to bless and heal others, and may our unity as Your people reveal Your Glory to the world. In Jesus' Name, Amen.

When God's people walk in unity, His Presence flows like living fire through every heart.

Day 306
Hearts Knit Together

Scripture:

"That their hearts might be comforted, being knit together in love, and unto all riches of the full assurance of understanding, to the acknowledgement of the mystery of God, and of the Father, and of Christ."

Colossians 2:2 (KJV)

Reflection:

When God joins hearts, He does so with threads of love that no distance or trial can easily unravel. The phrase knit together paints a picture of strength woven through tenderness, a bond crafted not by human effort, but by the Spirit's hand. Hearts knit together in love bring comfort, not confusion; unity, not striving. In such connection, joy multiplies, burdens divide, and faith deepens. The body of Christ becomes stronger when its members are bound by love rather than preference, by purpose rather than personality. This Divine weaving is how community becomes covenant secure, steadfast, and sustained by Grace. The mystery of God's love is that it draws us closer to Himself by drawing us closer to one another. What He knits together carries eternal purpose. Each friendship, each prayer partnership, each shared tear or triumph   He uses it all to reveal the richness of His wisdom and the beauty of His design. Beloved, allow the Spirit to knit your heart to others in the household of faith. Such bonds are more than friendship; they are Divine threads forming a tapestry of love that reflects the heart of Christ.

Prayer:

Father, thank You for knitting my heart together with others in Your Love. Strengthen every bond You have formed and let our unity reflect Your Grace and truth. Help me to cherish, protect, and nurture the relationships You have woven into my life. May every connection glorify You bring comfort to those around me. In Jesus' Name, Amen.

Hearts knit together in love form the tapestry of God's Grace upon the earth.

Day 307
The Unity of the Spirit

Scripture:

"Endeavoring to keep the unity of the Spirit in the bond of peace."

Ephesians 4:3 (KJV)

Reflection:

The unity of the Spirit is not something we create; it is something we protect. It already exists wherever Christ reigns in hearts surrendered to Him. The Holy Spirit binds believers together in peace, knitting differences into strength and turning diversity into harmony for the Glory of God.

This unity is fragile when guarded by pride but unbreakable when sustained by love. It thrives in humility, patience, and gentleness, which are the fruit of a heart that values peace over preference. The unity of the Spirit does not demand sameness; it celebrates surrender. It is the holy ground where Grace flows freely, and Truth stands firm. When we walk in the unity of the Spirit, we become a living testimony to the world that Jesus is Lord. Our love becomes our witness, and our peace becomes our power. The enemy's schemes falter where unity abides, for nothing defeats darkness more effectively than hearts joined together in the light. Beloved, strive to keep this sacred unity. Choose peace when others choose pride. Forgive quickly, pray faithfully, and let the Holy Spirit rule every word and action. For where He reigns, harmony reigns also, and Christ is glorified.

Prayer:

Holy Spirit, thank You for the unity You bring to the body of Christ. Teach me to walk in humility and peace, guarding the bond of love You have established among believers. Let my heart be a vessel of reconciliation and Grace, reflecting Your gentleness to all. Keep me aligned with Your Spirit so that unity may flourish wherever I go. In Jesus' Name, Amen.

The unity of the Spirit is Heaven's peace woven through hearts that walk in love.

Day 308
Bound Together in Peace

Scripture:

"And let the peace of God rule in your hearts, to the which also ye are called in one body; and be ye thankful."

Colossians 3:15 (KJV)

Reflection:

Peace is not just a feeling; it is a force. It is the Divine bond that holds the body of Christ together when differences arise, misunderstandings occur, and seasons shift. The peace of God is both shield and glue, guarding hearts and binding them in harmony under His rule. When peace rules within, division cannot reign without. The Spirit of peace teaches us to listen before we speak, to understand before we assume, and to forgive before bitterness can take root. In a world of conflict, those who are bound together in peace stand as living testimonies that Christ's love is stronger than any disagreement. Peace does not mean the absence of struggle, but the Presence of the Prince of Peace Himself. When His Peace rules, pride yields, and gratitude grows. Unity becomes effortless where hearts are ruled by calm surrender instead of control. Beloved, let peace be the cord that binds you to others in love. Guard it with prayer, preserve it with humility, and allow it to flow like still waters through every relationship. For where peace abides, Christ dwells richly.

Prayer:

Lord, thank You for the peace that surpasses understanding. Let it rule in my heart and flow into every connection You've given me. Help me to walk in patience, forgiveness, and love, maintaining unity through the bond of Your Peace. Make me a vessel of calm in every storm and a reflection of Your gentleness to others. In Jesus' Name, Amen.

Peace is the sacred bond that holds hearts steady in the love of Christ.

Day 309
Fellowship in the Light

Scripture:

"But if we walk in the light, as He is in the light, we have fellowship one with another, and the Blood of Jesus Christ His Son cleanseth us from all sin."

1 John 1:7 (KJV)

Reflection:

True fellowship thrives in the light. It cannot flourish where shadows linger, where fear, pride, or hidden pain dwells. Walking in the light means walking in truth: open, honest, and sincere before God and one another. It is here, in this sacred transparency, that real love grows and genuine unity is born. The light of Christ exposes not to shame but to heal. It reveals what's broken so it can be restored, what's hidden so it can be made whole. In that honesty, fellowship becomes deep and holy where masks fall, Grace flows freely, and hearts are truly known.   When believers walk in the light together, they create a refuge of purity and trust. The blood of Jesus continually cleanses, covering imperfections with mercy and washing away every trace of darkness. In such fellowship, joy blossoms, forgiveness reigns, and love becomes unbreakable. Beloved, choose to live in the light. Let your words be true, your heart be humble, and your love be unfeigned. For in the light of His Presence, fellowship becomes not just a connection, it becomes a communion.

Prayer:

Lord, thank You for calling me to walk in Your light. Cleanse my heart from anything that hinders true fellowship. Teach me to love with honesty and to walk with integrity before You and others. Let my life reflect Your brightness, drawing others into the warmth of Your Grace. In Jesus' Name, Amen.

Fellowship flourishes where hearts walk together in the light of His Love.

Day 310
The Grace of Reconciliation

Scripture:

"And all things are of God, who hath reconciled us to Himself by Jesus Christ, and hath given to us the ministry of reconciliation."

2 Corinthians 5:18 (KJV)

Reflection:

Reconciliation is one of the most beautiful pieces of evidence of Grace. It is the miracle of God taking what sin and sorrow have divided and weaving it back together through love. What begins as His gift to us, our own reconciliation through Christ, becomes a calling placed within us: to be instruments of peace in a fractured world.

To reconcile is to restore a relationship, not by ignoring the wound, but by allowing the cross to heal it. Jesus bridged the greatest divide between God and man so that we might learn to build bridges, too. His Spirit teaches us to forgive, to listen, and to reach out when pride says stay back. Reconciliation does not erase the past, but it redeems it, turning pain into purpose and bitterness into blessing. When we choose reconciliation, we reflect the very heart of God. The courage to forgive, the humility to apologize, and the willingness to begin again are sacred acts of worship. In such moments, Heaven smiles, for peace has triumphed over division. Beloved, let the Grace that reconciled you to the Father flow through you to others. The same love that restores your soul has the power to mend any broken bond surrendered to His Hands.

Prayer:

Father, thank You for reconciling me to Yourself through Jesus Christ. Teach me to walk in that same Grace toward others. Heal every wounded relationship, soften hardened hearts, and let Your Peace reign where strife once lived. Make me a vessel of reconciliation, reflecting Your mercy to the world around me. In Jesus' Name, Amen.

Reconciliation is the Grace that turns brokenness into bridges of peace.

Day 311
Love That Restores

Scripture:

"He restoreth my soul: He leadeth me in the paths of righteousness for His Name's sake."

Psalm 23:3 (KJV)

Reflection:

Love does what time cannot; it restores. God's love not only forgives the past; it rebuilds what was lost, heals what was torn, and breathes new life into weary hearts. The same Shepherd who restores the soul also restores relationships, leading us gently into the paths of peace that reflect His righteousness. Restoration is rarely quick, but it is always complete in His timing. The Lord's love repairs in layers, Truth upon trust, Grace upon Grace, until what was once wounded becomes stronger than before. He does not merely return what was broken to its former state; He makes it better, deeper, more rooted in His Presence. When Divine love rules our hearts, bitterness loses its hold and hope finds its way back in. The same love that restored Peter after his denial still reaches for us today, whispering: Feed My sheep, walk in My Grace, love again. Restoration is the song love sings over every broken place; it is the proof that redemption always has the final word. Beloved, let God's restoring love work freely in you and through you. His Love can rebuild what disappointment dismantled and breathe beauty into what once felt barren.

Prayer:

Lord, thank You for Your Love that restores all things. Heal every part of my heart that has been wounded and teach me to extend Your restoring love to others. Make me an instrument of renewal, One Who rebuilds in faith and loves with Grace. May Your restoration bring Glory to Your Name. In Jesus' Name, Amen.

Restoring love rebuilds what was broken and redeems what was lost.

Day 312
The Ministry of Compassion

Scripture:

"Finally, be ye all of one mind, having compassion one of another, love as brethren, be pitiful, be courteous."

1 Peter 3:8 (KJV)

Reflection:

Compassion is love in motion. It sees the pain others hide and responds not with pity, but with presence. When Jesus looked upon the crowds, Scripture says He was moved with compassion. Every miracle that followed every healing, every act of mercy was born from that Divine stirring of the heart. The ministry of compassion belongs to every believer. It begins in the quiet willingness to feel what another feels and to let love lead the response. It is listening when words are few, giving when needs are many, and comforting when hope feels faint. Compassion transforms suffering into a sacred space where human hearts meet the kindness of Heaven.

Restored hearts make the best vessels of compassion. Those who have tasted mercy know how to pour it out. Every wound healed by Grace becomes a well from which others can drink. In showing compassion, we mirror the heart of Christ the Healer who still bends slow, still wipes tears, and still whispers peace. Beloved, let compassion flow through you like living water. It is the fragrance of Christ to a world in need and the evidence that His Love has taken root within your heart.

Prayer:

Lord, fill me with Your compassion. Help me to see others through Your eyes and to respond with gentleness and Grace. Let my words bring comfort, My Hands bring healing, and my presence brings peace. Teach me to serve through love, and may Your mercy flow through me to all who are hurting. In Jesus' Name, Amen.

Compassion is the gentle ministry of love flowing through a restored heart.

Day 313
Carried by Love

Scripture:

"Bear ye one another's burdens, and so fulfil the law of Christ."

Galatians 6:2 (KJV)

Reflection:

Love carries. It lifts when strength has run dry, it steadies when faith feels faint, and it holds fast when life trembles beneath the weight of trial. In Christ's design, no one is meant to bear their burdens alone. He calls us into a community where hearts intertwine, where prayer becomes the shoulder beneath another's cross, and where compassion becomes strength shared between souls.

To carry one another's burdens is to fulfill the very heart of Jesus. He, the ultimate burden-bearer, carried the weight of our sin, sorrow, and shame to the cross, and still today, He carries us in Grace. When we extend that same mercy to others, we step into His rhythm of love, becoming His Hands in motion and His Heart in action.

Being carried by love is not weakness; it is wisdom. It is the humility to receive help when pride would rather hide. It is the courage to lean when the load feels heavy. Love is at its purest when it carries quietly, patiently, and without condition. Beloved, when you feel weary, remember: love will find you and lift you again. And when you see another faltering, be the One Who carries with prayer, kindness, and Grace. In this sacred exchange, Christ Himself walks among us.

Prayer:

Lord, thank You for surrounding me with love that carries. Help me to bear the burdens of others with patience and compassion. When I grow weary, remind me that I am not alone, for Your Love and the love of Your people will lift me again. Let my life reflect the strength of shared faith and the beauty of selfless love. In Jesus' Name, Amen.

Love fulfills its highest purpose when it carries another's weight in Grace.

Day 314
The Gift of Empathy

Scripture:

"Rejoice with them that do rejoice, and weep with them that weep."

Romans 12:15 (KJV)

Reflection:

Empathy is the bridge between hearts; it closes the distance that pain, pride, or misunderstanding can create. To empathize is to step quietly into another's story, to see through their eyes, and to feel with their heart. It is love that listens before it speaks and understands before it advises.

Jesus walked in perfect empathy. He wept at Lazarus's tomb, not because He lacked power to raise him, but because He shared the sorrow of those who mourned. He felt the hunger of the crowd, the loneliness of the outcast, and the weariness of those burdened by life. His empathy was the doorway to His miracles–He felt before He healed.

Empathy requires presence more than answers. It is found in the tears shed beside a grieving friend; the prayer whispered in quiet solidarity, or the simple act of showing up when words fall short. Through empathy, the love of Christ becomes tangible, and the comfort of Heaven touches human pain.

Beloved, empathy is a gift--a reflection of a heart softened by Grace. Ask the Lord to enlarge your compassion, to make you sensitive to the needs of others, and to let His Love move through you not in sympathy alone, but in shared understanding. For where empathy flows, healing follows.

Prayer:

Lord, thank You for the gift of empathy -- the ability to feel with others as You do with us. Soften my heart and make me attentive to the unspoken needs around me. Let my presence bring comfort, and my compassion reflect Your Love. Teach me to rejoice with those who rejoice and to weep with those who weep. In Jesus' Name, Amen.

Empathy is love that listens, feels, and heals through understanding.

Day 315
The Fellowship of the Heart

Scripture:

"That which we have seen and heard declare we unto you, that ye also may have fellowship with us: and truly our fellowship is with the Father, and with His Son Jesus Christ."

1 John 1:3 (KJV)

Reflection:

Fellowship in Christ is more than shared faith it is shared life. It is the quiet miracle that happens when hearts knit together in love and commune with the same Lord in spirit and truth. In that sacred circle of Grace, joy is made full, peace is multiplied, and Heaven's presence dwells richly among His people.

The fellowship of the heart is not limited by distance or time; it is eternal. It connects saints across generations and believers across boundaries, uniting all who are redeemed beneath one Name and one cross. Within such fellowship, souls find rest, purpose, and strength because every connection flows from Him, the true Vine who gives life to every branch.

This is the beauty of God's design: that we never walk alone. His Spirit lives within and among us, binding hearts together in a love that cannot fail. Every prayer shared, every tear joined; every joy celebrated becomes worship when offered in fellowship with Him.

Beloved, treasure the fellowship of the heart. It is the whisper of eternity within community, the reminder that what unites us is stronger than what divides us, and that in His Presence, we are forever one.

Prayer:

Father, thank You for the sacred gift of fellowship in Christ. Knit our hearts ever closer to You and to one another. Let our relationships be marked by love, humility, and joy, reflecting Your unity within us. May our fellowship bring comfort to the weary, strength to the weak, and Glory to Your Name. In Jesus' Name, Amen.

True fellowship is Heaven's heartbeat shared among hearts made one in His Love

Section Eight:
Victory And Overcoming

Day 316
The Battle Belongs to the Lord

Scripture:

"The Lord shall fight for you, and ye shall hold your peace."

Exodus 14:14 (KJV)

Reflection:

Every believer will stand at a Red Sea moment when the way forward seems impossible, and the enemy presses hard from behind. In that place of fear and uncertainty, God whispers the same Truth He spoke to Moses: The battle is not yours - it's Mine.

The victory does not come by striving, but by surrender. God does His greatest work in stillness, not panic. When we step aside and let Him lead, His Power moves mountains we could never move and parts seas we could never cross. The posture of peace is not weakness; it is faith anchored in the unchanging strength of God.

When the Israelites stood before the waters, they had no weapons, no plan, and no strength left, but they had His Promise. And that was enough. The same God Who fought for them fights for you today. He goes before you, stands beside you, and guards behind you. Your only task is to trust and obey, to hold your peace while He holds your victory.

Beloved, let your heart rest in His Truth: the outcome has already been secured. Every battle surrendered to God becomes a stage for His Glory.

Prayer:

Lord, I surrender every battle into Your Hands. Teach me to trust Your Timing, to stand still in faith, and to let Your Peace guard my heart. Fight for me as only You can and let my life testify that the victory belongs to You alone. In Jesus' Name, Amen.

When you stop striving and start trusting, God begins to fight on your behalf.

Day 317
Strength Made Perfect

Scripture:

"And He said unto me, My Grace is sufficient for thee: for My strength is made perfect in weakness."

2 Corinthians 12:9 (KJV)

Reflection:

Heaven's strength is revealed in the very place we'd rather hide our weakness. The world teaches us to appear strong, to never falter, to stand tall. But God whispers a different truth: Let Me be strong for you. His Power is not displayed in our perfection, but in our dependence.

Paul's thorn was never about defeat; it has always been an invitation. When he cried out for relief, God responded with Grace, not removal. The Lord didn't take away the trial; He transformed it into a testimony. Our weakness becomes sacred ground when surrendered–it is the space where His Strength settles and His Glory shines brightest.

Beloved, you do not have to hide the fragile places of your heart. Bring them into His light. For every place you feel insufficient, His Grace abounds all the more. You are not disqualified by your weakness; you are a candidate for His Power. The cracks in your vessel do not diminish its worth–they make room for His light to shine through.

Let the weight you carry become the altar of your surrender, and watch as His Strength perfects what you cannot control.

Prayer:

Lord, thank You that Your Grace is enough for me. In every place I feel weak, let Your strength be made perfect. Teach me to rely not on my own power, but on Your faithfulness. Let my life become a testimony that Your strength is revealed through surrender. In Jesus' Name, Amen.

Weakness surrendered becomes strength perfected in His Grace.

Day 318
The Power of His Name

Scripture:

"Wherefore God also hath highly exalted Him, and given Him a Name which is above every name: That at the Name of Jesus every knee should bow, of things in heaven, and things in earth, and things under the earth."

Philippians 2:9 -10 (KJV)

Reflection:

There is no name like the Name of Jesus. It carries authority in Heaven, dominion on earth, and power over all darkness. Every fear, every sickness, every storm bows before it. His Name is not merely spoken; it is lived, breathed, and proclaimed by hearts that know His Lordship and trust His sovereignty. When you speak the Name of Jesus, you are not using words; you are invoking the Presence of the One Who conquered death, silenced the grave, and reigns forever. Demons tremble, chains break, and peace floods in where His Name is lifted. His Name is both refuge and weapon; it comforts the weary and conquers the enemy.

The early church understood His Power. They healed the sick, cast out spirits, and preached boldly not in their own strength, but in the Name above all names. That same authority rests upon you, beloved. The same Jesus who walked among the broken now walks within you.

Call upon His Name when the battle feels fierce. Whisper it in the dark, declare it in the storm, and sing it in your victory. For the Name of Jesus is not only your defense, it is your destiny.

Prayer:

Jesus, Your Name is power, peace, and victory. I thank You that in every circumstance, Your Name prevails. Teach me to walk in the authority You've given me and to speak Your Name with faith and reverence. Let every word of my life bring Glory to You and reveal the strength of Your great Name. Amen.

Every victory begins with one declaration: Jesus is Lord.

Day 319
Standing in Authority

Scripture:

"Behold, I give unto you power to tread on serpents and scorpions, and over all the power of the enemy: and nothing shall by any means hurt you."

Luke 10:19 (KJV)

Reflection:

Authority in Christ is not arrogance; it is alignment. It is the quiet confidence of a heart that knows who it belongs to and what has already been conquered through the cross. When Jesus gave His followers authority, He was entrusting them with His Power, not their own. That same authority rests upon every believer who walks in obedience and faith.

The enemy thrives where ignorance reigns. When you know your authority in Christ, fear loses its footing. You are not a victim of circumstance; you are a vessel of Divine Power, backed by Heaven itself. To stand in authority means you no longer fight for victory, but from it. You enforce what Jesus already accomplished. Authority does not shout; it stands. It does not panic; it prays. It speaks Truth when lies whisper loud. It lifts hands in praise when pressure mounts. The same Spirit that raised Christ from the dead dwells in you, making you more than capable to stand firm, resist the enemy, and walk in victory. Beloved, put on your armor and remember who you are: a child of the King, sealed by His Spirit, empowered by His Word. You were not created to cower; you were commissioned to conquer.

Prayer:

Lord, thank You for giving me authority through Your Name. Teach me to walk boldly, not in pride, but in faith. Let me stand firm in Your Word, resist the schemes of the enemy, and carry Your Peace wherever I go. Remind me that my victory is not in my strength, but in Your finished work. In Jesus' Name, Amen.

Authority stands not in pride, but in the Power of the risen Christ.

Day 320
More Than Conquerors

Scripture:

"Nay, in all these things we are more than conquerors through Him that loved us."

Romans 8:37 (KJV)

Reflection:

Victory in Christ is not earned, it is inherited. It is the assurance that no trial, no loss, no storm can undo what His love has already secured. To be more than a conqueror is to walk through battle knowing the outcome is already written. Jesus has overcome, and His victory is now ours.

The world defines victory by avoidance of pain or visible success. Heaven defines it by perseverance, peace, and unwavering trust in the midst of trial. You are not merely surviving what has come against you; you are conquering through the love that never fails. The cross stands as eternal proof that what was meant to destroy has been turned into redemption's song.

"More than a conqueror" means that even in loss, love wins. Even in weakness, grace abounds. Even in warfare, peace prevails because Christ's presence within you is greater than the pressure around you. You carry His triumph in your spirit, and no weapon formed against you can undo what His blood has already declared: You are victorious.

Beloved, lift your head and take heart. The battle belongs to the Lord, and in His Name, you already stand on victory ground.

Prayer:

Lord Jesus, thank You that Your victory is mine. Teach me to walk in confidence, not in my strength but in Yours. Help me to see every challenge as an opportunity to reveal Your overcoming power. Let Your love be the banner over every battle and Your peace the crown of every triumph. In Your Mighty Name, Amen.

Victory is not won by strength, it is received through abiding love.

Day 321
Dressed for Battle

Scripture:

"Put on the whole armour of God, that ye may be able to stand against the wiles of the devil."

Ephesians 6:11 (KJV)

For He put on righteousness as a breastplate, and helmet of salvation upon His head; and He put on the garments of vengeance for clothing, and was clad with zeal as a cloak.

Isaiah 59:17 (KJV)

Reflection:

Victory begins before the battle is ever fought. Each morning you awaken, Heaven offers you armor not of metal, but of Spirit; not for fear, but for faith. To put on the WHOLE armor of God is to clothe yourself in His Truth, righteousness, peace, faith, salvation, and the living Word.

Without it, the heart is vulnerable; with it, you are immovable. The armor is not symbolic; it is a spiritual reality. The belt of Truth secures integrity; the breastplate of righteousness guards the heart; the shoes of peace keep your steps steady when the path is rough. The shield of faith quenches fiery lies, and the helmet of salvation protects the mind from despair. And with the sword of the Spirit, the Word of God, you do not retreat, you advance. Every battle you face is not fought in the natural but in the unseen. And your victory, beloved, is not found in striving but in standing. To be dressed for battle is to be clothed in Christ Himself. His Truth becomes your strength; His Peace becomes your protection. Before the day begins, pause to put on the armor. Speak His Word, claim His Promises, and remember you are fighting from victory, not for it!

Prayer:

Lord, thank You for the armor You have provided. Help me to put it on daily and to walk clothed in Your Truth and righteousness. Guard my heart, steady my steps, and strengthen my faith. Let Your Word be my weapon and Your Peace my defense. I am fully equipped in You. In Jesus' Name, Amen.

Clothed in His armor, you are covered in victory before the battle begins.

Day 322
The Shield of Faith

Scripture:

"Above all, taking the shield of faith, wherewith ye shall be able to quench all the fiery darts of the wicked."

Ephesians 6:16 (KJV)

Reflection:

Faith is your defense against every lie the enemy launches. It is the shield that stands between your heart and the fire meant to wound it. When fear whispers, faith answers. When doubt presses in, faith declares, My God is still faithful. The shield of faith is not fragile; it is forged by trust and strengthened through endurance. The enemy's darts come in many forms: discouragement, anxiety, temptation, accusation, but faith extinguishes them all. Not because the believer is unshakable, but because God is unchanging. Each time you lift the shield through prayer and declaration of His Word, Heaven responds. Your faith may be tested, but it will not fail when anchored in the One Who cannot lie.

Faith is not a denial of reality; it is confidence in a greater truth. It sees beyond what the eyes behold and clings to the promises of God even when circumstances roar. A raised shield is not passive; it is active resistance, declaring: I trust God's Word more than what I feel.

Beloved, keep your shield lifted high. Let praise be your stance and the Word your weapon. No dart of darkness can pierce the faith that is forged in His light.

Prayer:

Lord, strengthen my faith so that it remains firm in every battle. Teach me to lift my shield with confidence and to trust Your Word above every fear. Let my faith quench every fiery dart and stand as a testimony that You are greater than anything that comes against me. In Jesus' Name, Amen.

Faith raised high turns every attack into an opportunity for victory.

Day 323
The Sword of the Spirit

Scripture:

"And take the helmet of salvation, and the sword of the Spirit, which is the word of God."

Ephesians 6:17 (KJV)

Reflection:

The Word of God is not just ink on a page; it is breath and power. The Sword of the Spirit cuts through deception, destroys strongholds, and silences the lies of the enemy. It is living, active, and eternal, sharper than any double-edged blade. Every time you declare His Truth in faith, Heaven moves, darkness trembles, and victory advances. Jesus Himself wielded this sword in the wilderness. He did not argue with the tempter; He answered with Scripture: It is written. The same authority He carried, you carry now. When fear rises, when the mind is assaulted with doubt, when weariness sets in, draw your sword. Speak His Word aloud. Truth spoken in faith becomes the weapon that drives back every shadow. This sword is not meant to remain sheathed. It must be drawn daily in prayer, in praise, and in perseverance. Each verse hidden in your heart is a blade sharpened by the Spirit. Each declaration of Truth pushes the enemy further from your territory and draws your soul closer to peace.

Beloved, wield your sword with confidence and humility. You are not powerless; you are armed with the Word that formed the universe. Speak it, believe it, and stand upon it your victory is already written.

Prayer:

Lord, thank You for the power of Your Word. Teach me to wield it with wisdom, boldness, and faith. Let Scripture be my weapon against fear and my guide in every battle. Strengthen me through Your truth, and let my life be a living testimony of the victory found in Your Word. In Jesus' Name, Amen.

The Word of God is both the weapon and the victory of every believer.

Day 324
The Helmet of Salvation

Scripture:

"But let us, who are of the day, be sober, putting on the breastplate of faith and love; and for an helmet, the hope of salvation."

1 Thessalonians 5:8 (KJV)

Reflection:

The enemy's greatest battlefield is often the mind. Doubt, fear, and discouragement strike hardest there, but God has provided protection: the Helmet of Salvation. It guards your thoughts with the Truth of who you are and whose you are. When the mind is covered in assurance, the heart remains unshaken.

Salvation is more than a moment; it is a continual covering. To wear this helmet is to walk in the constant awareness that you are redeemed, forgiven, and sealed for eternity. When lies whisper that you are unworthy, the helmet declares: I am saved. When fear says you will fail, it answers: I am His. Salvation is the anchor of identity that no storm can uproot.

The mind renewed in Christ is a fortress the enemy cannot breach. Every thought aligned with His Truth strengthens your resolve, clarifies your vision, and restores your peace. The Helmet of Salvation doesn't just defend, it transforms, replacing anxiety with assurance and confusion with clarity. Beloved, keep your mind guarded in the hope of your salvation. You are covered by Grace, crowned with mercy, and secure in Christ forever.

Prayer:

Lord, thank You for the Helmet of Salvation that guards my mind and anchors my heart in hope. Help me to think with clarity, to resist every lie of the enemy, and to rest in the assurance of Your saving power. Let my thoughts reflect Your Truth and my peace reveal Your Victory. In Jesus' Name, Amen.

Salvation is the crown of assurance that guards the mind and steadies the soul.

Day 325
The Belt of Truth

Scripture:

"Stand therefore, having your loins girt about with truth, and having on the breastplate of righteousness."

Ephesians 6:14 (KJV)

Reflection:

Truth is the foundation upon which every other piece of armor rests. Without it, faith falters, righteousness wavers, and peace becomes fragile. The Belt of Truth is what holds everything together. It centers your life, steadies your spirit, and strengthens your stance in battle.

The enemy's oldest weapon is deception. He twists the Truth just enough to confuse and divide. But when you are girded with God's truth, lies lose their power. Truth doesn't change with emotion or circumstance; it stands eternal, because it flows from the unchanging character of God. His Word is truth. His Promises are true. His Son is Truth personified.

To wear this belt is to live with integrity, to let your words and actions align with His Word. It is choosing honesty over comfort, conviction over compromise. When Truth is wrapped around your life, you walk in freedom; for Jesus said, Ye shall know the truth, and the Truth shall make you free.

Beloved, fasten Truth around your heart every day. Let it be your anchor when the world shifts, your compass when confusion calls, and your confidence when the battle presses close. For when you stand in truth, you stand in victory.

Prayer:

Lord, clothe me daily in Your truth. Let Your Word be the belt that strengthens my resolve and steadies my steps. Guard me from deception and help me to walk in integrity and sincerity of heart. May Your Truth shape my thoughts, my words, and my life. In Jesus' Name, Amen.

Truth holds the armor together and the heart steadfast in every battle.

Day 326
The Breastplate of Righteousness

Scripture:

"Stand therefore, having your loins girt about with truth, and having on the breastplate of righteousness."

Ephesians 6:14 (KJV)

Reflection:

The heart is the seat of devotion, the wellspring of life, and the battlefield of faith. The enemy knows that if he can wound the heart, he can weaken the believer. But God, in His Mercy, provides a perfect defense: the Breastplate of Righteousness. It covers the heart with the holiness and integrity of Christ Himself.

This righteousness is not earned; it is received. It is not a self-made virtue but a Divine covering. Through Jesus, you are declared righteous, justified, and made clean. When accusations rise and shame whispers, this breastplate reminds you: You are covered by the Blood, not condemned by the past.

Righteousness guards the heart from compromise and keeps your love pure. It empowers obedience, strengthens conviction, and aligns the soul with the will of God. When you walk in righteousness, darkness cannot dwell near you, for your life reflects the holiness of the One Who redeemed you. Beloved, protect your heart well. Wear the breastplate daily, not as armor of pride, but as a garment of Grace. You are not fighting to prove your worth; you are standing in the worth Christ already gave you.

Prayer:

Lord, thank You for covering me in Your righteousness. Guard my heart from corruption and compromise. Let my desires reflect Your purity and my actions reveal Your holiness. Clothe me in Your Grace, that I may walk uprightly and shine with the light of Your truth. In Jesus' Name, Amen.

"Righteousness guards the heart and anchors it in the holiness of Christ.

Day 327
The Shoes of Peace

Scripture:

"And your feet shod with the preparation of the Gospel of peace."

Ephesians 6:15 (KJV)

Reflection:

Peace is not the absence of battle; it is the Presence of Christ in the midst of it. The Shoes of Peace equip you to walk steadily when the ground shifts beneath you. They anchor you in the assurance that wherever you go, you are guided, guarded, and grounded in His Love.

The Gospel of peace is both a message and a movement. It is the good news that reconciles hearts to God and restores harmony where chaos once ruled. When your steps are ordered by His Word, you walk with purpose. When your path grows uncertain, His Peace steadies your stride. These shoes are not for retreat; they are for advancing the Kingdom with gentleness and Grace. Peace protects against panic. It allows you to move wisely, respond calmly, and carry hope into fearful places. Every step taken in peace is a declaration of trust, saying, I will not be moved, for my footing is found in Him.

Beloved, let the peace of Christ be both your foundation and your fragrance. Walk boldly, knowing that wherever your feet tread in obedience, His Presence will follow, and His Gospel will speak through you.

Prayer:

Lord, thank You for the peace that keeps me grounded and gives me courage to walk forward in faith. Let my steps be guided by Your Spirit and marked by Grace. Help me to carry Your Peace into every place I go and to stand firm when the storms rise. May Your Gospel of peace flow through my life as a living testimony of Your goodness. In Jesus' Name, Amen.

Peace is the firm ground beneath the feet of those who walk with God.

Day 328
The Armor of Light

Scripture:

"The night is far spent, the day is at hand: let us therefore cast off the works of darkness, and let us put on the armour of light."

Romans 13:12 (KJV)

Reflection:

Every day you rise, you are invited to wear light. The Armor of Light is the radiant Presence of Christ shining through your life, a visible declaration that darkness no longer defines you. It is purity that guards, Truth that protects, and holiness that illuminates. Where His light dwells, shadows must flee.

This armor is not forged by effort but by intimacy. The more time you spend in His Presence, the brighter you shine. When the world grows dim with fear, faith-filled hearts become beacons of hope. Your kindness becomes your sword, your integrity your shield, your peace your protection. The Armor of Light is the outward expression of an inward transformation, a life wrapped in His Glory and walking in His Truth.

To cast off the works of darkness is to release every burden of guilt, shame, and compromise that dims your reflection of Him. You are called to shine, beloved, not with borrowed light, but with the brilliance of the One Who lives within you.

Let your light so shine that it points others to the Savior. For when you walk clothed in His light, you carry the dawn into every dark place.

Prayer:

Lord, thank You for clothing me in the Armor of Light. Let Your Presence radiate through my words, my actions, and my heart. Drive away every Shadow that would try to dim my testimony, and fill me with Your holy fire. May my life reflect Your Glory and lead others to the light of Your truth. In Jesus' Name, Amen.

To wear the Armor of Light is to walk clothed in His Presence, untouchable by the night.

Day 329
Victory Through Praise

Scripture:

"Let the high praises of God be in their mouth, and a two-edged sword in their hand."

Psalm 149:6 (KJV)

Reflection:

Praise is more than a song; it is a weapon. It lifts the soul above the battle and places it in the atmosphere of Heaven, where victory has already been declared. When you choose to praise in the midst of the storm, you invite the Presence of the Almighty to fight on your behalf. Darkness cannot dwell where praise resides, for God inhabits the praises of His people.

The enemy despises praise because it shifts your focus from fear to faith, from the problem to the promise. It silences doubt and stirs Divine confidence. Praise doesn't deny pain; it declares that pain does not have the final word. It is the sound of surrender and strength intertwined with the voice of One Who knows that God is greater.

In Scripture, walls fell through worship, chains broke through song, and armies fled at the sound of praise. Heaven still moves when believers lift their voices in thanksgiving. Every hallelujah release Power. Every Glory to God shakes the foundations of despair. Beloved, your praise is not wasted, it's warfare. When words fail, lift your hands. When tears fall, whisper His Name. Let praise rise from the ashes, and watch as God turns your worship into victory.

Prayer:

Lord, I praise You not only for what You've done, but for who You are. Teach me to worship through every battle and to see praise as my greatest weapon. Fill my mouth with thanksgiving and my heart with faith. Let my song of victory rise to Heaven and break every chain that tries to bind me. In Jesus' Name, Amen.

Praise turns battles into breakthroughs and sorrow into songs of triumph.

Day 330
The Sound of Triumph

Scripture:

God is gone up with a shout, the Lord with the sound of a trumpet.

Psalm 47:5 (KJV)

Reflection:

Heaven has a sound, and it is triumph. It is not the noise of struggle but the song of victory; not the cry of defeat, but the shout of faith. The Sound of Triumph is the echo of God's authority reverberating through the earth, declaring that darkness has been defeated and the King reigns forevermore. There are moments when the Spirit stirs within you to shout, not from pride or emotion, but from revelation. This is not noise, it is agreement. When faith rises, praise finds its voice, and that sound carries the weight of Heaven's Power. Jericho's walls did not fall from the shout alone; they fell because the shout came after obedience, after trust, after silence that was filled with faith. Your victory has a sound too. Sometimes it's a whispered Thank You, Jesus, in the midnight hour. Sometimes it's the joyful cry of a heart that knows the battle is already won. Whether quiet or thunderous, your declaration of faith shifts the atmosphere and calls forth a breakthrough. Beloved, don't hold back your triumph. Let your praise be heard in the heavenlies. Let the world know that your God reigns. For when you lift your voice in victory, you join the eternal song, the anthem of the redeemed.

Prayer:

Lord, let my life resound with the sound of triumph. Fill my mouth with praise and my heart with faith. When I face battles, remind me that victory has already been declared in Heaven. Let my worship carry the sound of Your Power, and my faith releases the echo of Your Glory. In Jesus' Name, Amen.

Triumph has a sound, the voice of faith declaring, The Lord reigns!

Day 331
You Are Who God Says You Are

Scripture:

"For we are His workmanship, created in Christ Jesus unto good works, which God hath before ordained that we should walk in them."

Ephesians 2:10 (KJV)

Reflection:

There will always be voices that try to define you, your past, your fears, your failures, and even the opinions of others. But none of these voices hold authority over your identity. Only God does. And He calls you His workmanship, His masterpiece, His intentional creation, His beloved design.

You are not a random collection of strengths and weaknesses. You are crafted with purpose. Formed with destiny. Designed with eternal significance woven into every detail of your life.

Before you took your first breath, God ordained good works for you to walk in. Not works rooted in striving, but in calling. Not born from pressure, but from purpose.

When you embrace who He says you are, every lie loses its grip. You are not broken beyond repair; you are being shaped. You are not behind, you are becoming. You are not overlooked, you are ordained.

Stand in His Truth today:

Your identity is not determined by who you were, but by the One Who is shaping who you are becoming.

Prayer:

Lord, silence every voice that contradicts Your truth. Help me see myself through Your eyes, chosen, purposeful, and wonderfully made. Lead me into the good works You have prepared for me, and let my life reflect the beauty of Your design. In Jesus' Name, Amen.

Identity is not discovered through comparison; it is revealed through Christ.

Day 332
Pierced Within

Scripture:

"A reminder that God heals what the world cannot touch the wounds of the heart. He healeth the broken in heart, and bindeth up their wounds."

Psalm 147:3 (KJV)

"Surely He hath borne our griefs, and carried our sorrows."

Isaiah 53:4 (KJV)

Reflection:

There are wounds unseen by human eyes, piercings of betrayal, loss, and disappointment that only the hand of the Healer can reach. These inner places, though tender, are not forgotten. When your heart aches beneath the weight of memory or regret, remember: the One Who was pierced for you understands every pain that pierced you. Jesus never wastes a wound. Each tear becomes a seed watered by Grace, producing compassion for others who suffer. The world may tell you to harden and move on, but Heaven whispers, Be still while I bind you up. Healing in God's Presence is not a moment; it's a process of being remade in His Love. Allow Him to touch what you've guarded. Invite His light into the shadows. For every place that once bled will one day bloom, and the scars that remain will testify: I have seen the goodness of the Lord in the land of the living.

Prayer:

Lord Jesus, You know every place where I've been pierced within. Thank You for carrying my griefs and binding up my wounds. I lay before You every memory and every ache, trusting You to heal what I cannot fix. Make my scars shine with Your mercy so that others may know the power of Your Love. In Your holy Name, Amen.

The places once pierced now pulse with His Presence and peace.

Day 333
Heaven Is Stepping Into Your Life

Scripture:

"Surely the Lord is in this place; and I knew it not."

Genesis 28:16 (KJV)

"Thy kingdom come. Thy will be done in earth, as it is in heaven."

Matthew 6:10 (KJV)

Reflection:

Sometimes Heaven's movement begins quietly, an answered prayer disguised as a delay, a closed door that shelters you, a whisper that redirects your steps. We often expect the miraculous to arrive with thunder, but most days it slips in on the breath of His peace. Heaven is not far away; it is present wherever Jesus reigns. Each moment you choose faith over fear, forgiveness over offense, worship over worry, you make room for Heaven to step closer. What looks ordinary becomes holy ground when you recognize His nearness.

Jacob awoke to discover that God had been with him all along. So it is with you. The unseen help, the quiet comfort, the sudden knowing in your spirit, all are evidence that Heaven is already at work. Look again. The light you seek is shining in the place you stand. A reminder that God's Presence is already moving where your eyes are just beginning to see.

Prayer:

Father, open my eyes to see the evidence of Your Kingdom all around me. Let me discern Your Presence in every moment and rejoice that Heaven is not distant but dwelling within me. Teach me to recognize Your Hand in the hidden things and to live aware that You are always near. In Jesus' Name, Amen.

From the revelation of His nearness to the renewal of our strength... Heaven is nearer than I thought; His Glory is already here.

Day 334
Hearing Leads to Faith

Scripture:

"So then faith cometh by hearing, and hearing by the word of God."

Romans 10:17 (KJV)

"My sheep hear My voice, and I know them, and they follow Me."

John 10:27 (KJV)

Reflection:

Faith is not born in noise but in nearness. It begins when the heart turns its ear toward Heaven and listens. The Word of God was never meant to be skimmed; it was meant to be heard. When His Voice becomes your source of truth, fear loses its authority and faith takes root. Hearing precedes believing. When you take time to listen, you are training your spirit to recognize the rhythm of His Heart. The more clearly you hear His Word, the more boldly you will walk it out. Every miracle begins with a moment of hearing, whether whispered in Scripture, stirred in prayer, or spoken in stillness.

Faith is the natural response of a heart that has encountered His Voice. You do not have to force belief; you only need to listen and obey. What you hear in the secret place will sustain you in the public battle. His Word will become your weapon, your compass, and your peace.

Prayer:

Father, teach me to hear You with the ears of my spirit. Silence every distraction and let Your Word speak life into me. Strengthen my faith through what You say, and help me to walk in obedience to every word that proceeds from Your mouth. In Jesus' Name, Amen.

When I hear His Voice, my faith takes flight. A reminder that faith grows not from effort but from intimacy, listening to the Voice of God.

Day 335
The Call to Abide: A Deeper Journey into God's Voice

Scripture:

"Abide in Me, and I in you. As the branch cannot bear fruit of itself, except it abide in the vine; no more can ye, except ye abide in Me.

John 15:4 (KJV)

"Be still, and know that I am God."

Psalm 46:10 (KJV)

Reflection:

The Voice of God is not reserved for the few; it is available to every heart that abides. When you live in communion with Him, His whisper becomes the rhythm of your soul. Abiding teaches you to discern not only what He says, but how He says it, His tone, His peace, His timing.

Many seek a word from God, but few seek to dwell with God. Abiding transforms your relationship from visitation to habitation. It is not an event; it is a lifestyle of continual awareness. The more you remain in His Presence, the clearer His guidance becomes, and the more naturally obedience flows. Abiding requires stillness. In a world that values noise, Jesus calls you to quiet. The vine does not strain to produce fruit; it simply remains connected. Likewise, when you stay close to Him, fruitfulness becomes effortless, and revelation flows without striving.

God's Voice anchors the abiding heart. It steadies you through storms, reminds you of who you are, and calls you back when distractions pull. Every whisper draws you nearer, every word builds your faith, and every encounter deepens your love.

Prayer:

Father, teach me to abide in Your Presence and to hear Your Voice above all others. Let my heart remain connected to You, bearing fruit that glorifies Your Name. Speak through Your Word, guide me by Your Spirit, and let my life be a testimony of communion with You. In Jesus' Name, Amen.

A reminder that abiding in God's Presence opens our ears to hear His Voice with clarity and Confidence. Abiding is not the absence of noise; it is the awareness of His nearness. From hearing His Voice to resting in His stillness...

Day 336
The Beauty of Stillness

Scripture:

"A reminder that peace and clarity are found not in striving, but in resting before the Lord. Be still, and know that I am God: I will be exalted among the heathen, I will be exalted in the earth."

Psalm 46:10 (KJV)

"In quietness and in confidence shall be your strength."

Isaiah 30:15 (KJV)

Reflection:

Stillness is not the absence of movement; it is the presence of trust. When we choose to quiet our hearts before God, we discover that He was never silent; we were simply too hurried to hear. The beauty of stillness is found in surrender, where striving ceases and peace reigns.

The world shouts for attention, yet God whispers. His Voice rarely competes with noise; it waits to be invited into the silence. In stillness, revelation is born. Strength is renewed. Confusion fades beneath the weight of His Presence. To be still is to declare, GOD, You are enough. It is a statement of faith that releases anxiety and welcomes assurance. The One Who learns to rest in Him becomes a vessel of calm in a world of chaos. When you practice stillness, you are not withdrawing from life; you are anchoring yourself in the One Who holds it all together.

Prayer:

Father, teach me the beauty of stillness. Quiet every anxious thought and fill me with the peace of Your Presence. Help me to rest in the knowledge that You are God, and You are near. May my calm confidence in You be a light to those around me. In Jesus' Name, Amen.

In stillness, I find His Strength; in His Presence, I find my peace. From the stillness we embrace to the steps He ordains…

Day 337
The Steps of a Good Man Are Ordered

A reminder that every path of obedience is marked by Divine direction and steady Grace.

Scripture:

"The steps of a good man are ordered by the Lord: and he delighteth in his way."

Psalm 37:23 (KJV)

"In all thy ways acknowledge Him, and He shall direct thy paths."

Proverbs 3:6 (KJV)

Reflection:

Every step of faith is a response to God's unseen map. We may not understand the route, but we can trust the One Who charted the course. God's guidance is not random; it is relational. When we walk with Him, our pace and direction become synchronized with His Purpose. The good man's steps are not ordered because he never stumbles, but because even in his stumbling, he is held. Divine order does not mean the absence of detours; it means the assurance of arrival. When your path winds through valleys or pauses in waiting, remember that the Lord delights in your journey as much as your destination.

To walk in step with Him is to rest in the rhythm of Grace. His direction is often discovered one obedient step at a time. You don't have to see the whole staircase, just the next step lit by His Word. Each move forward, made in trust, becomes an act of worship.

Prayer:

Father, thank You for ordering my steps even when I cannot see the way. Help me to walk in humility, faith, and obedience. When my path seems uncertain, remind me that Your Hand steadies my every move. Lead me by Your Spirit, and let my life bring delight to Your Heart. In Jesus' Name, Amen.

My path may twist, but His Purpose never wavers. From the steps He orders to the hearts He calls...

Day 338
Make You Fishers of Men

Scripture:

"And Jesus said unto them, Come ye after Me, and I will make you to become fishers of men."

Mark 1:17 (KJV)

"Ye have not chosen Me, but I have chosen you, and ordained you, that ye should go and bring forth fruit."

John 15:16 (KJV)

Reflection:

Discipleship begins with a call, not a choice. Jesus sought out His followers and invited them to follow Me. Long before you ever said yes to Him, He had already chosen you. Yet following Jesus requires more than hearing His call; it requires surrendering your own. To be a disciple of Christ means denying yourself, taking up your cross, and walking daily in obedience. It is a life of continual learning, humility, and growth in the knowledge of His Word. The Bible is the disciple's textbook, the weapon, the map, and the mirror. Without it, faith becomes fragile, and witness grows lukewarm. We become disciples of whatever we devote ourselves to. What we give our time and attention shapes who we become. But when we fix our hearts on Jesus, He transforms us into fishers of men, people who carry His Heart for the lost, His compassion for the weary, and His courage to reach the world. Discipleship has a cost, but it also carries eternal reward. Those who follow Him closely will know the power of His resurrection and the fellowship of His sufferings. The more we know Him, the more we reflect Him, and through our lives, others are drawn to His light. A reminder that true discipleship is a daily choice to follow Jesus, learn His Ways, and lead others to His Truth.

Prayer:

Lord Jesus, thank You for calling me to follow You. Help me to lay aside every distraction and take up my cross daily. Teach me to live as a true disciple to love Your Word, to walk in obedience, and to lead others to Your saving Grace. Make me a fisher of men who reflects Your Heart in all I do. In Your Name, Amen.

I will follow where He leads and draw others by His Love. From following His call to teaching His Truth...

Day 339
7 Things the Bible Teaches About Discipleship

A reminder that discipleship is not a title we wear but a life we live daily, humbly, and faithfully.

Scripture:

"If ye continue in My word, then are ye My disciples indeed."

John 8:31 (KJV)

"Go ye therefore, and teach all nations... teaching them to observe all things whatsoever I have commanded you."

Matthew 28:19-20 (KJV)

Reflection:

Discipleship is the heartbeat of the Gospel. It's the invitation not just to believe in Jesus but to become like Him. The Bible shows that discipleship is a daily process of following, learning, growing, and teaching others to do the same.

Here are seven truths Scripture reveals about what it means to be a disciple:

1. A Disciple Follows Jesus Wholeheartedly.

"True disciples don't follow from a distance. They walk closely behind their Teacher, trusting His steps even when the path is uncertain."

Luke 9:23

2. A Disciple Abides in His Word.

The Word of God shapes the heart of every disciple. To remain in His Word is to remain in His will.

John 8:31

3. A Disciple Bears Fruit.

"Obedience produces fruit character, love, and good works that reflect His nature to the world."

John 15:8

4. A Disciple Loves Others as Christ Loves.

"Love is the mark of true discipleship. It is not optional but essential."

John 13:34-35

5. A Disciple Denies Self and Carries the Cross.

"Surrender is the soil where transformation grows."

Matthew 16:24

6. A Disciple Serves with Humility.

Jesus washed feet to show us that greatness in His Kingdom begins with service.

Mark 10:44-45

7. A Disciple Makes Disciples.

Discipleship multiplies. The life of a disciple is not complete until it reproduces, leading others to follow Christ.

Matthew 28:19-20

These seven truths form the foundation of a faithful walk. To follow Jesus is to be ever learning, ever growing, and giving. The more you walk with Him, the more you'll reflect His Heart, and your life will become a living invitation for others to do the same.

Prayer:

Lord, thank You for calling me to be Your disciple. Teach me to follow You with my whole heart and to live a life that bears lasting fruit. Help me to love as You love, serve as You served, and share the Gospel with boldness and Grace. Make me a vessel through which others can see and know You. In Jesus' Name, Amen.

Discipleship is not learned by watching; it is lived by walking with Him. From the lessons we learn to the lives we lead...

Day 340
Leading in Discipleship

Scripture:

"Follow me as I follow Christ."

1 Corinthians 11:1 (KJV)

"Whosoever will be chief among you, let him be your servant."

Matthew 20:27 (KJV)

Reflection:

Leadership in the Kingdom of God is not a title to attain; it is a life to embody. Jesus redefined greatness by kneeling to serve. He led not with demands, but with devotion. Those who lead in discipleship must first learn to sit at His feet, for leadership without intimacy becomes empty labor.

A disciple who leads must model what they teach. The greatest influence comes not from eloquence, but from example. When others see consistency between your words and your walk, they are drawn not to your ability, but to His anointing within you.

Leading in discipleship means guiding others toward transformation--not imitation. It is helping others hear His Voice, discern His will, and grow in their own relationship with Him. As you pour into others, remember: the strength to lead comes from the secret place. The more you abide, the more you overflow. True leaders in Christ are not recognized by crowds, but by fruit, lives changed, hearts healed, and faith strengthened. To lead is to love. To love is to serve. And to serve is to reflect the humility of the One Who came to serve us all. A reminder that true leadership begins with servanthood and is sustained through abiding in Christ.

Prayer:

Lord Jesus, thank You for the privilege to lead others in Your ways. Keep my heart humble, my motives pure, and my eyes fixed on You. Teach me to lead from the overflow of abiding in Your Presence. May my life point others to You alone, the true Shepherd and Teacher of our souls. In Your holy Name, Amen.

From those who lead to those who live as true disciples... The best leaders are first faithful followers.

Day 341
Are You a Disciple of Jesus Christ?

A reminder that discipleship is not defined by what we know, but by how we live and who we follow.

Scripture:

"Then said Jesus to those Jews who believed on Him, If ye continue in My word, then are ye My disciples indeed."

John 8:31 (KJV)

"By this shall all men know that ye are My disciples, if ye have love one to another."

John 13:35 (KJV)

Reflection:

Being a disciple of Jesus is more than calling ourselves Christians; it's living a life that looks like Him. The word disciple means learner or follower. It's not a one-time decision but a daily devotion to grow, to change, and to walk in obedience. True discipleship is revealed not in titles, positions, or words, but in fruit. It's seen in how we love, how we serve, and how we respond when no one is watching. A disciple is One Who allows the Holy Spirit to shape every area of life, the thoughts, the tone, the choices, and the character. Jesus never said, Come and be comfortable. He said, Follow Me. The call to discipleship is a call to leave behind self-will and live surrendered to Him.

It is costly, but it is also the only life that leads to true freedom and joy. Ask yourself today: Am I following Him out of convenience or conviction? Do I love like He loves? Do I obey even when it's hard? The more we walk with Him, the more His reflection becomes visible in us until the world no longer sees us, but Christ in us, the hope of Glory. The best leaders are first faithful followers.

Prayer:

Lord, make me a true disciple, One Who not only believes but follows. Help me to walk in Your Word daily, to love others as You have loved me, and to live a life that bears fruit for Your Kingdom. Let every step I take bring Glory to Your Name. In Jesus' Name, Amen.

Discipleship is not perfection--it is persistence in His Presence. From the life we live to the harvest He gives...

Day 342
God Is the Beginning

Scripture:

"In the beginning God created the heaven and the earth."

Genesis 1:1 (KJV)

"I am Alpha and Omega, the beginning and the ending, saith the Lord, which is, and which was, and which is to come, the Almighty."

Revelation 1:8 (KJV)

Reflection:

Everything that exists began with God, every breath, every sunrise, every heartbeat. Before you were formed, before the world was spoken into being, He already had a plan and a purpose for your life. When you start with Him, you find order. When you center your thoughts on Him, you find peace. When you trust Him to lead, you find purpose.

Discipleship begins and ends with God because He is both the Author and the Finisher. We cannot move forward in our own strength without first acknowledging the Source. To begin without God is to build without a foundation. But when He is the cornerstone, everything aligns every season, every assignment, every step. Remember: your beginning may look small, but it is sacred because He is in it. The same God Who created light out of darkness is still speaking life into what feels uncertain. He does not need perfect conditions to begin with, only a surrendered heart willing to believe.

Every time you start something new, a prayer, a season, a dream invites Him to speak the first word. When God is the beginning, He will also be the ending, and everything in between will carry His Glory.

A reminder that everything starts, sustains, and succeeds in the Presence of God.

Prayer:

Father, thank You for being my beginning and my end. You are the foundation of my faith, the center of my purpose, and the strength of my days. Start every work in me and through me with Your wisdom and finish it with Your **Grace**. May everything I do begin and end with You. In Jesus' Name, Amen

When God is the beginning, every ending leads back to His Glory. From the God Who begins all things to the One Who sustains them…

Day 343
The Power of the Gospel

Scripture:

"For I am not ashamed of the Gospel of Christ: for it is the power of God unto salvation to everyone that believeth."

Romans 1:16 (KJV)

"For the kingdom of God is not in word, but in power."

1 Corinthians 4:20 (KJV)

Reflection:

The Gospel is not a story to be remembered; it is a power to be demonstrated. It is not theory or theology; it is the very breath of God that brings dead things to life. When the Gospel is preached under the anointing of the Holy Spirit, chains break, hearts are healed, and eternity shifts.

The early Church did not persuade with eloquence but with evidence. Miracles followed the message. The lame walked. The bound were delivered. The lost were found. That same Gospel still carries the same power today. It has not weakened with time nor diminished with culture. The Word that spoke galaxies into being still speaks freedom into every soul who believes.

We have not been called to present a powerless Gospel. We are called to demonstrate it to live in such surrender that His authority flows through us. When we carry His Word with faith, the atmosphere must respond. Light invades darkness. Hope confronts despair. Heaven touches earth. The world does not need more opinions; it needs an encounter with the POWER of The Living God. And that power is within you. When you open your mouth to proclaim the Name of Jesus, the Gospel itself moves, breaking, healing, restoring, and redeeming.

A declaration that the Gospel is not only words, but it is the living power of God that transforms hearts, heals lives, and conquers darkness.

Prayer:

Lord, thank You for entrusting me with the power of Your Gospel. Let Your Word be alive in me, burning with conviction, authority, and compassion. May I never shrink back in fear or shame, but boldly declare that Jesus saves, heals, and delivers. Let my life become a testimony of the Gospel's transforming power. In Jesus' mighty Name, Amen.

The Gospel is not a message I carry...it is the power that carries me. From the Glory revealed to the promise fulfilled...

Day 344
Relentless Authority in Christ

Scripture:

"Behold, I give unto you power to tread on serpents and scorpions, and over all the power of the enemy: and nothing shall by any means hurt you."

Luke 10:19 (KJV)

"As for God, His way is perfect: the word of the Lord is tried: He is a buckler to all those that trust in Him."

Psalm 18:30 (KJV)

Reflection:

Every battle fought in faith refines the authority we walk in. True authority in Christ is not born from ease, but from endurance from facing the storm and declaring, It is written, until the waves obey His Word.

The believer who has been tested and found standing is not just strong; they are established. When the enemy comes in like a flood, they rise with the confidence of One Who knows the Word is tried and proven. They have seen God keep His Promises, heal what was broken, and restore what was lost. Their authority is not arrogance; it is the fruit of abiding in the One whose power has never failed.

To walk in relentless authority is to speak with Heaven's assurance: the victory has already been won, and every promise of God stands undefeated. Trials may roar, but the tried Word of God roars louder. A reminder that trials reveal the power and authority of those who stand on the proven Word of God.

Prayer:

Heavenly Father, thank You for the battles that taught me to trust Your Word. When the enemy whispers doubt, remind me that Your Promises have been tried and proven in my life. Clothe me in the authority of Jesus Christ, not to boast, but to boldly declare Your Victory. Let my words carry the weight of Heaven, and may my life testify that Your Word always prevails. In Jesus' mighty Name, Amen.

Faith walks in the authority of the Risen King.

Day 345
Great Wonders Are Coming!

A reminder that God is preparing to reveal His Power and Glory through a purified and obedient Church.

Scripture:

"Sanctify yourselves: for tomorrow the Lord will do wonders among you."

Joshua 3:5 (KJV)

"For the earth shall be filled with the knowledge of the Glory of the Lord, as the waters cover the sea."

Habakkuk 2:14 (KJV)

Reflection:

The Spirit of God is stirring in the earth, and Heaven is preparing to display great wonders once again. These will not merely be signs and miracles for spectacle's sake, but demonstrations of His holiness, justice, and mercy through a people made ready. Before every Divine outpouring, there is a Divine cleansing. The Lord is purifying His Bride, separating her from the noise of the world, so that His Glory can be revealed without mixture. Do not be disheartened by shaking or pruning; both precede the unveiling of His Power. As the Church surrenders pride for purity, comfort for calling, and fear for faith, the atmosphere of Heaven will invade the earth. You were not born for complacency, you were born to carry Glory.

God is preparing to move in ways that will silence doubt and ignite awe. What He does next will not just change circumstances; it will change hearts. Stand ready, sanctified, and steadfast, for great wonders are coming, and they will flow through those who have learned to abide.

Prayer:

Father, thank You for the promise of Your coming wonders. Purify my heart and prepare my life as a vessel of Your Glory. Let Your Presence move through me in power, humility, and holiness. Use me to carry the fire of revival into every place You send me. In Jesus' Name, Amen.

Faith waits expectantly for the wonders of God.

Day 346
When Heaven Touches Earth

A reminder that God's Glory is not a distant light but a Presence that desires to rest upon you.

Scripture:

"Arise, shine; for thy light is come, and the Glory of the Lord is risen upon thee."

Isaiah 60:1 (KJV)

"The earth is the Lord's, and the fulness thereof."

Psalm 24:1 (KJV)

Reflection:

There are moments when worship deepens into wonder when the veil seems to thin and the atmosphere shifts. Heaven draws near, and the soul can almost feel eternity breathe. This is the Glory of the Lord, His tangible Presence revealing that you were created to dwell with Him, not merely serve Him from afar.

When Heaven touches earth, peace overshadows fear, tears become holy, and silence speaks louder than songs. The Glory of God is not reserved for mountaintops; it meets the surrendered heart in kitchens, cars, and quiet rooms where His name is whispered with love.

The Father longs to rest His Glory upon yielded lives. It is not earned by striving but received by surrender. Ask Him to take you there to the place where worship becomes encounter, where your heart becomes His dwelling, and where every breath says, Here am I, Lord let Your Glory fall.

Prayer:

Heavenly Father, I long for Your Glory. Take me beyond words into the weight of Your Presence. Let Your Spirit rest upon me until everything lesser fades away. Teach me to host Your Glory with humility and holiness, and to shine so that others see You in me. In Jesus' Name, Amen.

Take me there, Lord, where Heaven touches earth, and I am found in Your Glory.

Day 347
The Power of a Testimony

Scripture:

"And they overcame him by the Blood of the Lamb, and by the word of their testimony; and they loved not their lives unto the death."

Revelation 12:11 (KJV)

"Come and hear, all ye that fear God, and I will declare what He hath done for my soul."

Psalm 66:16 (KJV)

Reflection:

Your testimony is more than a memory; it's a weapon. Each time you share what God has done, you remind Hell that its grip has been broken. Your story carries the fragrance of deliverance and becomes an invitation for others to believe again.

Testimonies are living proof that God still moves, still heals, still restores. They tear down walls of doubt and ignite faith in those who listen. When you speak of His Goodness, Heaven bears witness; angels rejoice, and hearts are strengthened.

Never underestimate what God can do through your story. It was born in battle, shaped by Grace, and sealed by victory. Your scars now shine as evidence of His Mercy, and what once hurt now heals others. Speak boldly, for your voice carries the sound of a breakthrough.

A reminder that your story of redemption carries Heaven's authority to set others free.

Prayer:

Lord, thank You for turning my story into a testimony of Your faithfulness. Give me the boldness to share it so others may find hope. Use my words to reveal Your Power and to draw many to the saving knowledge of Jesus Christ. Let my life forever proclaim You are good, and Your mercy endures forever. In Jesus' Name, Amen.

My story belongs to Him; through it, others will see His Glory.

Day 348
Blessed Be the God and Father of Our Lord Jesus Christ

Scripture:

"Blessed be God, even the Father of our Lord Jesus Christ, the Father of mercies, and the God of all comfort; Who comforteth us in all our tribulation, that we may be able to comfort them which are in any trouble, by the comfort wherewith we ourselves are comforted of God."

2 Corinthians 1:3–4 (KJV)

Reflection:

There are moments when the soul bends beneath the weight of sorrow, and the heart longs for quiet refuge. It is in those moments that we come to know Him as the Father of mercies and the God of all comfort. His compassion is not distant; it draws near, wrapping itself around every wound and whispering peace into the ache of the soul.

Suffering does not disqualify us from His Grace; it deepens our capacity to carry it. The very places that once felt shattered become vessels of comfort to others when filled with His Love. In every trial, He is both the One Who sustains and the One Who sends us forth to sustain others. What the enemy meant for harm becomes a ministry of healing in His Hands.

When you have tasted His Mercy in your pain, you carry within you a sacred testimony, the evidence that even in affliction, His Presence abides. You are proof that comfort has a name, and His name is Jesus.

Prayer:

Father of mercy, thank You for comforting me in every place of pain and teaching me to comfort others through Your Spirit. Let my life reflect Your compassion. Use my scars as reminders of Your faithfulness and as pathways through which others can find healing. In Jesus' Name, Amen.

His Mercy comforts the wounded and empowers the healed to comfort others.

Day 349
My Alabaster Box

Scripture:

And, behold, a woman in the city, which was a sinner, when she knew that Jesus sat at meat in the Pharisee's house, brought an alabaster box of ointment, and stood at His feet behind Him weeping, and began to wash His feet with tears, and did wipe them with the hairs of her head, and kissed His feet, and anointed them with the ointment.

Luke 7:37–38 (KJV)

Reflection:

There is something sacred about the moment when a heart fully breaks before the Lord - not in despair, but in surrender. Like the woman with the alabaster box, we come carrying the weight of all we have been through: the regrets, the losses, the mistakes, and the memories that still sting. Yet in His Presence, our brokenness becomes an offering.

The fragrance of true worship is not found in perfection but in surrender. It is the perfume of a repentant heart poured out in love. Every tear becomes oil, every sigh a song, and every scar a vessel of gratitude. She did not wait until she was whole to come; she came because she knew that He alone could make her whole.

What she poured out that day could never compare to what she received in return: peace, forgiveness, and the freedom of being known and loved by the One Who saw her not for who she had been, but for who she was becoming. So bring your alabaster box, beloved. There is no fragrance more precious to Heaven than your poured-out worship.

Prayer:

Jesus, I bring You my alabaster box, all my pain, all my praise, all that I am. Let my life be a fragrance that fills the room with Your Presence. Heal what has been broken within me, and let my worship rise as a testimony of Your Grace. I am Yours, completely and forever. In Your holy Name, Amen.

True healing flows where surrender meets worship.

Day 350
Crowned with Righteousness

Scripture:

"Henceforth there is laid up for me a crown of righteousness, which the Lord, the righteous judge, shall give me at that day."

2 Timothy 4:8 KJV

"And when the Chief Shepherd shall appear, ye shall receive a crown of Glory that fadeth not away."

Peter 5:4 (KJV)

Reflection:

The race of faith is not won by speed but by endurance. It is not the fastest who finish strong, but the faithful, those who keep believing, keep trusting, and keep walking even when the path grows steep.

For those who remain steadfast, there is more than a reward awaiting them; there is recognition from the King Himself. The crown of righteousness is not earned by human effort; it is bestowed through the Grace that carried you, sustained you, and kept you running when you wanted to stop.

Righteousness is the garland Grace weaves through every act of obedience, every surrendered yes, and every quiet moment of perseverance. Heaven sees what no one else sees. And one day, the Chief Shepherd will place upon your head the unfading crown reserved for those who loved His appearing and lived unto His Name.

Prayer:

Lord, keep my eyes fixed on the eternal crown. Strengthen my heart to finish faithfully and to live worthy of Your Name each day. Let Your Grace empower every step of my journey. In Jesus' Name, Amen

Faith runs for the crown that never fades.

Day 351
The Victory of Faith

Scripture:

"For whatsoever is born of God overcometh the world: and this is the victory that overcometh the world, even our faith."

1 John 5:4 KJV

"Nay, in all these things we are more than conquerors through Him that loved us."

Romans 8:37 (KJV)

Reflection:

Faith is not fragile; it is forged in fire. Every trial you endure becomes the very place where faith reveals its true strength. What the enemy designed to break you becomes the tool God uses to build you. The pressure that tries to crush you only produces a deeper confidence in the God Who sustains you.

Faith does not retreat in fear; it advances in assurance. It rises in the face of impossibility, not because circumstances are easy, but because Christ has already secured the victory. Faith refuses to bow to what it sees, because it is anchored in what God has spoken.

You are not fighting for victory; you are fighting from victory. The battle may be fierce, but the outcome is already sealed. You stand as more than a conqueror, covered by the love of Christ, strengthened by His Spirit, and upheld by His Word.

Victory is not a distant hope; it is your present inheritance. Every act of faith, every prayer whispered in the storm, every step taken in trust is a declaration that you belong to the undefeated King.

Prayer:

Father, let my faith rise stronger than fear. Remind me daily that through Christ, I have already overcome. Strengthen my spirit, steady my heart, and anchor my confidence in the victory You have secured for me. Help me walk boldly in the triumph of Your Love. In Jesus' Name, Amen.

Faith never loses when it trusts The Victor.

Day 352
The Fire Still Falls

Scripture:

"Then the fire of the Lord fell ... and when all the people saw it, they fell on their faces: and they said, The Lord, He is the God."

1 Kings 18:38-39 KJV

"For our God is a consuming fire."

Hebrews 12:29 (KJV)

Reflection:

The same fire that fell for Elijah still falls today. God's power has not weakened; His Glory has not faded. His fire still answers where there are surrendered altars. When a life is yielded fully and without reservation, He responds with fire that purifies, empowers, and reveals His Presence in unmistakable ways.

The altar is your heart. The fire is His Presence. The offering is your surrender. God is not looking for perfect vessels; He is looking for willing ones. When you place your desires, your will, your plans, and your pride on the altar, His holy fire consumes what is fleshly and kindles what is holy.

His fire burns away compromise. His fire refines motives. His fire ignites passion for His Name.

The fire of God does not come to destroy you, but to transform you, burning away what cannot remain so that what is eternal can shine through. A heart marked by His fire becomes a testimony that causes others to say, The Lord, He is God.

Prayer:

Lord, send Your fire again. Place Your holy flame upon the altar of my heart. Burn away all that is not of You, every impurity, every distraction, every divided affection, and fill me with a holy passion to see Your Glory revealed. Let my life be a living altar, wholly surrendered and fully ablaze for You. In Jesus' Name, Amen.

Faith builds the altar; God sends the fire.

Day 353
The Banner of His Name

Scripture:

"We will rejoice in Thy salvation, and in the Name of our God we will set up our banners."

Psalm 20:5 KJV

"The Name of the Lord is a strong tower: the righteous runneth into it, and is safe."

Proverbs 18:10 (KJV)

Reflection:

Ancient armies marched under banners declaring who they belonged to and who they fought for. A banner wasn't just fabric; it was identity, confidence, and courage. Your banner is the Name of Jesus, Your protection, your covering, your triumph, and your unshakable strength. When you lift the Name of Jesus over your battles, you are declaring that you do not fight alone. You fight under Divine authority and heavenly power.

His Name is not merely spoken, it is raised. Raised over fear. Raised over sickness. Raised over confusion. Raised over every attack of the enemy.

Where His Name is lifted, His Presence is revealed. And where His Presence stands, no darkness can remain. When you raise His Name, fear loses ground, hope rises again, angels are dispatched, and Heaven's victory goes before you.

Faith lifts the banner high not because the battle is easy, but because The Victor is present.

Prayer:

Jesus, Your Name is my banner of victory. I lift it over my home, my family, my mind, and every battle I face. Let Your Name silence every fear, shift every atmosphere, and stand as my strong tower. Be glorified in me and fight for me as I stand under the covering of Your mighty Name. Amen.

Faith fights under the banner of the King.

Day 354
Unshaken

Scripture:

"Those that trust in the Lord shall be as mount Zion, which cannot be removed, but abideth for ever."

Psalm 125:1 KJV

"He only is my rock and my salvation; He is my defence; I shall not be greatly moved."

Psalm 62:2 (KJV)

Reflection:

When everything around you shakes, faith reminds you Who holds you. Life shifts. People change. Seasons rise and fall. Emotions waver. Circumstances stretch you. But God Your Rock, your Fortress, your Defender remains the same. Those who trust in Him do not stand on shifting soil; they stand on a mountain that cannot be moved. Mount Zion is not famous for its height, but for its permanence. It endures storms, winds, and centuries because its foundation is unshakable.

So it is with the believer. Your stability is not found in the calmness of life but in the unchanging character of God. Faith does not deny the shaking; it simply refuses to be defined by it. The earth may tremble around you, but you stand anchored because God Himself is your ground, your guard, and your guarantee. To trust in the Lord is to be rooted where fear cannot uproot you, where storms cannot undo you, and where circumstances cannot destroy what God sustains.

Prayer:

Lord, make me unshakable in Your truth. Let my confidence rest in Your unchanging love, and my heart anchor itself in Your eternal faithfulness. Strengthen me to stand firm when life trembles and to trust You when everything else feels uncertain. In Jesus' Name, Amen.

Faith stands firm when everything else falls.

Day 355
The Lion of Judah Reigns

Scripture:

Weep not: behold, the Lion of the tribe of Judah, the Root of David, hath prevailed.

Revelation 5:5 KJV

"The Lord shall roar out of Zion, and utter His Voice from Jerusalem…"

Joel 3:16 (KJV)

"The Lord is a man of war: the Lord is His Name."

Exodus 15:3 KJV

Reflection:

The Lamb who was slain is also the Lion Who rules and reigns with unchallenged authority. The cross revealed His humility, but the resurrection unveiled His dominion. The Lion of Judah is not silent He speaks with the thunder of victory, power, and sovereignty. Your victory does not come from your strength but from His Roar. Every battle you face bows to the One whose blood broke the power of sin, whose voice shatters darkness, and whose reign is eternal.

When the Lion of Judah roars, fear loses its vocabulary. Confusion scatters. Intimidation collapses. His Voice establishes order, restores courage, and releases heavenly confidence.

Hope rises not because the battle is easy, but because your King has already prevailed. Heaven is not nervous, and neither should you be. Your Defender is the roaring, ruling Lion of Judah.

Prayer:

Lion of Judah, roar over my life. Let the sound of Your Authority silence every fear and overthrow every scheme of darkness. Speak into every place of confusion and command Your Peace to reign. Roar over my family, my mind, my future, and every battle I face. Let Your victorious power drive out discouragement and strengthen my spirit. Remind me that I am protected, upheld, and secured by the King who has already prevailed. I worship You, my mighty and victorious King. In Jesus' Name, Amen.

Faith rests in the roar of the Lion.

Day 356
The River of Life

Scripture:

"And He shewed me a pure river of water of life, clear as crystal, proceeding out of the throne of God and of the Lamb."

Revelation 22:1 KJV

"He restoreth my soul."

Psalm 23:3 (KJV)

"Ho, every one that thirsteth, come ye to the waters…"

Isaiah 55:1 KJV

Reflection:

From the throne of God flows a river that never runs dry, pure, life-giving, and unmarred by human striving. This river is the very expression of Heaven's heart toward you: renewal, restoration, and continual refreshing.

Wherever the River of Life flows, dry places awaken, broken places heal, and weary souls regain strength. This river carries everything you need: peace for anxiety, clarity for confusion, healing for wounded places, and joy for the heavy-hearted.

Every promise God has ever spoken is carried in the current of this living water. Jesus Himself is the Source of the Living Water who satisfies every thirst and revives every part of you touched by His Presence.

When you drink deeply of Him, what was dormant comes alive again. Hope returns. Vision rises. Strength is restored. You do not have to live dehydrated in your spirit. He invites you to the waters of renewal every single day.

Prayer:

Lord, let Your river flow through every part of my life. Wash away all that is dry, weary, or weighed down. Restore what has been broken and breathe new life into my soul. Let the waters of Your Spirit refresh my mind, renew my strength, and revive every dream that has grown faint. Draw me closer to Your Presence, where living water flows freely and endlessly. Make me a vessel that carries Your life to others. May Your river flow through me, not only to me. In Jesus' Name, Amen.

Faith drinks deeply from the river that never runs dry.

Day 357
The Crown of Life

Scripture:

"Blessed is the man that endureth temptation: for when he is tried, he shall receive the crown of life."

James 1:12 KJV

"Be thou faithful unto death, and I will give thee a crown of life."

Revelation 2:10 (KJV)

Reflection:

Endurance is the evidence of genuine love for God. It is the quiet strength that keeps following Jesus when the road grows difficult, when the battle intensifies, and when answers seem delayed. Those who remain faithful through trial are promised a crown not made of gold or jewels but of life. Eternal, unshakable, overflowing life.

The Crown of Life is Heaven's affirmation that your suffering was not unseen and your perseverance was not forgotten. He has watched every tear, every prayer prayed through pain, every moment you stood when giving up felt easier. None of it is wasted.

Trials do more than test your faith -they refine your devotion. They purify your motives, deepen your trust, and anchor your hope in the One Who cannot fail. The crown is not a reward for perfection but for faithfulness. For choosing Jesus again and again. For loving Him in the valley as much as on the mountaintop.

Your endurance today is weaving eternal Glory for tomorrow.

Prayer:

Lord, sustain me with holy strength to endure with joy. When trials press in, steady my heart. When I grow weary, breathe fresh courage into my spirit. Fix my eyes on the promise You have set before me and keep me faithful until the very end. Let my perseverance honor You. Let my steadfastness reflect my love for You. Shape me into One Who finishes the race with devotion that does not waver and faith that does not retreat. And when my journey is complete, may I receive the crown of life from Your Hand with gratitude and worship. In Jesus' Name, Amen.

Faith endures for the crown that lasts forever.

Day 358
Rekindle the Fire Within

Scripture:

"Wherefore I put thee in remembrance that thou stir up the gift of God, which is in thee by the putting on of My Hands."

2 Timothy 1:6 (KJV)

"Not slothful in business; fervent in spirit; serving the Lord."

Romans 12:11 (KJV)

Reflection:

There are seasons when the embers of our faith seem to dim beneath the weight of trials, distractions, or delay. Yet the fire has not gone out; it only awaits the breath of God. He is calling you to stir again the flame within, to remember His Promises, and to walk forward in the power of His Spirit. What He placed within you was never meant to be buried under fear, doubt, or fatigue. Fan it into flame, beloved. Faith that once flickered can burn bright again when surrendered to the wind of His Presence.

Prayer:

Lord, breathe Your holy fire upon my heart again. Let every place that has grown cold be consumed by Your Love. Rekindle my faith, my zeal, and my devotion until I burn with a steady flame that brings You Glory. In Jesus' Name, Amen.

The flame that once flickered now burns with holy purpose.

Day 359
The Song of the Redeemed

Scripture:

"They sung a new song, saying, Thou art worthy to take the book, and to open the seals thereof: for Thou wast slain, and hast redeemed us to God by Thy Blood."

Revelation 5:9 KJV

"Let the redeemed of the Lord say so, whom He hath redeemed from the hand of the enemy."

Psalm 107:2 (KJV)

Reflection:

Heaven's anthem is not sung by angels -it is sung by the redeemed. Those who know the weight of sin and the wonder of Grace. Those who understand the power of the cross and the cost of redemption.

There will be a day when no voice remains silent, when every redeemed heart joins in the song that belongs only to those washed in the Blood of the Lamb. This song is your inheritance. It is the melody born from mercy, the sound of gratitude shaped by Grace.

You were created for this song. For worship that rises from remembrance. For praise that springs from redemption. For a voice that joins the eternal chorus declaring: Worthy is the Lamb!

Prayer:

Worthy are You, Lamb of God! Let my life be a melody of Your mercy. Teach me to worship now as I will forever before Your throne. Amen.

Faith ends where worship never does.

Day 360
Reinforcements Are Coming

Scripture:

"Though an host should encamp against me, my heart shall not fear: though war should rise against me, in this will I be confident... I had fainted, unless I had believed to see the goodness of the Lord in the land of the living. Wait on the Lord: be of good courage, and He shall strengthen thine heart."

Psalm 27:3, 13 -14 (KJV)

Reflection:

You are not fighting alone. Heaven has heard your prayers, seen your perseverance, and dispatched reinforcements on your behalf. The Lord of Hosts commands legions, and His Word never returns void. When you feel surrounded, remember you are surrounded by a Kingdom that cannot be shaken and an army that cannot be defeated.

In prayer, the Spirit reveals glimpses of Heaven's movement visions of warriors armored in light, horses charging forth, swords clashing in triumph. You may not see it yet, but victory is already in motion. The Lord is declaring, Do you hear the gallop of the horses? Do you hear the clanking of swords? The reinforcements are coming! The enemy may roar, but the Lion of Judah roars louder. Just as Aslan arose in victory and led His army to triumph, so too does your risen Savior lead you. His Presence brings courage; His promise brings strength; His Power brings deliverance. Hold the line. Stand in faith. Heaven is backing you. What you've been battling is about to break because your reinforcements have been released.

A reminder that Heaven's armies still move at the command of our Mighty God, who never leaves His children defenseless.

Prayer:

Heavenly Father, thank You for never leaving me to fight alone. Thank You for the armies of Heaven that You send to strengthen and protect Your people. Open my ears to hear the sound of Your reinforcements coming. Let courage rise as I wait on You. You have never lost a battle, and I trust that victory is already secured in Jesus' mighty Name. Amen.

It may look like I'm surrounded... but I'm surrounded by Him. From the battle He wins to the Glory He reveals...

Day 361
Heaven's Gavel

A reminder that God still rules from His throne, rendering verdicts of justice, mercy, and victory on behalf of His people.

Scripture:

"Shall not the Judge of all the earth do right?"

Genesis 18:25 (KJV)

"For the Lord is our judge, the Lord is our lawgiver, the Lord is our king; He will save us."

Isaiah 33:22 (KJV)

Reflection:

There are moments when Heaven holds court. The prayers of the righteous rise as petitions before the throne, and the Judge of all creation renders His verdict. It is finished. The gavel strikes, not in wrath, but in righteousness. What was once delayed is decided. What was once hindered is released.

Heaven's gavel declares that every accusation spoken against you by the enemy has been overruled by the Blood of Jesus. The adversary may roar with lies, but Truth has already spoken. The Judge stands, the verdict is read, and the case is closed. When the gavel falls in Heaven, authority shifts on earth. Angels are dispatched. Justice is executed. Peace is restored. You do not fight to win; you stand to enforce what has already been decreed. The gavel that fell at Calvary still echoes through eternity: It is finished. You are not forgotten, silenced, or forsaken. The ruling is in your favor. Heaven's gavel has fallen, and it declares your freedom, your healing, and your vindication.

Prayer:

Righteous Judge, I thank You for ruling on my behalf. Let every false word, accusation, and assignment of the enemy be overturned by the Blood of Jesus. I receive Your verdict of victory and walk in the authority of Your Word. Let Your justice reign in my life, and may Your Glory be revealed through every decision You render. In Jesus' mighty Name, Amen.

When Heaven's gavel falls, every other voice is silenced.

Day 362
Show You His Glory

Scripture:

"And he said, I beseech thee, shew me Thy Glory."

Exodus 33:18 (KJV)

"Moses said, 'Please show me Your Glory."

Exodus 33:18 (ESV)

Reflection:

There comes a moment when the soul that has wrestled, waited, and withstood the fire begins to cry not for more answers, but for more of Him. This was Moses' cry not for provision or power, but for Presence. And God, in His Mercy, answered. You have known His work in you, the refining fire, the stretching, the sanctifying process that shaped your faith. But now the Spirit whispers: I have worked for you long enough. Watch now as I work through you and show you, My Glory. What has been hidden in preparation will soon be revealed in manifestation. God is ready to take you places you've never been, to use you beyond what you imagined, and to display His Power in ways that confound the wise. Nothing can hinder what He has ordained. This is the moment where faith matures into Glory, where your surrendered life becomes the stage for Heaven's light to shine. You are being moved from faith to faith and from Glory to Glory until you stand in eternal Glory with Him. A reminder that God is not finished revealing Himself, His Glory is still being shown through the lives of those who believe.

Prayer:

Heavenly Father, thank You for faithfully working in me through every season. Continue to perfect the work You have begun and let Your Glory be revealed through my life. Use me as a vessel of Your Presence, a reflection of Your Goodness, and a testimony of Your Power. In Jesus' mighty Name, Amen.

I have seen His work within me; now I will behold His Glory through me. From the Glory revealed to the promise fulfilled...

Day 363
Great Wonders

A reminder that God is still a wonder-working God, faithful to perform what He has promised.

Scripture:

"This is the Lord's doing; it is marvelous in our eyes."

Psalm 118:23 (KJV)

"For Thou art great, and doest wondrous things: Thou art God alone."

Psalm 86:10 (KJV)

Reflection:

We serve a God of great wonders. He is not limited by time, circumstance, or impossibility. When He moves, creation responds to the sea's part, walls crumble, and hearts are transformed. Every miracle, seen or unseen, bears His fingerprint of Divine purpose. The wonders of God are not only found in the grand and visible, but in the quiet and continual. The breath you draw, the peace that surpasses understanding, the doors that open in impossible places all testify to His Hand at work. Sometimes, the greatest wonder is not the miracle itself, but the timing of it. When all hope seems gone, Heaven intervenes. God is never late, never weary, and never uncertain. He orchestrates every detail so that His Glory is revealed and our faith is strengthened.

You are standing on the edge of something wondrous. What you have prayed for in private, you will soon witness in power. The same God Who spoke to Moses from the burning bush, who stilled the storm for His disciples, and who raised Jesus from the dead still moves today. Watch for His wonders; they are nearer than you think.

Prayer:

Lord, You are the God of wonders. Let my life become a testimony of Your Power and faithfulness. Open my eyes to see the marvels of Your Hand and let awe rise within me again. Perform great wonders in my midst, not for my Glory, but that Your Name may be exalted in all the earth. In Jesus' mighty Name, Amen.

I will not only believe in miracles, but I will expect great wonders from my God. From the wonders we behold to the promises we carry...

Day 364
My Times Are in Your Hands

A reminder that seasons may change, but God's Hand remains steady upon your life.

Scripture

"My times are in Thy hand."

Psalm 31:15 (KJV)

"To everything there is a season, and a time to every purpose under the heaven."

Ecclesiastes 3:1 (KJV)

Reflection:

Every moment of your life rests safely in the palm of God's Hand. He holds not only your future but your seasons, every transition, every quiet waiting, every breakthrough. Though time moves, He never does. The Spirit whispers: Your times and seasons are in My Hand. They change according to My plan. I know where you are, and I know where I am taking you. Every season is important, for in each one you learn more about Me and who you are in Me.

Do not rush the seasons. In winter, He draws you close to receive His warmth. In spring, He makes all things new. In summer, His protection keeps you from the heat of weariness, and in autumn, when things fall away, His unshakable Kingdom remains. God's faithfulness is not seasonal; it's eternal. Though your surroundings may shift, His Hand does not. You have been planted on a firm foundation, rooted in His Promises, unmovable in His peace.

Prayer:

Father, I trust You with every season of my life. Teach me to rest in Your Timing and to see Your Hand in every change. When I cannot see the reason, help me to remember the rhythm that You make all things beautiful in Your time. My life, my moments, and my future are Yours. In Jesus' Name, Amen.

Though the seasons change, the hand that holds me never does. From the hands that hold our times to the triumph that never ends...

Day 365
Resting in Triumph

Scripture:

"But thanks be to God, which giveth us the victory through our Lord Jesus Christ."

1 Corinthians 15:57 (KJV)

"The Lord shall fight for you, and ye shall hold your peace."

Exodus 14:14 (KJV)

Reflection:

Triumph in the Kingdom doesn't come through striving; it comes through surrender. The battles you have faced were never meant to wear you down but to reveal His Strength within you. Every trial, every tear, every test has been working toward this moment: rest. Rest is not passive; it is powerful. It is the position of those who know that Jesus has already overcome. You don't have to keep fighting battles that He has already won. The cross was the battlefield, and the empty tomb is the proof. Heaven has already ruled in your favor.

Resting in triumph means living in the awareness that the victory is finished and the promise is fulfilled. The enemy's greatest strategy is to keep you exhausted, but God's greatest gift is to keep you established. You are not striving to become victorious; you are standing in victory already purchased by His blood. Let peace reign where fear once lingered. Let praise rise where worry once ruled. The sound of triumph is not always a shout, sometimes it's the stillness of knowing He is God, and He has done it all. A reminder that the battle belongs to the Lord, and every victory is secured in His finished work.

Prayer:

Lord, thank You for every battle You've won on my behalf. Teach me to rest in Your Victory, not my effort. Let Your Triumph become my peace, and Your Presence is my resting place. I lay every weight at Your feet, knowing You are faithful to complete what You began. I rest in You, my conquering King. In Jesus' Name, Amen.

I no longer strive to win, I rest in the victory already won.

The Secret Place

Psalm 91:1

Scripture:

"He that dwelleth in the secret place of the Most High shall abide under the Shadow of the Almighty."

Psalm 91:1 (KJV)

There is a place beyond striving for a sanctuary where peace cannot be shaken, and fear has no voice. It is the secret place, the stillness beneath His wings, where hearts are steadied, and faith becomes sight. In this hidden communion, God reveals Himself not through noise, but through nearness. It is here we learn that abiding is not simply visiting His Presence but dwelling in it; not rushing in and out but resting under the Shadow of His Love. Every word within This Call to Abide was birthed here in moments of prayer, surrender, and Holy quiet. These pages are proof that His shelter is real, His Promises are tried and proven, and His Shadow is the safest place on earth. When the world trembles, remember the secret place. When your heart grows weary, return to it. For the same Presence that carried you through these devotionals is waiting to carry you still.

The call to abide begins in the secret place… and there it continues.

Afterword

This Call to Abide

by Starrla Riordan

There are moments in life when the noise fades, the striving ceases, and all that remains is His Presence, gentle, steady, and near. That's where this journey began for me, not in a season of certainty, but in one of surrender. This Call to Abide was born from quiet mornings, tear-stained prayers, and the unwavering whisper of a Father who kept calling me closer.

For years, I believed abiding was something I needed to do, another form of discipline, another spiritual task. But as I walked through seasons of breaking and rebuilding, I discovered that Abiding was never about effort; it was about being. It was about learning to rest, to trust, and to let God write the story when I couldn't see the next line.

Every word in this book was written from that sacred place, the secret place where faith is refined and His Voice becomes unmistakably real. These pages are not just reflections; they are reminders of His nearness. They are proof that God meets us not only on the mountaintop but in the still, unassuming valleys. To the One Who reads this: you are seen, loved, and chosen. Your journey may not look like mine, but your calling is the same: to abide. Stay near Him when the world calls you away.

Trust His Timing when your heart longs for answers. And remember: His Presence is the prize, not the destination. As I close these pages, I offer this final prayer: May every word draw you nearer to the heart of our Heavenly Father and deepen your call to abide.

With all my heart,

Starrla Riordan

Acknowledgments

Every word within these pages is a testimony of the faithfulness of God and the people He has woven into my life to help me walk out this call. None of this would exist without His Divine guidance, yet He so graciously surrounded me with those who encouraged, prayed, and believed along the way.

To my spiritual mothers and Pastor: your wisdom, prayers, and unwavering faith have been my covering. You have poured into me with Truth and tenderness, teaching me what it means to abide through both battle and blessing. Your lives have modeled the beauty of steadfast faith, and I am forever grateful for the strength you have spoken into mine.

To my family: Thank you for your patience, love, and understanding as I withdrew into the quiet to listen and write. You have allowed me the space to meet with God, and in doing so, you became part of every page.

To my brothers and sisters in Christ: Your encouragement has been a lifeline. Each testimony shared, each word of prayer, each moment of unity has been a spark of strength that helped this vision come to life.

To my dear friends: Thank you for reminding me to rest, to breathe, and to keep believing. Your kindness has been a reflection of His Heart.

And to the One Who called me to abide: Jesus, You are the Author and the Finisher. Every word, every thought, every revelation belongs to You. This book is Yours. May it bring Glory to Your Name and draw every heart that reads it closer to You.

With deepest love and gratitude,

Starrla Riordan

The Call of the Shield Maiden

Arise, daughter of strength. Take your place in the armor of light.

There is a sound rising, the call of the Shield Maiden. It is not a call to battle in the natural, but a summons to stand firm in the spirit. This call is not given to the timid, but to the faithful, to those who have been forged in the secret place, refined by fire, and taught to war in prayer.

You have been hidden, but not forgotten. Prepared, but not passed over. You were never meant to blend in; you were born to stand out as a living testimony of His Glory. The world may not understand your strength, but Heaven recognizes your armor.

The Lord is calling forth His Shield Maidens, women who guard peace through prayer, who wield the Sword of the Spirit with wisdom, and who stand clothed in the whole armor of God.

Twice it is written:

Put on the WHOLE armour of God, that ye may be able to stand against the wiles of the devil. For we wrestle not against flesh and Blood, but against principalities, against powers, against the rulers of the darkness of this world, against spiritual wickedness in high places. Wherefore take unto you the whole armour of God, that ye may be able to withstand the evil day, and having done all, to stand.

Ephesians 6:11 - 13 (KJV)

Daughter of God, rise in righteousness. Let your prayers be as arrows, your worship as warfare, and your peace as a fortress. This is not the time to retreat; it is the time to arise, clothed in His strength and shielded in His Truth.

Heaven is calling: Arise, Shield Maiden… and abide in My strength.

Soli Deo Gloria

To God alone be the Glory.

Every page, every prayer, every revelation within This Call to Abide exists for one purpose: to exalt the Name of Jesus Christ. It was His Spirit Who inspired, His Hand that guided, and His mercy that sustained.

May this work never point to the pen, but always to the Author. May every testimony born from these words return as praise to Heaven. May every heart that reads feel the invitation to draw nearer still.

This is not the end of a book; it is the beginning of deeper abiding. The call continues. The invitation remains. And through it all, one Truth endures forever:

He is worthy. He is faithful. He is enough. All Glory, all honor, all praise to the King of Kings and Lord of lords.

Soli Deo Gloria.